A
Casanova's
Code

The Basics of Being a Lover

First Edition

By Javier A. Ocasio

ISBN: 978-80-11-08164-5

Why Write This Book?

For almost four decades, the majority of women, and many men, have been telling me the same things about us men. One woman suggested I write a book about it a decade ago. Well, here it is. I hope you find it fun and worthy of telling others.

Thanks for the suggestion and the encouragement, Wendy. This book is all thanks to you.

Some Suggestions About How to Get the Most Out of This Book:

1. **Be open-minded**. A humble desire to improve as a lover is key. Or to laugh through all the shenanigans.

2. **Explore at your pace**. Skim chapters, read highlights, or jump around. This book is not purely linear.

3. **Reflect on what you learn**. Let it sink in before moving on. Unless it clicks, or you already knew.

4. **Personalize your copy**. Annotate freely! Highlight, dog ear, bend pages, whatever you feel like.

5. **Review regularly**. Refresh your memory as needed. Especially if you have little to no experience.

6. **Self-reflection is key**. Journal about your experiences. You never know how it can help you.

7. **Agree to disagree**. It's okay to have different perspectives. My goal is to share fundamental knowledge, not convince you. Take what works and adapt the rest. Or, ignore what's not of use to you and go forth!

PART IV – The Basics of Being a Better Lover

A Casanova's Code picks up where book two left off. Here, we'll be diving into everything from the magic of holding hands to steamy make-out sessions, all the way to sex and oral sex. I'll be sharing my thoughts and ideas about what to do or not to do with every lovely lady part (hair, neck, back, you name it) – from foreplay to the big finish, the whole nine yards. I'll even share some of my pleasant wins and hilarious blunders in each area, just for fun.

I want you, my fellow lover, to test out these ideas (if you haven't already) and see what works for you. Maybe you're already a pro, and this can validate some of your moves. Or maybe you know someone who could use a little guidance. Either way, this book is all about starting with the basics and building from there. Remember, this isn't 12 moves to blow her mind in bed or how to reinvent sex. A Casanova's Code is simply a guide to the basic things you need to master (if you haven't already in your own way) in order to clearly and pleasantly navigate getting all feely touchy with a girl in a way that maximizes the probability that the experience will be pleasant for you both. No harm, no anger, no trauma. The code to this Casanova's madness is all about making you a smoother lover. Hope you enjoy the ride!

Chapter 0: Selfishness in Sexual Things, Sexual Aggression, The Two-Way Street

The default idea I embody, to prevent myself from becoming selfish, is to pay equal attention to both of our needs in each moment, regardless of the original intent or plan. As necessary, I use my words like a big boy, and I encourage her to use hers. That way, communication is open and fun, and selfish greed isn't an issue. And most of the time, just because of that consideration, I get to do all I want anyway, except it's with my lover's blessing.

Upon reading this part, if you immediately recognize that it doesn't apply to you because you're:

- ✓ A considerate lover with self-control.
- ✓ Have a woman who loves to let you be as greedy as you want because satisfying you also satisfies her.
- ✓ You're a man who communicates openly with your woman about preferences, or…
- ✓ Have a balanced give-and-take dynamic.

Then consider yourself one of the lucky few. In that case, this doesn't apply to you, and you can skip this chapter. But if you have never really stopped to care or ask about what the girl likes, wants, or desires, or you're the type to sex your woman then roll over and go to sleep, or you're the type that scoffs at the idea of not getting everything you want each and every time you have sex, I highly recommend you read on.

Not being greedy about sexual things can be tough for some, so here are some things to consider.

The Highlights:

1. Not having had sex in a while is not a reason to lose yourself and just hump away like some animal.

2. You are not entitled to any woman's body. Just because she chose to have consensual sex with you doesn't entitle you to only think about your animalistic pleasure.

3. Hollywood, porn, popular culture, and advertising all play a role in shaping our expectations and the intensity of our desire.

4. Challenge your discomfort.

5. Be mentally prepared to face what is mentally uncomfortable about not thinking of only your pleasure.

6. Imagine all the things you'd like to do with a woman. Now imagine that she may say yes to half of those things if you're willing to do at least half of what she wants.

7. While the idea of spontaneous sex when you desire it might be pleasing to imagine, warming her up first will always be appreciated.

8. Women have a different idea of sex than we do for the most part. Get acquainted with that if you don't already know.

9. As the man of the relationship, it's usually advisable that you lead the way on sexual things to encourage and create a pleasurable experience for you both.

10. There are sexually greedy women out there as well.

11. Your anger about various things in life has no place in sex, as sexual aggression can be extremely harmful.

12. Do not mistake anger for passion. Angry sex and passionate sex are completely different things.

13. There are times when a woman will indeed give you permission to do whatever you want with her body in sex, but there are still limits.

14. Being sexually frustrated for one reason or another can quickly turn into sexual aggression.

15. Sexual things are two-way streets. It's not her way or just your way.

16. Just like women cannot be in the mood, neither do you always need to be hard or horny. And don't let anyone put you down for having those moments.

The main problem with being sexually selfish and greedy is that you want way more than might be considered reasonable by the woman that you are with. You want your dick sucked more than you want to eat pussy (you know who you are). You might also like to get yours, and then when you're done, you like to leave the girl hanging. Or you might only like everything your way every single time. The ultimate inconsiderate, greedy lovers are those in a long-term relationship who just have sex with their partner and then roll over and pass out. Day after day. Year after year. There is more to it than that, though, as we are about to explore.

1. Now, let's be honest: When you haven't had sex in a while, it's your first time, your sex drive is peaking, or your hormones are raging, things can get primal. It's consensual, the clothes come off, and everything feels great. But once you're in, that intense pleasure and urge can take over, and you just start humpin' away. You might get caught up in the moment, focused solely on your own satisfaction and orgasm (while she patiently lies there, rolling her eyes, waiting for you to finish). This impulse can be overwhelming, especially for those without sexual experience or those experiencing a dry spell, or for those who just don't care what a woman wants and only care about what they/you want. That doesn't change the fact that you are supposed to be an intelligent human being. That means that not having had sex in a while is not a reason to lose yourself and just hump away on a woman like some animal.

2. Add to that a sense of entitlement – wanting "what you deserve" after finally getting a chance – and it's easy to become selfish in the heat of the moment. Hence, selfishness in sexual things. You get access to her body, and now it's all about your pleasure. In those situations, just take a breath, lover, and try to control your urges. Remember, you are not entitled to any woman's body. Just because she chose to have consensual sex with you doesn't entitle you to only think about your animalistic pleasure.

Women can be guilty of this, too. But right now, we're focusing on us men and how we can strive to be better lovers. I'll talk about the ladies in a bit.

Breaking Free from Influences

3. (As I mentioned in book 1, chapter 3, the sex industry, but for those who haven't read that yet.) Hollywood, porn, popular culture, and advertising all play a role in shaping our expectations and the intensity of our desire. These influences can create a sense of sexual entitlement, which often clashes with what women actually want. Try to understand that you are indeed under some influence, whether it's movies, books, internet porn, parents, family, religion, work atmosphere, or a friend's group, whether you acknowledge it or not. For many of you, your biggest challenge might just be your own biology.

Breaking free from those types of things isn't easy, and I'm sure there are books out there on how to do such a thing. The important thing to remember is to at least recognize which ideas were introduced to you and which you came up with on your own, and why. Then explore from there as to why you feel it's ok to operate as you do. If you have a partner to talk to, that will help, but if you have a lady friend, try to confide in her. That could be a great help too. The point is to acknowledge what influences you to be selfish in sexual things so that in the process of becoming more aware, you begin to ask yourself the right questions.

Challenge Your Discomfort

4. So, what now? There's no magic formula in facing your sexual selfishness (again, if that applies to you). But if the idea of meeting your partner halfway or of listening to her say that her desires and needs aren't the things you like and that makes you squirm because it involves things you're not used to, then that's your starting point – discomfort with fairness. Everything isn't about you/your pleasure.

If you're in between sex partners or just don't like relationships and prefer to just have random hook-ups, at least take the time to analyze whether or not your approach is all about you. If it is, no matter how you justify it, challenge yourself to explore how transformative it might be to not make sexual things all about you.

Your sexual greed can look very different from someone else's as well. One woman told me how almost every night after a shower and lying in bed, her husband would come up and have sex with her missionary style till he came. Then he'd roll over and go to sleep. This continued – until she divorced him 20 years later. Now, as a divorced woman, she's having the best sex of her life and can't believe she lived a life like that sexually, where someone else only ever cared about their own pleasure.

Another woman I met told me about how her man loved to get his dick sucked and asked for it all the time. Yet he hardly went down on her – even though she desired it and asked for it.

5. Here's the key: be mentally prepared. Think about what scares you about pleasing or thinking about your partner's needs and desires. Consider why you prefer to receive and not give pleasure, or why only the thought of doing the things you like does it for you sexually. In other words, do you think that solely pleasing yourself should somehow also satisfy her in the same way? Preparing yourself to experience things outside of what does it for you is the only way to have the courage to go through with new things enough times to get used to them. And maybe even learn to like them.

Try to stay open. If you have a lover or partner, create an atmosphere for the conversation that is devoid of judgment and where sexual ideas may be expressed safely without ridicule. And make especially sure that you won't make fun of anything she might say later. Unless, of course, your relationship is awesome enough to where that type of humor is cool. You'll be making yourself vulnerable, so you might feel insecure tackling how to include her more in the pursuit of your pleasure, and by not making fun of or ridiculing her, you make it easier to not be ridiculed in return.

Not all women can relate to or be open to having that type of conversation, though. This definitely needs to be said. So, having a neutral third party or even seeing a therapist could be the way to go. But you have to make that judgment call as to whether or not the girl you are with is in a place where you can discuss desires and sexual exploration together. If you, for whatever reason, decide not to talk to her about it, then at least work it out with someone else. Then maybe the results of your efforts to become a better lover may surprise her and speak for itself.

6. If you do not have a partner, then just take the time to map out what it is you like or love to do with the opposite sex. Or if you have yet to be with a woman or haven't been with one in a long time, what do you dream or fantasize about doing with them? Map that out in either case, then anticipate that maybe she might say no to 50 percent of these sexual desires. Then imagine that the only way she will

entertain the things you really desire to do is if you entertain the things she desires – or if you bring out those desires from within her.

Allow me to illustrate an example. The number one complaint I have heard from ladies for decades is oral sex. For decades now, I have heard about how we men of all ages, young to old, love receiving oral sex way more than we like to give it (or just put zero effort into it or are 'meh' at it). I've surveyed a lot of the men I've come across in my life (from my teens till now), and I can say with clarity that the majority of those men aren't a fan of oral sex. They only usually do it because they either want to get their dick sucked – or to reluctantly reciprocate. Of those in the category that do eat pussy regularly, many will do it if asked, but not genuinely enjoy it. Those of us who genuinely enjoy it or love to go down on our partners, and our partners love it, are in the minority, though we may seem like the majority due to how vocal we can be about it.

This general attitude manifests in a unique way in porn because the focus is always on the man getting his dick sucked and not eating pussy (or just a little bit). This, of course, creates the illusion that not only do women love it as much as we desire it, but that they look forward to doing it to us as much we look forward to having that done to us.

I know many of you love getting head. For some of you, it might even be your favorite thing a girl can do for you. For others of you who have yet to be with a woman, it might be something you are super curious about and look forward to. Regardless, you have to think about the flip side of that coin. That is, you, going down on her, learning to enjoy it to some degree, and being dedicated enough to figure out how to get her off.

When turned on or starved, our male, sexually greedy brain really does empower one to think more about one than the other, and I feel for ya. But, like I've said before and, like I will continue to say in this book, if you want to be a better lover, if you want to really make things even better for us men by improving yourself, one male at a time, and our male to female sexual relations, you gotta, for pussies' sake, stop being so damn greedy about getting your dick sucked and eat more pussy. I help you learn to like it more in the oral sex chapter.

7. This is more than just about oral sex though. We men have our way of wanting sex, visualizing sex, and even of starting sex. Oftentimes, we're hard, we find a wife or partner, and then try to have

sex with little to no regard for properly warming her up; I'm guilty of that one. Or, we even go so far as to have her warm herself up before we go in for the full thing.

8. Women have a different idea of sex than we do, for the most part. That isn't to say that there aren't women out there who don't view sex or like sex the way we men do. It's just that women are inherently different to us men, and typically they favor romance, relinquishing control, being submissive, and or being dominated in the ways that they individually like. Talking to them, whispering to them, painting a picture, teasing, and all that before sex are things they generally love. Whereas most of you guys, in being so caught up in your desire, just go right for it, bypassing many of these crucial elements that would enhance the experience for her and not coincidentally, for you as well. Cuz, you know, a well-hydrated and turned-on woman usually will tend to have a wet pussy and an excited body in contrast to the opposite when you do nothing, and she isn't turned on.

Here is a clear example. A girl and I are texting each other. We are getting into it because we haven't seen each other in a while. Sultry, sexy messages start getting exchanged. We suddenly take a sharp turn in our texts and start talking about what turns us on. Naturally, I love sexy pictures of this type, that type, videos, and surprises. Although sexy and kinky messages are great too. When she starts telling me about what turns her on, guess what she says? Was it pics? Videos? Nudes? Dick pics? Nope. None of the above. She loved imagining me working out with heavy weights, being sweaty and doing hard work, watching my muscles work hard, and even being kind and caring.

Talk about a real difference, right? That's not to say all women are like that, nor is it to say that they don't like nudes or seeing us topless. That is just one of many real-world examples that exemplify a fundamental difference in what turns them on versus us.

Listen, I'm not saying we need to do everything to please the woman and to forget our needs or desires, I'm all about balance and eliminating selfishness in sexual things both ways, but to whom this applies (and you know if it's you or not) if you don't expand your horizons to greater possibilities of sex that include her, and you expect her to be happy in the long term (or short term) with your same ole shit, then you're in trouble. Chances are that if someone shows up randomly who offers and displays these types of things missing from her sex life, she will be tempted to go for it, if not outright jump on that chance (maybe). With this in mind, this is more about guaranteeing that you don't become stale, that you include her needs and desires, and that you create an atmosphere of giving and sharing so that you can both have more pleasure and joy, which may make it so that she is happier being with you.

9. As the man of the relationship, it's usually advisable that you lead the way on these things: fairness, sexual openness, and selflessness. And if you can't get all the experience necessary in order to keep your sexual greed in check with your first partner or first few partners before you settle down, then you need to read...and watch.. .and listen...and learn from every source possible. That way, you can apply and improve each time in order to eventually transition from selfishness to selflessness. One of the key things to learn in that journey, by the way, is to experience joy, pleasure, and gratification from giving and doing.

10. All that said, there are some greedy women out there as well. They might make demands, seduce you in ways that are all about them getting what they want, or even be willing to give you what you want, but everything has to be their way with zero room for deviation. I'm sure that there are more manifestations out there than I can cover. The thing to keep in mind is to notice the sexual selfishness on the flipside when it presents itself.

I've experienced sexual selfishness in various ways with women. It typically doesn't manifest in the same way as it does in us men. I was with one woman who was into pretty much everything you can imagine, but it all had to be done exactly the way she wanted. Another knew exactly what she liked – and how she liked it. She'd only do those things and nothing else. No room for discussion or experimentation. Then there was another woman who loved to receive but hated to give in any capacity.

The most important thing that I can share is that unless you like to be submissive, or you get off on letting her be selfish sexually, you need to lay down some boundaries. Be clear about what you are comfortable with and what you aren't comfortable with. Create balance with her demands by either mirroring them or clearly stating your own. If she threatens to just walk away if she can't get her way, let her walk. You don't need the headache and the games. But if she is willing to engage and see where you can meet each other, that would be great! It's a start. Worst case scenario, if you have never encountered a woman that is sexually selfish and then one day you do but don't know how you feel about it, just go for the ride and then decide. Could be fun.

A sign of a good woman – if you are sexually selfish but trying to be better – is if she sets some boundaries and calls out your behavior swiftly.

Sexual Aggression

11. There are some of us men out there who are frustrated. Some are angry. It can be because of a myriad of things. Could be you. Could be a friend or a family member. Work, family, life problems, tragedy, trauma, women treating you badly or ignoring you, unhappy with your life in general – I get it. The thing is that a portion of us men who hold onto that kind of emotion usually tend to also take it out on our women in some way or another, including but not limited to when we have sex. That can translate into sexual aggression and angry sex. I touch on this in several ways in the first few chapters of Book 1: The True to Yourself Man.

Obviously, angry sex can result from anything that makes you mad, and you decide to take out your frustrations during sex. Sure, there may be some women out there who are into that, but I assure you that it's the minority. Not to mention, angry sex is a slippery slope to sex becoming plain ole violence or worse. So please, always take the time to compose yourself and vent your anger or deal with your anger in another way before engaging in sex or anything sexual. That energy is strong and can have a real negative effect on the girl you are with. You shouldn't treat another human being like that, much less someone you take on as a lover.

Hit the gym, go for a run, ride a bicycle, meditate, scream into a pillow, or do whatever you need to do that can help. Just get it out of your system before you get with a girl. If you can't get it out for some time, then that's ok. Just wait until you feel better.

I've had angry sex before, and each time the experience was different but always ended poorly. I never got violent, but my emotions were so strong that they directly affected my sex partner at the time. Those very real effects woke me up because I felt terrible afterward. Due to that, I swore to never do that ever again, or to even allow myself to be close to a situation where that might be a possibility.

12. There are other men out there who aren't angry or upset about anything, and yet they, too, display aggression in sex. Porn influence can be part of it, but often I find that it's because aggression and roughness replace passion and genuine desire. There can be a bit of not knowing how to express that desire properly, so aggression is the easiest way to do so, especially if you are muscular or are naturally strong. Overall, there is a significant difference.

When you have passion and desire as a man, there is an innate hunger that goes beyond just being horny and in the mood. Your body and spirit not only seek the sights, scents, warmth, and feels of a woman, but you also seek the connection, the breath, her reactions, her moans, and her gratification. Essentially, when you have passion, you crave the discovery of a woman's body in a way that is not based on anger or aggression but more on hunger and an appetite to both experience and discover her in a certain way. You subconsciously want to become one with her. When done right, that creates mutual pleasure and gratification. Not to mention that women generally love a passionate man.

When you are just being aggressive, sexually selfish, and fierce, there's no real connection there. You are just using her body for your own desires and to satisfy yourself while you vent. I've been told stories many times by women who, for one reason or another, ended up having consensual sex with men who showed they only cared about their pleasure with the aggression that they displayed. That aggression is scary and, when left unchecked, has caused and will continue to cause harm to women. The worst result of that is rape. The most extreme result cam be murder. Don't be that guy.

13. And yes, there are times when a woman may want you to, and give you permission to, have your way with her body however you like. But even in those scenarios, there are limits. I can't tell you the number of times that I have heard horror stories from women about the shit we do in bed to them that they just endured in order to get it over with. What can add a bit more injury to that is when you are well hung, and you think that just stabbing it in there as hard as you can is perfectly ok, despite her obvious pain or negative reactions.

Aggressive sex is something that some women like. However, you have to acknowledge the chemistry and mutual agreement or verbalize it before you indulge in aggressive sex, and even then, you need to test limits as you go. I've honestly been told by plenty of women that I could do whatever I wanted, or that I could be as rough as I wanted. With very few exceptions, I was actually able to carry that out before having to tone it down because they expressed pain or discomfort, or I did something they didn't like. That speaks to the limits of what they actually meant without saying it as much as it speaks to me not stopping the second time and asking for specifics.

14. Sexual frustration can have something to do with angry sex as well. Maybe you can't get it up as well anymore? Maybe she isn't responding to your hard efforts as you would like her to. Maybe she's taking forever to cum. Maybe she doesn't reciprocate in the ways you'd like. Perhaps when you're having trouble getting it hard, she does nothing about it and just looks at you like something is wrong with you instead of doing something about it. Maybe you've just been rejected a lot. When you feel sexually frustrated, regardless of the reason, it's usually better to call yourself out and then stop things or just not start to begin with. Better that than accidentally getting all aggressive and unintentionally harming the woman you are with, with your words or your actions.

No matter the cause, the intent, or how justified you might feel, you have to learn to let the sexual aggression go. Better to make it a joyful and fun occasion than to have it devolve into the opposite.

The Two-Way Street

15. The short premise of this part is really simple: everything in sex and lovemaking is a two-way street. If you look at it from that standpoint, it nullifies sexual selfishness altogether. Just as women don't need to turn themselves on or work themselves up for you, it is not your job to be instantly hard all the time or turned on, contrary to popular belief. There's a difference between you being horny and a girl taking the time to turn you on. You getting her excited is just as important as her getting you excited.

You can be completely horny and not be hard—it happens. In those circumstances, there are three types of women: the ones who see that and wonder why you aren't hard and look at you like, "What's wrong with you?", and then there are the ones who see you aren't hard and get right to work on trying to get you hard without question. Lastly, there are the ones that maybe try to help you out, or not, but just accept that an erect penis isn't always necessary and focus on just enjoying things in other ways.

Never let a woman make you feel bad, talk down to you, or make you feel like it is your job and your job alone to get yourself hard for sex, or anything sexual for that matter. It really says a lot about a woman, depending on what she says and what your experience is with her, so keep that in mind. All these things go both ways. The expectations frequently lie solely with the man, on you. But a good woman will also joyfully do things for you and be attentive to your desires and needs.

Just as we men don't appreciate being shamed for not being hard, or for not having a big dick, don't shame a woman for being dry down there or super wet. If she's dry, the simplest reason for that is she's either dehydrated or not turned on enough. However, there are some women who just don't get wet much, if at all, and that may be normal for them. So long as you're doing your part to excite her and turn her on, and she responds positively to what you do, it'll be fine. A little lube will buff it out, or if she's super wet, lick some of that up and then keep going. Even if you prefer things one way or another, do not make put-down comments or say negative things about her privates, and don't put up with a woman doing the same just because she has other preferences. It goes both ways.

Just like we men appreciate no teeth when a woman is giving us a blow job, so too must you not bite or grind her pussy with your teeth. This can also apply to breasts, nipples, and areolas (these are all things I cover later), but you have to take that on a case-by-case basis and ask to be sure. Some women love to jump right in and start biting and shit during foreplay and sex too; don't let them get away with that unless you actually are into it. Some think that is a turn-on, or it's fun for them, but if it isn't for you, don't put up with it and speak up.

So, no shit, there I was…going down on this girl. She was tasty and smelled good, and I was having a great time when, all of a sudden, as she climaxed, she wrapped her legs around my head and neck and grabbed a fistful of hair, thereby locking me in place, unable to breathe or free myself. She starts to roll left and right as she orgasms at a high rate of speed, and not only did I almost suffocate and break my neck, but I also hurt my jaw, and it hasn't been the same to this day. What's the point of that story? Don't grab a girl's head and shove her onto your dick without her permission and then hold her there while trying to get it deeper into her throat while you orgasm, especially if she isn't a fan of cum. That goes both ways, trust me. You wouldn't want a strong girl to lock you in, so don't push her head down without clear consent or indication that she's into it. And no, she didn't do that to retaliate, as I've never shoved a girl's head down onto my dick without her asking me to.

16. Lastly, if a woman is not in the mood for sex or sexy things, the same can apply to you too. There are ladies out there who can feel entitled and get greedy as though you were some machine that needs to perform when it suits them. Women tend to internalize rejections, so when you say no to a woman, even in a simple home scenario, if she is entitled, selfish, needy, has issues, or if she doesn't understand men but rather has her own assumptions about men, she might be hurt by this. She might be confused and might even retaliate in some way or another. Those are teaching moments as much as they are important in order to set up boundaries and learn about each other. You are allowed to not be in the mood for sex or sexy things—it's perfectly okay and part of the two-way street. Just don't shrug it off and ignore the scenario; address it in a healthy manner when these things happen. The simplest and healthiest way I know of is to just ask, "Am I not allowed to NOT be in the mood when you are?" or "Do I have to always be in the mood when you are in the mood?' Making her think in a way that establishes a sense of what is fair can usually do the trick. Sometimes. Maybe. If she isn't a narcissist. If it turns into a fight when you aren't in the mood, and it's happened more than once, then you might need to walk away and reconsider that relationship.

Look, the overall point is that if you are putting everything you can into the sexual part of your relationship and you are not getting similar or anything of equal effort in return or in some way that makes you feel like you aren't doing everything, then you need to re-evaluate whether or not this can continue. Accordingly, if she is always sucking your dick, and on top during sex doing all the work or initiating sex, and you are just taking everything without giving her anything in return, how long do you think that can last if she isn't getting something she values or enjoys in equal measure in return?

There are some situations, and indeed some women, in which it can be all about you or all about her in turn. That is to say that you can have a partner who is willing to let you be as greedy and selfish as you want in turn. Today, it's all about you. The next time, it's all about her. So even in the face of that type of sexual greed, in turn, it's ok because it's balanced.

Everything goes both ways, lover. Don't get too selfish and greedy. Don't make it all about you, and don't let it be all about her. Sex is more than just about you getting your nut off or getting boobies in your face. Otherwise, you can't keep things in balance. So, even if you can't or don't enjoy the exact same things with each other, at least do something that is equally valued or complementary so that smooth traffic flows on that two-way street. You are dealing with a whole separate being who has her own needs and desires. Acknowledge that, and controlling your own desires to make room for hers just might become easier.

Chapter 1: Arms and Hands: When Innocent Passion Starts With Touch

I always approach hand-holding, hand touches, and hand caresses with a childlike mentality and innocence. Even if I know that the girl and I like each other, that we are both interested, and that we are already gravitating close as we walk and talk, I make sure she can see and feel the joy of the first touch of her hand as my excited heart beats in my chest. Allow the gravity that draws you to each other to do the work. Please don't force it, nor try to hold on too tightly.

There are times when you meet a lovely lady, and at first touch—and possibly well into the relationship as well—where mere touches of the hands and arms can be electrifying and very sensual. I never ignore those moments and their potential. I try to be attuned to these things in order to enjoy them as they happen because they are often not repeatable and are different with each girl. So, I am not in a hurry to move beyond that as it happens. I want to live in that moment in as many ways as possible, even if they are just simple and childlike, before moving on to something else. Or, even in conjunction with something else, like kissing or making love.

I adore hand chemistry and electricity, so I never skip it, and neither should you, lover.

The Highlights:

1. Remember that not everyone likes or enjoys holding hands the way you might.

2. Never force a hand touch or hold. Let it be an organic moment.

3. If a girl tries to hold your hand or touch your hand, and you don't like it or don't want that from her (maybe you like someone else or for any reason), never yank your hand away or be rude if you can help it. Lead with kindness.

4. If you try to hold or touch a girl's hand and she pulls it away, regardless of how she reacts to your gesture, if you get upset or

butt-hurt about it, contain yourself. Be respectful. Don't respond harshly. Lead and be kind.

5. If the hand-holding doesn't work for one reason or another, don't overthink it. It's ok.

6. If it does work out and you end up holding hands with a girl, don't let your excitement result in a death grip!

7. Don't be a lame/limp hand holder. If you're gonna hold hands, actively do so in a relaxed way.

8. Gently using your fingers to stroke her fingers, hands, and arms is usually intuitive and can feel pretty amazing if you haven't moved on to other things yet.

9. Beyond just touching, stroking, and caressing, you can (but you don't have to) use your lips to place a kiss on the hand, palm, fingers, or arm when the moment is right.

10. When you hold a girl's hand, do so in the way that places your forearm ahead/in front of hers when walking side by side. Gently guiding her shows a respectful lead.

11. Your height and her height, if very different, will have a direct impact on your ability to hold hands. If it isn't possible, then just have her hold your arm as though you were escorting her.

I'm sure that some of you are thinking of a chapter on arms and hands. Really? What could be so intimate or basic about arms and hands that it would need its own chapter with basic dos and don'ts? I mean, there are more important areas to pay attention to, right? And how could knowing anything about this possibly make me a better lover? Most men already know this stuff or at least can figure it out. Well, sit back, lover, because when it comes to a woman's body, you have to have all your bases covered and leave no area unloved without the knowledge to properly pay attention to it when consent is given or when desire is expressed. Not to mention that not all men get the basics of these things. If I hadn't run into that many men who didn't know, I wouldn't have felt the need to even include this chapter. So, if this chapter has insight for you, don't feel bad, as most of this chapter comes from my own direct experience of mistakes I made or awkward things I did due to my nervousness or lack of instinct at times.

Consent, consent, consent and respect, respect, respect. For most of us, the very first physical move that happens between us men and women is usually hand touching or hand holding. So, before you go and get all grabby or too excited, be certain that it's mutual. When in doubt, what? That's right, ask. Talk about it. Just don't be like me and…well, I'll save that epic fail for the end of this chapter.

Remember, girls are not your property, and you have no rights over them or their parts. If a girl doesn't like you, never is it ok to grab her hands or wrist and demand answers with a refusal to let go unless you get them. But when it is a mutual thing, those first touches can be so exciting and magical! So be patient, don't force it, be respectful, and if you want more details as well as my stories, read on. (Otherwise, for those who already are well-versed, onto the next chapter).

Something else needs to be said – so please pay attention. I fully understand that there is a lot of excitement when you see a woman you like, and you finally get to spend some time with her. When the excitement is mutual, we often rush right into bed, and it's awesome. But I gotta tell ya, there have been many times when I was super excited about a girl, and I chose not to engage super-fast despite the obvious chemistry and desire. Why? Because there are many things that you can miss when you bypass certain things. And holding hands is one of those things.

The Basics in More Depth

1. Not everyone likes to hold hands, so if either you or the girl doesn't like to, for whatever

reason, talk about it. See if you can find some middle ground that satisfies you both. I've actually run into this scenario before, even though it was rare.

In one experience, it turned out that the girl just wasn't a huge fan of public displays of affection. In the dark, indoors, and at home or around friends and family, it was no problem. But walking around in public areas with lots of people, nope. Another example was of a close friend who had chronically sweaty palms. We would hold hands for less than a minute (yes, I would hold hands with my friends sometimes), and her palms would just be drenched in sweat. That made it so that we rarely did that, but I didn't hold it against her, nor did it bother me. It's just how it was for her.

The bottom line is that you just never know, even when it comes to simple hand-holding. Take the time to find out and be considerate if it isn't instantly obvious.

2. Never force a hand touch or hold. It's the organic moments that truly make it special. There have been times when I have seen men grab a woman's hand and not let go, even when it was clear that she didn't want to. In other situations, I've seen men misread signals and go for the hand hold, get rejected gently, and then proceed to try to force it. Look, I get it, rejection sucks but that isn't the way to handle it. Be a man, take the rejection like a grown true to yourself man (ahem, book one), don't let it bother you, and move on.

3. If a girl tries to hold your hand or touch your hand, and you don't like it or don't want that from her (because maybe you like someone else), never just yank your hand away or be rude. Gently clasp her hand in yours, thank her for her affection, speak gently but truthfully about your feelings, and kindly return her hand to her lap or side, depending on whether it happened sitting or standing.

I feel like it should always be taken as a compliment when a girl likes you and has the courage to make a first gentle move like that. Take it as an honor, respect her, her feelings, and her gesture, and do not dishonor or disrespect yourself by responding in a fashion that will affect her from ever wanting to do something like that again. Your actions could very well affect her ability to muster the courage to do this in the future to someone she may like who also likes her, and you do not want to be the reason that diminishes her heart's courage.

And yes, of course, sometimes women can be cold and harsh, even rejecting simple things like a hand touch from a man. The question is, do you want to be like that? I hope not. Because if you do react like that, you aren't contributing to making dating, or the world for that matter, better for anyone. And each drop of goodness in the world counts, for what is the ocean made up of if not a multitude of drops? (Guess the movie for that one.)

4. If you try to hold or touch a girl's hand and she pulls it away, regardless of how she reacts to your gesture, if you get upset or butt-hurt about it, do not lash out. Allow yourself to feel what you feel, but be in control of how you express it by choosing your words carefully. Also, choose to remind yourself that these things happen. Furthermore, it is an opportunity to show the depth of your patience and best self, an

opportunity to display your kindest and most understanding self. Can you do that, lover?

I know that some of us men can be afraid of intimacy as well. Maybe you weren't with a loving family, maybe you have had bad experiences and rejections from women, or maybe something else entirely. But either way, sometimes it's easier to start with touch rather than words. And I know that if you are afraid of intimacy, you might also be afraid of rejection, and that's ok. Try to shift your perspective a bit and see it from the view of what a wonderful opportunity to grow my courage.

5. If the hand-holding doesn't work out one way or another, don't overthink it. It's ok. Sometimes you both may like each other and start to hold hands, and there's just no spark. No electricity. It feels fine, and her hand is nice, but it doesn't excite you. Though the conversation and interaction started off with some excitement, they quickly faded or fizzled out. In these moments, you and her usually end up letting go of hands and leaving it at that. Or if it's purely one-sided, it can still happen. Just be honest with the moment and how you feel. Sometimes things just fizz out and remain normal. It's ok.

6. If it does work out and you end up holding hands with a girl, remember not to let your excitement result in a death grip! Some girls are tough, and some require a gentler touch. Try to always start off with gentleness.

I've been with a girl who was so excited to hold hands that she constantly had a death grip, and I had to remind her all the time to ease up until she learned to have a relaxed grip. On the flip side of that coin, I have also been with a woman whose hand I enjoyed holding, and I definitely over-gripped it a bit. We men tend to be stronger than women, on top of having more manly bone structure and hands, so if you get excited, hold her hand, but go easy. Save the death grip for the gym.

7. Don't be a lame or limp hand holder. Don't just limply keep your fingers intertwined with hers so that the only reason the hand holding is happening is because she is holding onto your hand. A gentle, relaxed grip that moves and explores her hand is usually nicer.

It is likely that some of you men aren't big on hand-holding, and that your girl or future girl will be. Many women feel great pride at being alongside their man and enjoy this simple act of hand-holding. I find that the men who limply hand-hold are mostly the ones who think nothing of it or who just don't enjoy doing that for their own reasons. And listen, I'm not telling you to hold hands if you don't want to. All I'm saying is that if you do, even if you don't like it, actively hold her hand. Don't limply do it. It's a simple activity that you can manage with almost no energy consumption and minimal effort. Even if you only do it for a short while before you stop doing so, engage, and if she's attentive, she'll notice and appreciate the effort.

8. Gently using your fingers to stroke her fingers, hand, and arm can feel pretty amazing in the right situations. Especially if you haven't moved onto other things yet. Generally, this is pretty instinctive as the desire to touch and explore usually comes naturally, but I included that here because there are times when we freeze up or get so nervous that we get stuck in our heads.

Gentle hand touches are awesome. These usually come very naturally as two people are close and share affection with each other. While gently touching can be awesome, do not over-rub the same area

s of skin for too long! Then it becomes irritating. I've experienced this way too often in my youth and even in adulthood, and I have no idea why I didn't say anything and instead just let the woman keep on rubbing my arm or hand in the same spot till it became aggravating. So, pay attention to how much time you spend rubbing or gently caressing an arm, a hand, or whatever. It can get irritating, and that is not the effect you want to have.

9. Beyond just touching, stroking, and caressing, you can use your lips to place a kiss on the hand, palm, fingers, or arm. But when you do so, be sure to keep your lips relaxed. You want to do a more sensual, appreciative kiss rather than a firm or hard one. That should be pretty self-explanatory unless you have a thick mustache or beard. In which case, ensure your lips touch and that it just isn't a facial carpet rub on her hand, arm, or finger.

10. When you hold a girl's hand, do so in the way that places your forearm ahead/in front of hers when walking side by side.

This should come pretty naturally. It places you as the leading one while holding hands when walking side by side, which, as a man, you should do. There may be circumstances when a woman may yank you here or there, and she'll be the one with her hand in this position momentarily, but otherwise, it should be you who is in the front position over her arm overall. Take the lead.

Additionally, when walking with a woman, keep her shorter legs and pace in mind. That matters because if you are trying to get to know a girl or to establish a connection, you don't want to walk one or two steps ahead of her the whole time. Keep pace with her. If you were a soldier at any point in your life, or a trainee, then you should know how to keep pace with someone who isn't in your natural step and rhythm. If you weren't a soldier or trainee, then this is your opportunity to practice. Walking beside her so she doesn't have to super stride to keep up is something she will appreciate, especially if she's in heels or uncomfortable shoes.

11. Your height and her height, if very different, will have a direct impact on your ability to hold hands. If it isn't possible, then just have her hold your arm as though you were escorting her. This too can happen very intuitively when you're with a girl, despite your desire or hers to hold hands. But if you like the feeling of her holding you for whatever reason, you can have her grab onto your arm, or you can bend your arm at the elbow and have her hold you that way – just like in the movies when two people go on a fancy date.

Look, lover, I know that a lot of this seems pretty obvious or simple to figure out. Thing is, I wouldn't even be writing this if all the men I knew, have met, or been told about, all had the capacity and presence of mind to navigate these things. I mentioned it earlier, but I'm repeating it here. While this may be more useful to the inexperienced youth, this also applies to the men out there who think they know what they are doing, but actually don't.

What's obvious to you might not be to someone else, and I'll never make fun of anyone for that. Instead, I want to support and help if possible, so if you read this chapter and already know, great! If not, then I hope it helps, but either way, pass this on to those you definitely know that need it.

The Epic Fail

As a young adult, I definitely enjoyed handholding. But of all the circumstances in which I held hands with a woman, one stands out above the rest, and that was the one with the girl whose hands would sweat. Granted, there was more than one, but this particular one stood out.

We were on a date at the movies. Our hands inched closer and closer until our hands connected. And boy, did her hands feel amazing! The problem was: we continued to hold hands very tightly to the point where our hands not only started to sweat, but they also started to drip sweat from in between. And for some reason, neither of us were letting go. I'm not sure if we were seeing who could hold out the longest or what, but eventually, we both let go almost simultaneously. We got a chuckle out of it and laughed, and after that, we switched to holding hands gently. Thank God – because I'm certain her hand was as sore as mine at the movies. Lesson learned.

In this example, I only really missed a couple of the tips I shared. I didn't really speak up and I held on too tight for too long. It was harmless otherwise because we both laughed about it, and she held my hand tight in return.

The Epic Success

Sometimes an epic success in relations with women just comes naturally. Once upon a time I had a girl as a best friend. We truly were just best friends – with the addition that we loved to hold hands. Or should I say more accurately that I loved to hold her hand. For some reason, her hand felt so perfect in my hand that I wanted to hold her hand all the time.

We never got into a relationship in any way. Never kissed, nothing, just held hands as friends. And yeah, maybe this isn't a truly epic relationship story, but when it comes to hand-holding, does it need to be? What truly made hand-holding with her so epic was that no one else's hand felt or fit my hand better than hers at that time. So epic and wonderful was that hand-holding that we would even take naps that way. And hardly ever did our hands get all sweaty either. It was so natural and such a good fit that it felt weird if we didn't hold hands when we hung out.

It didn't matter where we went or what we did, most of the time we were holding hands. It was always so easy and effortless that most of the things that it felt natural from the very first time we held hands. Pretty much everything that I wrote about here in this chapter were no-brainers between her and I. Almost completely intuitive. For some reason, it wasn't always that with other women, but when you are both on the same page without having to think about it, everything is easy. This was even more reason to keep some of the things in this chapter in mind. Not everything, including hand-holding, will always occur intuitively, so it might be of some use to keep some of these things in mind just in case. Ok lover?

Chapter 2: Kissing: No-One Likes to Kiss Bricks

I've always approached kissing nervously and excitedly. I never really knew exactly what a girl's lips would feel like, how they would move, how they would kiss, or how it would feel to me. I only knew: (a) I love how girls' lips and tongues felt, and (b) I wanted to do it all the time because it turned out to be my favorite thing to do, and it really turned me on.

My philosophy started out as just being as adaptable and fluid as possible due to inexperience. I learned quickly that most girls liked their own kissing style, so I would just adapt and mimic whatever they did in the beginning. That helped me learn about what I liked and didn't like, and then I developed my own preferences in kissing. Eventually, I realized that you can influence kissing by thinking of it as a passionate dance of hunger and appetite. I then made sure how I held the girl and how I kissed her would wordlessly communicate to her the hunger and passion that was within me for her.

My philosophy then evolved into waiting for the moment when our eyes and faces would come close, and the gravity was undeniable. To make the first kiss nothing fancy or sloppy, but rather a soft, relaxed meeting of our lips as we inhaled each other deeply. After that, to go with the flow and let the dance begin, while never forgetting what an honor and a blessing it is to get to be that intimate with this person.

Or, if I was too unsure or nervous about when or how to kiss, I would just ask if I could kiss her. Either way works.

Highlights:

1. Whatever you do, keep your lips relaxed. No one likes to kiss bricks, hard surfaces, or really hard and rubbery things. (Except for maybe the Blarney Stone).

2. Remember, kissing is a dance! Do the same dance and things will go great. If you wanna bachata and she wants to mambo, it's not gonna work out. Pick the same dance, even if it isn't your favorite, or create your own together.

3. Absolutely no darting of the tongue into a girl's mouth no matter how hard the urge. Who does this when first kissing a woman? Really?

4. Drippy wet lips are a no-go. That means, don't freaking slobber over your lips and make a slurpy wet mess before you go for a kiss.

5. Caballeros, please, for the love of lips, do not think that someone else's lips are a chew toy.

6. Do not kiss with your eyes open. Generally. Some women think this is creepy.

7. Keep your cake hole clean. (Cake hole = your mouth/mouth hole). This basically means practicing good oral/facial hygiene.

8. Don't overthink kissing. And while you are at it, take away your ego. You're not the world's greatest kisser, nor is your kissing style the right/only one.

9. If a girl has lipstick of any type, only go for simple pecks or simple kisses on the lips. No fancy kissing. And if she has lipstick on her teeth, gently whisper it into her ear discreetly so she doesn't get embarrassed.

10. If you know you're going to eat together, come prepared to clean your potentially dirty mouth.

11. If the girl has braces, keep gentleness in mind and be considerate.

12. If you have a ton of facial hair, don't rub a woman's face off with lots of face-twisting while kissing.

13. Don't try to suck on a woman's tongue early on. Just kiss normally.

14. Taking her cheeks or face gently into your hands before a kiss is a thing that can be nice to do, but only in the right moment.

15. If you get canker sores, or if you also get herpes sores (commonly known as cold sores), on your lips and mouth, do not kiss a woman until they are completely healed. Also, keep an eye out for them on her as well before you kiss.

16. When timing a kiss, if you have no idea when to kiss or go for a first kiss, it's always ok to ask, "may I kiss you?" How you ask matters. Starting with "may I?" or "would you like to?" are simple yet reliable ways to begin to ask.

Be aware of the fact that there are people who pierce their tongues, lips, and cheeks in various ways. This can complicate kissing for some of you in subtle ways and can also leave you confused as to how to kiss, should your instincts fail. Taking it one step further, there are also people who have their tongues split. As in, having their tongues cut down the middle in order to split them into two. Like a snake. If you happen to be to the point where you are about to kiss one of these people, be sure to casually talk about whether there are any differences, preferences, or if any special considerations should be taken.

Alrighty, if after reading the abbreviated version of my advice, it didn't make complete sense to you, lover, or you need more details in order to form a better mental picture, then read on!

The Basic Rules in Depth

1. Keep your lips relaxed! No one likes to kiss bricks, hard surfaces, or really hard and rubbery things. Think soft, like fluffy pillows or relaxed like May's lips in 'Dumb and Dumber' when a finger gets pressed against her lips while telling her to shhhhhhh. Had her lips been all flexed and hard, it wouldn't have turned out as funny. But because her lips were relaxed, they were flexible and malleable for that scene. Maybe your lips don't need to be that relaxed, but hopefully, you get the gist – relaxed but moving and alive.

2. Kissing is a dance! Just like dancing, you can't walk up to a dance partner and do the bachata while they're doing the tango. It won't work. Seriously won't work. Trying to force your kissing style on someone else won't cut it either. Kissing is about flow and harmony. If you're unsure or lack confidence in your kissing game, think of it as a dance. Learn the rhythm, follow each other's lead, and adapt. Let each kiss bring you closer until you create your own unique chemistry or style together.

Now, for those of you who are naturally talented and easily adaptable kissers, this might be a non-issue. However, for those who are unsure, lack confidence in their kissing game, have little to no clue, or are new to the art of kissing – or simply lack an underlying philosophy when it comes to interactions with females and their mouth holes – remember that kissing is like a dance.

If you don't know how to kiss and you don't know how to dance, you might not relate to those analogies. If you're the stiff type or not comfortable with dancing, being in the flow of the moment can be challenging. As a result, you might end up trying to force a kiss, applying too much pressure, using your tongue unnecessarily, or feeling disgruntled if the girl you're kissing doesn't respond as you'd like.

In such cases, consider what I wrote in Book 1: The True to Yourself Man, and specifically the chapter about learning to dance.

Learning to dance teaches you about rhythm in motion, how to follow, how to lead, and the basic steps. This repetition builds the foundation for instinct. Interestingly, these skills are directly translatable to kissing, albeit in a completely different context. Unless, of course, you're kissing while dancing!

And if everything else intimidates you or fails, communicate openly during those first kisses with a new girl, your first girl, or a girl you haven't kissed in a long time. Let her know: "Hey, I'm a bit nervous (or it's been a while), so I might need a little gentle coaxing or some kisses before I relax and get in the flow." You don't have to say it exactly like that; it's just an idea, but hopefully, you get the point.

Use your soft lips to remain flexible and adaptable. Flow with each other and treat each kiss as an opportunity to come closer in harmony until you create your own unique kissing chemistry or style together. That's what I want you to consider: when you kiss someone with different styles, focus on creating something new that works for both of you. It becomes special because you both contribute a bit of your individuality to create something unique between you.

When you achieve that with someone you kiss, it opens you up and helps you understand what the other person desires in a kiss. Rarely do you randomly encounter a girl where the chemistry is 100% on point. I've been fortunate enough to experience this, and it can be mind-blowing. However, don't count on it. Mind-blowing kissing isn't necessarily a precursor to a good relationship, but being flexible and adaptable is. I discuss this further in Book 2: Women & Relationships.

3. Absolutely no darting of the tongue, in a stab-like motion, in and out of a woman's mouth when kissing. No matter how intense the urge. The consensus is universal, my dear aspiring lover; not a single girl to date has come forth and said, "You know what I love? I love it when I first go to kiss a guy and the moment we are about to touch lips, his tongue darts out of his mouth and into my mouth like some pseudo penis trying to sex my mouth hole in search of my uvula…" Yeah, literally no girl says that. At all. Ever.

So, keep your flavor-sensing, muscular uvula searching device trapped between that great wall of teeth you got. The appropriate moment for using your tongue will most often be detectable when a woman opens her mouth in such a way that her tongue starts to instinctively come into play. Sometimes it happens right as that first kiss is about to happen. Sometimes it happens later, other times it happens only in extreme passion, and often, the girl you are kissing will initiate it. There are many scenarios. But under no circumstances are you, the human male, to think or be under the impression that somehow jabbing and thrusting your tongue into a woman's mouth is gonna set you up for success or impress the woman into somehow being wowed by your other worldly tongue stabbiness. Got that? Absolutely zero tongue darting/stabbing/probing/thrusting. It is one of the biggest turn-offs I know of when it comes to kissing for girls. The only exception is if the girl specifically requests it. Period. And the statistical probability of that happening is almost zero. Remember that lover because it's on the test. (Real life is the test).

4. Don't think that it's cool to have spongy, soft, drippy, wet lips upon initial kissing with a girl. That means, don't slobber over your lips and make a slurpy wet mess before you go for a kiss. Not cool. It's also a major turn-off for a lot of female humans out there.

Now I understand that some of you out there suffer from the dry lip. I get it, your chips are lapped. Fortunately, in this day and age, there is a magical invention called lip balm. Look it up, it's a real thing. Now, if your lips look like a tree that is shedding a shit ton of bark, you might wanna hydrate first and foremost. Then moisturize second. Maybe also exfoliate your lips. This isn't me saying that you can't lick your lips before a kiss, cuz I do it, and many women do it too. But there is a huge difference between a quick lick of the lip and straight-up waterfall out of your mouth hole, or a fully salivated mustache or beard, in order to prep for a kiss.

Worst-case scenario, barely moisturize your lips with your tongue and then gently rub your lips together. That can be quick and should suffice for a kiss. If you're lucky, the woman's lips are moisturized and it rubs off on ya, then it's a win-win! Unless it's lipstick, in which case, wear it proudly and do not wipe it with your sleeve. Be proud.

Oh, and if you look in the mirror and see dry, cracked lips with small chunks of dry lip skin peeling off your lips, you have no business even trying to kiss a girl like that. Go read the personal hygiene chapter of Book 1: The True to Yourself Man, then come back and try for a kiss.

There may indeed be more things out there that my fellow female humans of earth do not like when it comes to kissing in the beginning. Bad breath, having eaten something stinky like onions or garlic, food in the mouth, cigarette smell, alcohol taste, you name it. But let me address one that is truly noteworthy: biting.

5. Damas y Caballeros, my aspiring lovers, please…for the love of lips, do not think that someone else's lips are a chew toy. Only if you have discussed it, or asked the person if they are into biting, is that acceptable. There are many out there that just roll the dice and do it anyway. Well, I am here to tell ya, once again that the vast majority of human beings that partake in the mouth-to-mouth, don't like it when it is unwarranted, immediate upon the first kiss, overeager, or just plain too hard. Or, at the very least, announce that you would like to do that beforehand and see if the girl likes it too. Say something, anything. And if a woman does do that to you and you don't like it, speak up. Say something. Don't endure that crap just because you're thrilled to be making out with that person. Unless you like it, then endure away.

6. Do not kiss with your eyes open. This one isn't so much a deal breaker when kissing, so much as it can be a bit creepy to some women. I myself have caught plenty of women with their eye holes open at one point or another, but there has only ever been one who kept her eyes open the whole time. Didn't faze me at all. I just recommend that you don't do it. It's pretty natural to close your eyes as you go for the kiss, so don't resist it and be weird. Just try to remember that with your eyes closed, you can focus on the kiss and sense more of it as well. That's how the world can just melt away and become a world of kissing.

7. Keep your cake hole clean. This basically means practice good oral/facial hygiene. I already covered oral hygiene and how to keep

your cake hole well maintained In Book 1, Chapter 3, but to be super brief when it comes to being out and about with a woman, make sure you have a mini toothbrush, a toothpick, or a flossing stick with you so that after a meal you can go to the toilet and look at the mirror while you clean your mouth. You don't have to do this if you know your mouth and the amount of gunk that does or doesn't usually build up in it as you eat. So, if you are one of the lucky ones whose mouth is usually clean no matter what you stuff your hole with, then, as you were lover and carry on.

One more detail on this very issue is: don't let a woman walk around with stuff in her teeth either. Be polite and mention it discreetly, or if you have an extra thing to clean teeth with, like a toothpick, give her one and let her know what's where in her teeth.

8. Don't overthink kissing. And while you are at it, take away your ego. That way, you can get more intuitive with your kissing and see if you and the woman that you are kissing can find a good flow.

I do realize that some of us men have no instinct whatsoever when it comes to kissing and you think that puckering your lips like your grandma or mother does is the way to kiss. I'm tellin' ya, it isn't. That is called a pec on the lips. And while not unpleasant, it's usually not the kiss a girl is looking for.

While overthinking isn't something you want to do, some thought will help in the sense I just mentioned. This isn't an algebraic equation, it's lip to lip contact – so if all else fails, just mimic whatever the girl does. I've done this countless times, and sometimes I got it right, other times it took practice, other times I messed it up, and other times I was terrible. But overall, whenever I copied a girl's kissing style, things went great. Which was awesome because it meant more happy kissing, and who doesn't want that?

Some of you men will find, or already know, that you have your own kissing style and like to lead and take charge with your kissing. That's totally cool. There are many women out there who are into that. Just don't overthink it and delude yourself into thinking that any other way of kissing just isn't right.

And did I mention not to use a woman's lips as a chew toy?

9. If a girl has lipstick of any type, only pecks or simple kisses on the lips will do. No fancy kissing. And if she has lipstick on her teeth, gently whisper it into her ear discreetly so she doesn't get embarrassed.

The main reason why I suggest not to kiss if she has thick lipstick of any type, at least in the beginning, is twofold. One – if you kiss her without thinking, you will get lipstick all over your mouth, and/or beard. Sometimes it comes off easy, sometimes it doesn't. And sometimes that stuff is hard to take off your skin, not just from your lips. Two – there are times when a woman won't want her lipstick smeared or smudged or taken off by your mouth. And unless you know that ahead of time, her reaction might not be too pleasant. Especially if it's a special date or a special occasion. Some ladies can be particular, what can I say? Hopefully, though, they don't think it's a big deal and just laugh and roll with it.

There are times when a woman will tell you that it's the type of lipstick that doesn't come off with kissing. Then you're good to go. Even then, don't go for fierce, full-on kissing because sometimes you just never know until the kissing happens – regardless of what the lipstick brand label says.

Another very important aspect to consider is their make-up. Listen here, my fellow lovers, plenty of women out there spend a lot of time and money on make-up in order to look good for themselves and for the men whose attention they desire. So, when you are at a point where a kiss might be a real thing with a girl, please, pretty please, with heavenly sugar on top, pay attention to their make-up. If not for their sake, do it for your own sake…because we end up looking pretty silly with their make-up around our mouths and on our noses if kissing turns into a full-on make-out session.

At the same time, this isn't really a big deal, and easy-going women won't mind it at all and will likely laugh about it, so don't overthink this one. My point is to just be considerate to those women who wear make-up initially to see how they roll.

10. If you know you're going to eat together, come prepared to clean your potentially dirty mouth. If a kiss is in your future, food in your teeth or a dirty mouth or tongue can be a turn off. Either use a tooth pick or carry a small brush that you can use in the bathroom to make sure your cake hole is clean before lockin lips.

11. If the girl has braces, please keep gentleness in mind and be considerate. Some women, even as adults, decide to get their teeth realigned or fixed for their own reasons. When they do, braces are sometimes necessary. In that case, you should approach kissing a bit more gently than normal. Or at the very least, with more consideration.

When a woman has braces, her lips will stick out a bit farther than normal because the braces are now under her lips. This usually also means that her lips could be sore or at least more sensitive. If you kiss too hard or accidentally bump her lips with your teeth in the wrong way, chances are that you will end up hurting her lips and cause her to bleed. In order to avoid this, only a small amount of thought and attention is necessary. I'm confident you can manage that.

The forceful male kisser who likes to dominate and press too hard – you know who you are – is especially dangerous to ladies with the metal mouth. My dear lover, I get it. Some of you are over-eager or like to be dominant when it comes to kissing. You shove your face right into and onto the girl, thereby causing her to back up or lean back, etc. I don't recommend you be this way unless she specifies that she likes that kind of thing. Just never forget that if you do this with a girl who has braces, you will hurt her and make her bleed. Which is not cool at all in any way. But if it is she who shoves hard and cuts her own gums and makes herself bleed because she wants to kiss you so bad, that's a whole different thing. Then you gotta decide if you like it and whether or not you like bloody kisses. All I'm saying is for you to be the considerate one.

12. If you have a ton of facial hair, don't rub a woman's face off with it. Sometimes we men can really get into kissing, which is fine and good. Thing is, if your facial hair isn't soft or moisturized, chances are that it will be rough and prickly. If you move your head and mouth a lot when kissing, you will most likely leave her lips pink, red, and or raw afterwards. Now, not all women dislike this, and not all women are even noticeably affected by facial hair. But just in case they are, take the time to enquire in order to be sure. And if you don't enquire, the appearance of red rash-like marks around her mouth, or any other part you put your scruffy face to, will give you your answer.

13. Don't try to suck on a woman's tongue early on. This should be a no-brainer, but once again, it needs to be said. There are times when kissing, you both get into it to the point where you are practically devouring each other. In those moments, it may not be uncommon for

one or the other to stick their tongue into the other's mouth to get their tongue sucked on. It can be erotic and feel really nice. Just don't do it right away or at the beginning of kissing a woman, especially while still initially dating.

Also, take into consideration that not everyone has the same length tongue. So, whether it's tongue sucking or making tongue-to-tongue contact, pay attention to the differences in tongue length before attempting to suck on a girl's tongue or before letting her do so to your tongue. Otherwise, one of you could be in for a world of ache and hurt, and that will definitely impact kissing desires.

One time, long ago, in a faraway land, during a wonderful kiss, a girl sucked and pulled on my tongue so hard that the pain instinctively made me pull away. She held on to my tongue so tightly that the bottom of my tongue tore before I finally broke away. You heard that right. The flesh that attaches the bottom of my tongue to the bottom of my mouth tore. Big ouch. Don't do that to a girl.

14. Taking her cheeks or face gently into your hands before a kiss is a thing that can be nice to do – but only in the right moment. This is something that you typically see in movies. It just so happens to be something that is not only done in real life but that women enjoy when done in the right moments. It's hard to say exactly when you can do this, but if I had to really pinpoint the best time, it would be when your face and her face are really close together, and you have locked on eye contact for a few seconds at least. Maybe you are holding each other's hands as you face each other and as you inch towards each other's lips. You could then gently take her face into your hands as you both go for the kiss. If you have good instincts, this shouldn't be an issue, though.

If you don't have good instincts at all, then just wait until you have already kissed and you find yourself in a moment where you are looking into each other's eyes wantonly for a few seconds. Then, it should work.

15. No kissing of any type if you have active herpes sores on your lips or canker sores in your mouth.

I would bet that a lot of us have seen people with sores on their lips at one point or another. Whether or not you realize what those bumps or pimply things were on their lips is a different story. Most often, people refer to them as cold sores. Cold sores are, in fact, a form of herpes. Take the time to look that up and do some reading on it. Either way, cold/herpes sores are something that is transmissible to other people through kissing. Or even lip-to-body part contact. Because of that, I highly encourage you not to kiss a woman or any of her body parts if you feel a breakout coming on or if you already have a breakout going on. Wait until they are completely gone and healed before doing any kissing or sexual activity. That especially includes oral sex.

Sometimes you can get sores that can occur in the mouth as well or even on the tongue. These could also not be herpes sores, but rather canker sores. These types of sores can be caused by an overly dry mouth, biting accidentally on your cheeks or tongue and having that little wound turn into a sore, scratching or scraping your gums accidentally can do it, high acidity in the mouth, and even stress. These types of sores, especially under the tongue, can really suck in the amount of pain and discomfort that they can cause. Fortunately, there are several over-the-counter fluids/rinses/creams you can use to help them go away faster. I've had canker sores since I was a kid, so I am very familiar with them.

Of all the things I've tried to help against canker sores, the most effective is a mouthwash called Glyco Thymoline. It's a mouthwash that specifically reduces acidity in the mouth. No, this isn't a paid advertisement but rather a genuine recommendation after much trial and error with years of over-the-counter products. Until I figured out what causes the sores for me, I thought they occurred randomly, and nothing had ever seemed to work apart from hydrogen peroxide, but even then, hydrogen peroxide was only half effective. The Glyco has worked every single time to make them go away faster and to partially reduce the discomfort they cause. You can't really find the Glyco Thymoline mouthwash in stores, but you can order it online. Take the time to web search it and evaluate it for yourself.

Take the time to look up canker sores and the different types of herpes that you can get and what they look like. That too will be worth your while. I would show pictures and cite all kinds of sources, but the book would just get that much thicker, and I believe that you should not believe everything that I write here. Everything I write here is from my own experiences and life education…which of course includes random things I've been told, read, watched etc., over the decades. So, what I humbly request from you is that you web search on your phone the random things I mention here. Experiment and try things out. Don't just take my word for it. Make things real for yourself by making them a part of your experience.

Sores on your lips aren't something you should take lightly. It's also something that you shouldn't pass around to women. Please be considerate and restrain yourself long enough for them to go away before doing anything with a woman. And while canker sores aren't contagious, they are small open wounds in your mouth that can make you more vulnerable to other infections should your mouth come into contact with various feminine body parts that could be compromised in one form or another without you knowing. So be aware, protect yourself and protect others by allowing these things to heal before engaging in anything intimate or at the very minimum, let your partner or date know and talk about it.

Full disclosure up front is the best way to go about these things. None of that "I didn't know" crap or playing stupid. Part of being a true to yourself man is taking responsibility for yourself, and in this regard, it is no different.

16. When timing a kiss, if you have no idea when to kiss or go for a first kiss, it's always ok to ask, "may I kiss you?" How you ask matters. Starting with "may I?" or "would you like to?" are simple yet reliable ways to begin to ask.

I was in my mid 40's on a third date when I asked I girl for a kiss. I really wanted to kiss the girl I was on a date with but I was unsure of how to make the move given the circumstances and my urges giving me mixed signals. I decided to play it safe and asked her if she would like to kiss. Turned out she had never had a guy ask her before and she was 40. Not only did she love being asked before it happened, it's something she never forgot.

Overall, if you don't have a good instinct for kissing, these tips should help. Most importantly, if you can't recall anything else, focus on making kissing a dance and mimicking the style of kissing of the girl you are currently with. You both need to be flexible and flow and sway to see what feels natural…or create a new way of kissing by adapting to each other.

We all have our own way of kissing that feels instinctually good or easy but when it comes to kissing someone new, the excitement of feeling new lips, feeling a different flow, different mouth, lip and jaw proportions, along with the warmth and passion it brings, is something new and unique each time. And if you are lucky enough to find yourself someone whose lips make you never want to kiss another pair, let's hope that for your sake that it lasts a long time. Either way, just be grateful and considerate.

Here are two stories from my past about kissing. Both were fun because I wasn't stubborn. I just tried to go with the flow and see if I could learn more than I already knew about kissing.

The Epic Fail

A long time ago, in what now feels like a different life, I was in the middle of a South Korean club thinking about kicking my friends butt in Armored Core, a Playstation One game. The music, people dancing, all disappeared as I strategized in my mind different tactics and mech builds, when all of a sudden, a tall female Russian with blonde hair, piercing blue eyes, and an Angelina Jolie-like face with full lips approaches me. She wants me to dance. So, I did what any normal 21-year-old male human, who happens to be Puerto Rican, would do. I said ok.

We danced. It was a slow dance, and the next thing I knew, we were making out. Or at least I thought we were. You see, kissing a female that possesses lips with the fullness of a warm sunrise and the feel of the most comfortable mouth pillows, can make you lose sight of yourself when you're that young. Especially if you have never experienced lips like that before. Thusly, those lips in turn made me completely forget how to kiss.

Seriously.

Even though I had trained for years for such a scenario, I never imagined that I would get to kiss a woman's lips with such fruit-like fullness! It was like smooching cushiony clouds within slices of moist velvet that inspired pleasure.

After a few moments of kissing, she pulled back. I stood there kinda stunned, and still in a semi-state of bliss. She smiled ever so lovingly with her perfectly-crafted lip and jaw structure…and then proceeded to immediately slap me in the face.

Now, I know what you're thinking, say what? She slapped you!? Yep. She sure did. But it wasn't a malevolent slap. Nor was it one that was truly meant to harm me so much as it was a slap of endearing shock to wake me up. But still a slap nonetheless because of the sting I felt. To be honest, I broke all my rules for kissing, so it was no wonder that happened. My lips were too hard, I had no rhythm, I didn't flow or dance, I may have licked my lips a bit much and although I have never tongue thrusted, even my tongue was probably too hard and tense when we did touch tongues. As opposed to her tongue, which was soft and had rhythm and flow. Also, I had never ever, ever, ever, ever imagined that lips could feel like that. So, I was caught off guard and just drew a major blank! Essentially, I think I kissed like a fish would.

Then she looked at me while laughing/smiling, and said (in perfect Russian accent form): "That is not how you kiss."

I laughed and smiled and said something to the effect of: "Okay, well, if that's not how you kiss, then show me how."

She basically just told me to relax my lips and move softly or gently first, and not to make my lips so hard by flexing them so that they look like a hard puckered butt hole. I knew all of this already of course but, in that moment, I forgot. Even worse, I failed to apply it! I did my best to focus and follow her instructions like a new soldier learning how to march.

A couple more slaps later, I had it down and perfectly copied her style of kissing.

Even though that epic fail kissing story isn't nearly as bad as some of the others that have happened in my life, it was the only one in which I was slapped and then immediately corrected/retrained on how to do it properly. And me, acknowledging that I indeed did suck at kissing in this moment, I just adapted and learned a valuable lesson in kissing that actually improved my kissing technique while making my cheeks warm and toasty.

So, what's the moral of that story? Even when you think you know how to kiss, you can mess it up. It is totally ok, and maybe even more fun, if you call it out in the moment in a loving and endearing way. You can then talk about how to improve the kiss, sans slaps, and then immediately try again. Kissing is such a joy! It doesn't have to be all stressful, and most certainly nothing to be all serious about. Which means, my aspiring lover, if it doesn't magically work out that first time, laugh, smile, and try again.

The Epic Success

This particular example comes after having been with the same girl multiple times. We had been on several dates, we had sex already, we hung out, and obviously, we had kissed quite a lot. The kissing was great to me, and although her unique jaw structure, along with her unique lips and mouth, felt great, I had to adapt and stay on top of adjusting each and every single time we kissed.

I'm sure you have noticed that there are many different types of jawlines out there. I'm sure you have also noticed the many different types of lips and dimensions to people's faces. All obvious, right? Well, sometimes, those distinct differences can make kissing a bit challenging as the proportions of you and her may go well but not quite right either. In this instance, although I enjoyed kissing this girl, something was always just a bit off, which caused me to readjust constantly. It wasn't until a short time before I moved away, and we didn't see each other again, that we finally talked about kissing and our unique styles.

She opened up and commented that my way of kissing wasn't exactly what she liked or how she thought a guy should kiss her. When she said this, I asked her to show me exactly how she thought I should kiss her (or a guy in general). She gave me the example, and I tried to mimic her style. After successfully doing so, she was suddenly way happier with the kissing, but I had to tell her that although I could kiss exactly how she wanted me to, it wasn't how I naturally kissed. I further explained that in her thinking that I should kiss as she kisses, making it so that the guy now has to abandon how he kisses and then adopt her way.

She had never taken the time to think that maybe it was possible to create a whole new way with someone. Upon considering this for a few moments, she asked me what I would suggest we try. My response was simple: let's kiss and let go of our preferred ways of kissing, and let's get playful in order to see what we create. Well, we had a great laughing time kissing and playing, and eventually we came up with a new and mutual way of kissing that we both liked. It was short-lived since I moved away not long afterwards. But that was an epic moment in my kissing history because it was a genuine period of honesty and openness that prioritized creating something new together in order to get closer. This was much better than either of us trying to force the other person to adapt regardless of our feelings.

Remember, what I covered here are just the basics. You can never go wrong with mastering these simple things in order to create a healthy, tasty, and pleasurable foundation for all the different ways you can kiss in the future. Getting funky, kinky, or freaky is fine and all when you're both into it and like how each other kisses. But if your mouth stinks, you slobber too much, you bite irrationally, can't control your tongue fluidly, are too harsh at the wrong moments, have poor timing, and can't go with the flow or adapt, all that fancy kinkiness is for nothing. Chances are she won't enjoy it that much, my dear lover, and all you're doing then is pushing her towards someone else rather than bringing her closer to you.

Keep it fun. Keep it light. Keep it pleasant…and if all else fails, just copy her style of kissing.

Chapter 3: Ears: Sensitivity Without Fear

After much trial and error, my philosophy when it comes to ears is to first pay attention to whether or not the girl derives any pleasure from her ears being stimulated. If so, then I would only approach them if we have already kissed, and whispering naughty things in her ears has already been established as something she likes. And also, if I was near her neck or kissing her neck for any reason, I always approached it as an addition to other stimuli I was giving.

Highlights:

1. Be sure that the girl whose ears you are about to touch or approach is ok with you messing with her ears.

2. Make sure that the lovely woman's ears are clean and hygienic if you are about to use your lips or tongue.

3. Do not make any loud sounds in her ear.

4. Don't slobber or drool all up in her earlobe or ear hole. No matter how enjoyable it is, keep the bulk of your saliva in your mouth hole.

5. Nibbling gently is ok but straight-up biting is usually a no-go.

6. Watch out for piercings and perfumes.

7. Timing is key, and don't linger longer than necessary. This is a place to visit, not a place to camp.

8. Never underestimate the power of sweet whispers to the ear.

Giving attention to a girl's ears can be a very tricky thing. Sometimes the girl will just be too sensitive and pull away. Other times, a girl will be ticklish. And yet other times, you can do everything right, but her piercings and rampant use of sprays, perfumes, or even make-up, can get in the way unpleasantly. But if all goes well, it will be a very nice and pleasurable experience for her that can increase the passion/sexual desire within her. Just remember not to dwell there too long as there are other places to be.

The basics in depth

1. Be sure that the girl whose ears you are about to touch, or approach, is ok with you messing with her ears. Not everyone likes their ears messed with. And it can be for a plethora of reasons, so please, be sure to find out first unless she makes it obvious through body language. There are a few ways to do this, but the two simplest I can think of are to either ask directly if the conversation is turning more sensual or find out through casual touch if you two have already kissed. If you and this person are already close, friendly, or aren't afraid to touch each other casually, this is another way to find out so that you don't get embarrassed or trespass in an area that the other person might not be comfortable with.

There are some women who don't like their ears touched at all, so don't let that mess you up in any way. Nor should you use that as an opportunity to try to grill her as to why or to convince her to let you try. Just accept it and move on. It's one less thing to think about or worry about when it comes to intimacy. Not to mention that by just accepting that boundary and creating a feeling of safety, she might want you to give them attention in the future in her own time.

2. Make sure that the girl's ears are clean and hygienic. The last thing that you want to discover, if you start touching this girl's ear with your fingers or lips and tongue, is that her ears are full of chunky wax and blackheads or flaky skin or just plain dirty. Or, if they have any number of piercings, the holes in which their piercings reside also aren't clean, or maybe even infected.

I know that it might seem highly unlikely that a woman would have something like that going on but I'm here to tell ya, they can. And some do. Been there, witnessed that, done that, got the t-shirt, and the movie never made it past VHS. Women are human too, so they miss things. Because of that, it happens. Just pay attention so that you aren't caught unawares. Oh, and if she becomes your girl, then mention it because it's a hygiene issue.

3. Do not make any loud sounds in the person's ear. Both intentional and accidental. Use caution and be attentive. This matters because when you go to whisper, you almost always do it in very close proximity to someone's ear. That's because you know on some level

that anything loud while being that close is no bueno. Things like coughing, making squeaky kissy noises with your lips, breathing overly hard, or even moaning above a certain noise level will likely not be received well. Keep that in mind, lover – pleasant feels and pleasant sounds only.

If you have never played with a girl's ears, but one has played with your ears and made a loud noise in yours, use that as an example. Or if not, then I'm sure you have some kind of headset and that you have, at some point, listened to something that was so unexpectedly loud that it hurt your ears. Just remember this so that you keep your noises to a minimum. And don't forget about hard breathing through the nose too because it also makes constant noise directly into the ear – so breathe easy.

4. Don't slobber or drool all up in the woman's earlobe or ear hole. Your mouth and tongue naturally have saliva, so of course some wetness/moistness is unavoidable, and in many cases it's pleasant, but that doesn't mean that you get leave a big ole deposit of it all up in there. Try to keep it to a minimum if you can. Just remember not to make a loud sucking sound if you have to keep excess from coming out of your gullet.

The gentle warmth of the touch of lips is great and can be a very intimate thing. It's also very important to be aware that there is a fine line between a pleasant intimate moment and one that quickly goes south where the other person suddenly stops you because they feel nothing but wet slobber all over their ear hole. In fact, it is perfectly ok to use your fingers to gently wipe any excess from her ears or, if it is only a small amount of saliva there, you can even blow gently, not directly into her ear hole, around her ear to speed up the drying process. But better to just not get carried away.

5. Nibbling is ok, but straight-up biting is usually a no-go. Once again, this usually applies in the beginning. This is one of those things that you need to play by ear. (Pun intended). If your approach involves any amount of teeth, then at some point you are going to want to use those teeth to nibble some part of the ear. Just remember: nibble, don't bite. The exception to this is if the woman tells you that they want you to bite, in which case your response should be something like, "how hard?" If that is what ends up happening, just be sure to work your way up with the amount of gentle pressure you use. For the most part, though, I find that gentleness works best in this area.

Remember, the goal is to induce pleasurable sensations – not to take a chunk of flesh off.

6. Watch out for piercings. Piercings are pretty ornate when done well in a person's ear. But oftentimes, having piercings can make navigating the ear way more of a challenge from a lover's perspective. Because of this challenge, don't run away from it. Learn to observe for the simple signs of good hygiene. Eliminate the use of teeth when piercings are present because clanging your teeth against metal, or heaven forbid, you snag an earring on a tooth or something, this is definitely not a pleasant experience. And to make matters even more complicated, if you yourself have a tongue piercing then you really want to be careful! Like super-duper, extra careful. There is a probability that you may accidentally snag your tongue on a piercing on their ear, and that will only be funny in hindsight.

For most ladies, the ears can be a really powerful erogenous zone. I know that for me personally, it wasn't until the age of 19 that I encountered a lovely human of the female type who absolutely loved to mess with my ears. I quickly discovered that it was a direct line of intense pleasure to my lower back, right in line with my kidney area. It was so intense that often, I couldn't tolerate the intense pleasant feeling for very long at all. I could literally feel the line of sensation/pleasure/ energy go from my ear, around the back of my head, down my neck, down my spine and then feel the buildup of sensation on the side of my lower spine that also coincided with the ear that was being stimulated. I loved it and hated it all at the same time. It made it so there was always this internal struggle of "don't stop!" and yet simultaneously, "this is so intense! It's awesome, stop! Please don't stop!" Of course, it always made me laugh while I cringed and desperately tried to endure the horribly pleasurable sensation.

This is why I always encourage consensual play and exploration. You just never know what you might discover or how much fun you might have.

7. When it comes to messing with someone's ears, though, you really have to be careful because if your timing is off or just plain bad, the other person can react in a confused "what are you doing?" kind of way. So please, don't be in the middle of a conversation and then decide you want to dive right in and touch another person's ears. Or worse, be in the middle of an amazing kiss and then gamble by stopping and going straight for the ears (which can be a thing if you

have an ear fetish). A good rule of thumb for me has always been that if I find myself kissing the neck area and working my way up, it's usually a good opportunity to go for the ears.

8. Never underestimate the power of sweet whispers to the ear. Apart from all the physical touch highlights that I have emphasized here, quite possibly the most important one above them all is the effect you can have on a woman when you say the right things in the right way in her ear.

Don't forget that we men are the primary visual ones. Women are more easily stimulated by other things. One of those things is the power of words. While phone calls with sexy talk and messages with allure can be hot to either of us, nothing beats talking to a girl and then getting to whisper something in her ear. Doing this in such a way that makes her excited, alongside being filled with positive sensations from the reverberations of the sounds entering her ear, which can also make her get horny and wet.

So, what to say? Well, that is really difficult because girls from various places around the world are different. Add to that different cultures and language backgrounds, and then it becomes obvious to me that there are only two ways to have an idea as to what to say. The first is experience. If you have enough experience with girls, and of paying attention to what turns them on etc., you'll have a pretty good idea of what to say and can apply those words over time.

The second way is to pay attention. And you don't have to have a girlfriend to do this. If you aren't the type to want or need more than one woman, or to go through the time and painstaking process of multiple women over the years, then just make sure that you have genuine conversations with the woman you are interested in. Or, if you have never really been the sweet-talking and whispering in the ear type, finally start learning with the woman you are with. At least to such a degree that the things that she likes, loves, and is turned on by are clearly delineated in your head. That way, as you start to bond, get closer and mutual attraction and desire starts to manifest, you can heighten her experience and yours, by saying the right things. This is NOT to manipulate her into sleeping with you because you want a trophy fuck, but rather because you are genuinely interested and enjoy getting her turned on and wanting you before you get all sexual or have sex.

I'm sure you could go out there and find a whole list of things that, generically, men could say that women would like, but none of that would be exactly customized to the girl you are with. So, while there are some bits to learn by looking something like that up, or by surveying the women you know, I would encourage you to think about harnessing your attention to detail, alongside your wordsmithing and conversation skills. That way, if you are really into the girl, she can also see how you are paying attention by how you say certain things in ways that are enticing or exciting to her.

Now, as far as how to say those things in her ear and the timing: the first thing you will have to get evaluated is whether or not you have the kind of voice a girl, or the girl you like and or are with, actually enjoys. Hate to say it, but not all of us have the kind of voice that will have that kind of effect on a girl, even if you are sly with words. Just as an example, I feel like I don't have a particularly noteworthy voice. Nor do I think it's sexy when compared to other men who are noted for their impressive voice. But, since I am Puerto Rican, when I speak Spanish to a girl, even though I don't have that particular Puerto Rican accent and manner due to being raised all over the world, most women have reacted positively to me speaking Spanish to them close to their ear whenever the moment is right. Can that be universally said for most Spanish? Yes, because it's considered one of the sexy love languages. Now, take, for example, people who speak Hindi or Chinese. Those languages and their corresponding English accents aren't particularly known for their sexiness. Whereas a Spanish or Italian accent when speaking English are. If your inherent voice and language and accent aren't of the mostly universally sexy type, then whispering in the ear, even with the right words, might not have much of an effect. Or, at the very least, the odds are stacked against you depending on the girl you are with.

Is everything I've explained always true? Nah. I've seen plenty of women who, when they genuinely like you, these things don't matter much. Speaking to her kindly and sensually will work just fine. You whispering even normal things in her ear can work just fine. But what I've covered usually applies in some form until a strong connection is established with a girl.

Like I described from the outset, the way to say what you want to say to her in her ear is with a clear voice first and foremost. Speak confidently, enunciate, and if you ask a question, wait for her response. The response is everything. This will tell you whether you have had the desired effect and how to proceed after that…or if you had no effect and to leave it alone. At worst, the girl will laugh at your attempt either because it didn't work or because you tickled her ear.

You can follow up with the stated intention if indeed you intend to do something. You can follow up with a gentle caress or touch, or even with a gentle but firm kiss on the neck or ear area to drive the message of the whisper home. But the actual words that come out of your mouth all depend on the situation and the mood. For example, if you are both talking and enjoying each other, but then you hear her stomach grumble, you could whisper in her ear something to the effect of, "How about we get out of here and get some tacos?" She might smile and laugh, and respond with an enthusiastic "yes" while also positively affected by the closeness and subtle but quick intimacy of that action.

If you're kissing passionately but you haven't touched her anywhere private yet, whether it's your first time or your hundredth time in this situation, you could then work your way to her ear and say something to the effect of, "Are you hungry for more?" Or "where shall I touch you next?" When said with the right intensity and confidence during heated kisses, the answer will likely be a positive one.

There's room to play with how you do it and when. Just remember not to force it. These types of things usually have their way of making themselves known when the moments are ripe for closeness. Just don't ruin it by talking really dirty too fast or too much. Saying something like, "I really wanna fuck right now…" or "my cock is so hard! Wanna feel it?!" Or even, "I really want you to suck my dick!" These just aren't comments you whisper into a woman's ear – unless you are both bonded already or you two have that type of sexual understanding already. Keep it clean, suggestive, and simple at first. If you play with her imagination, the effect may even be better than you imagined.

The Epic Fail

So, no shit there I was, finally about to figure out the key to teleportation while playing a video game in my room, when all of a sudden, this girl walks through my door and wants my attention. Naturally, I stopped what I was doing because, you know, girls were always more important than dicking around with a game I'd played 3,069 times.

This girl and I had already messed around quite a bit. Since we had some sexual history, I knew how to read her and pretty much figured that we were going to end up making out. I also realized she was nervous for whatever reason, or was it excitement? Anyway, I interrupted her talking by planting one on her lips – and she instantly pounced on me. As we kissed and got hotter and heavier, I worked my way up to her neck and to her ear. Unfortunately, due to the intensity of the passion, I was a bit too eager and hungry (Not food hungry)! When my lips made contact with her ears, my teeth practically escaped out of my mouth with too much over-eagerness. Although she barely winced when my teeth made contact, what happened next killed the momentum and the intense passion of the moment.

I got a bit too excited and overestimated my knowledge of what she was into. Not only did I end up tonguing her ear way too much – and with too much saliva – but I was also breathing heavily right into her earhole! Almost simultaneously, I accidentally made a loud, squeaky kissing noise as a result of all of the above, plus my lips coming together in a weird way. She immediately pulled her head away from me and exclaimed a loud, "aaowww!!", while wiping the slobber off her ear.

Needless to say, I felt bad. I also couldn't help but laugh as well. I did apologize…profusely. Then she tried to tackle me and do the same thing to me – so that I could experience how it felt! We wrestled a bit, she got her way because I thought it was fair, and she did the same thing to me. Of course, because I saw it coming, and we were laughing the whole time, it wasn't as bad as an unexpected assault on your unsuspecting ear. Still wasn't pleasant because of her exaggerated licking, biting, and squealing, but it was funny. I seriously almost peed my pants.

Fortunately, we just skipped onto other things after all that. Still, she was a bit hesitant to let me near her ears afterwards, and it became a joke of sorts. She became more sensitized in that area due to her new awareness, which resulted in her being more ticklish there overall. A fun fact I quickly exploited, but that was pretty much it.

This scenario was epic in my failures but nowhere near as bad as it could have been had it not been such a fun, intense, but lighthearted interaction between her and I. Which, again, I mention because when intimacy isn't taken so seriously (as in do or die or deal maker or deal breaker) and can be morphed into fun play, then mistakes or mishaps can have a whole different impact. This also creates a safe space for each person not to be perfect, or get everything just right, when you don't yet fully know each other's likes and dislikes. That's a really healthy and freeing position to be in.

Here's an additional fail. I once knew a girl who was an acquaintance for a long time. Didn't really hang out or really take the time to get to know each other. We had seen each other around randomly, and I had cordially said hello to her. Then out of nowhere, and quite suddenly, we connected! After the mutual sudden interest, the first time we really hung out, we got pretty close fairly quickly. Next thing I knew, we kissed. After we kissed, we stayed close, and I kept my hand on her neck, gently rubbing it and softly touching her cheek. As I looked at her, I moved my hand to her neck and then her ear. I gently started to touch and rub it in a kind and adoring way, but little did I know that she did not like having her ears touched. Like, at all. She gently took my hand down from her ear and explained to me that ears are no bueno for her. She was also about to proceed to explain why, but I stopped her. I said, "You don't need to explain or justify it. Just telling me that your ears are off limits is enough."

We talked about it briefly, and she ended up sharing a little about her past and the why of it all. It was fascinating to say the least but, in retrospect, I did neglect something that I normally would have done. As I was caught up in the moment, it was easy to forget. Normally, when I start to get closer to someone, one of the first questions I ask is if there are any things that person does not like or areas on their body that are off limits.

Fortunately, the girl was very aware and ever present. She knew I meant no harm and acknowledged that she forgot to mention this preference, just as I had forgotten to ask.

The Epic Success!

I'll never forget one particular night I was with a heavenly specimen of a female, getting all passionate in bed and about to do the sex…when I decided to reach for the nape of her neck. Simultaneously, I leaned in so that I could also touch with my lips what my fingers and eyes were taking great delight in. For whatever reason, I spent but the briefest of seconds on her neck – and went straight for her ears.

The moment my lips reached her ears, she gripped the bed sheets, slightly tensed up and exposed her neck to make sure I had better access to her ear. I gotta admit, this was sexy as hell. I carefully reached with my other hand and, with just the right amount of pressure, traced my fingers up her neck and moved her hair onto her head. When her hair was in place, I gripped her hair firmly at the base of her scalp, thereby holding her head in place while simultaneously brushing my lips against her earlobe and working my way up slowly. All the while ensuring that my breath was light and gentle.

After getting to the top of her earlobe, my lips were already moist, so I pressed them together over her earlobe and worked my way back down. I also paused momentarily to press my teeth and give just the right amount of pressure to my nibbles, all the while enjoying her moans and writhing on the bed. I tugged on her ear a bit, both with my lips and just gently enough with my teeth, but I didn't linger too long. There is a whole body to explore after all. I turned her head to the other side and did the same thing to her other ear before she could no longer bear it…at which point she pounced on me.

Post sex, I commented on her bodily responses to some of the things we did. I mentioned my approach with her ears, and I was elated to hear that she loved it and that I had read and responded to her desires perfectly.

Woo-hoo! It's always nice to get a little validation about my instincts because it helps me to build confidence in my interpretations of what I feel and the impulses I get. I don't ask for a review, mind you. I wait for the right moment, or if it comes up in conversation, how pleasant this or that was. Sometimes this is greatly appreciated because it shows that I care enough about pleasing my partner and the best way to do that is through direct feedback after the fact – rather than asking in the moment. It's different for everyone. Sometimes talking about it isn't cool with certain women because they think that it takes away from the magic, or they question why we have to talk about it at all, so I've learned to anticipate that too. In this case, I got everything right. No squeaking sounds, no hard breathing, no biting too hard, slobbering, nothin'. I freakin' nailed it. Admittedly, her bodily responses and movements made it easier because she didn't try to hide her pleasure.

Good luck with the neck area, lover. It really is something else.

Chapter 4: Hair Play/Caress: The Windblown Waterfall

Women tend to feel many different ways about their hair. One thing is for certain, though, if they spend hundreds of dollars to make it look good, they will feel very unpleasant feelings towards you if you mess with it. That aside, when their hair is washed and brushed in a normal way, playing with their hair in and out of bed can be something they really enjoy. But only if they want that kind of attention from you.

Golden rules:

1. Do not mess with a woman's hair if she just had it done. Not sure if you knew this before, but now you can't claim ignorance. The majority of women's hairdos can be very expensive. Mess that up at your own risk.

2. On the flip side, a great deal of women love their hair played with. But you gotta know how they like it, which means you have to ask.

3. Not every girl has the type of hair that you can play with. If that's a thing you really like to do, be sure to date someone you can do that with.

4. Having rough nails, hangnails, and even rough calluses on your hands can snag hair randomly and accidentally.

5. Playing with hair does not mean yanking it or pulling on it. It is more like running your fingers through it by starting at the base of her scalp so that you can make contact with the skin, then gently slide your fingers through the length of the hair.

6. Pulling a woman's hair in sex is not something you should do belligerently or erratically. Getting it wrong can be the difference between her getting more turned on or completely turned off.

Hair, in and of itself, has no nerves. In that sense, it does not feel. When a woman says that they like their hair played with, it actually means that they like the sensation of the tugging of the hair root on the scalp. It's a nuanced thing, but accurate. I have found that the feeling of someone's fingers/hand going through another person's hair, while making contact with the scalp, to be the most pleasant sensation they like. If you find something different, then roll with that.

The basics in more detail

1. Do not mess with a woman's hair if she just had it done. Some of you might be oblivious to this but please do not mess with a woman's hair when it has been done up fancy or stylized at a hairdresser. They pay good money to get these things done, and they don't need you or me comin' along going, "wow, nice hair!" And then trying to touch it with our grubby hands or man paws. So, if you want to be a better lover, you had better pay attention to detail in this arena. Otherwise, you will find out quickly what can happen if you mess with a woman's hair when she does not want it messed with.

2. On the other hand, many women love having their hair played with. Sometimes your partner may even ask you to play with her hair. One simple way that I have learned to detect whether or not a girl likes her hair played with is a real no-brainer. Can you guess how? Just ask. Now don't go around asking any girl. That's considered creepy. But if you have been talking with someone and you two dig each other, while watching a movie, or just during an idle conversation, it might be a good time to bring it up or ask. Obviously, it's easy if you two are a couple already.

3. One more thing to keep in mind, though, is that not every girl has the type of hair that you can do this with. And some girls just plain don't like it. So please be sure to ask if your powers of discernment are not so good. But, above all else, do not try to convince a woman to let you do this. I am not a fan of coercion in any way to try to get another person to do something. There are circumstances in which coercion might be necessary (such as if someone is injured and in clear need of medical attention), but just because you want to play with a woman's hair does not equate to her needing to let you. And for the love of all that is holy, do not ask childish questions like, "Why not?" Sometimes knowing why is irrelevant. Just accept the no. She does not need to justify it in any way. And like I've said before, if that's the case, then it's one less thing to think about or worry about as a lover.

Straight flowy hair – usually good to run your fingers through. Slightly wavy to really wavy – takes a bit of attention but also shouldn't be too much to manage if it's moisturized and not too frizzy.

Really curly hair – yeah don't try to run your fingers through it (unless you have curly hair and know how to navigate it). Afro hair – not hair that you can play with in the sense of running your fingers through it, although it has a lot of fun styling potential.

4. Having rough nails, hangnails, and even rough calluses on your hands can snag hair randomly and accidentally. This one should be easily acknowledged. If you rub any of these things on your own skin, you can instantly recognize the roughness. That roughness doesn't always translate well into smooth sailing if you run your fingers through a woman's hair. It may not be a big deal, but it's worth mentioning. On that note, also take into account any bracelets, watches, or rings you may be wearing. Those things are almost always guaranteed to snag hair. Even when I scratch my head, they often will yank hairs out.

5. Playing with hair does not mean yanking it or pulling on it. The basics of playing with a woman's hair are really rather simple: I recommend that you always start with the hair at its base. You can do this at the forehead hairline, side of the head hairline, or at the bottom of the head/top of the neck hairline. You gently work your fingers into the hair while firmly but gently rubbing them into the scalp. When the hair in between your fingers reaches the back of the crevice between your fingers, you can then slowly pull your hand out towards the ends of her hair. You do this while creating a little resistance with your hand by slightly pressing your fingers together until the hair falls away from your fingers. Then you repeat this again on another part of the head.

Don't force your way through, and certainly don't yank through a hair knot. Sometimes hair becomes entangled and gets into knots. Unless you know how to detangle a hair knot, it's better leave it to the woman to detangle because she probably knows best. That's about it really. Remember, it's all a process. Whether it's your first time ever, or your first time with this person (even though you have done this many times before with others), it is ok to get feedback. You could say, "Hey, how does this feel?" And follow it up with more pressure? Less pressure? Then adjust as necessary. Heck you can even forego fingers and just use their favorite brush.

6. Pulling a woman's hair in sex is not something you should do belligerently or erratically. Getting it wrong can be the difference between her getting more turned on or completely turned off. And if

porn is your guide in how to pull hair, better stop that now, lover, because that's just entertainment.

Some women like their hair grabbed and pulled. Not pulled like in a catfight between two women – an important distinction. I have found that a good approach to this, when you learn what your partner is into (by asking or talking about it), is by running your fingers through their hair from the chosen hairline area. This can be the top of the forehead, back of the head, whatever…and once your whole hand, palm included, makes it into the hair and passes the hair line, you make a fist. When you do that, if you execute it right, you will have the exact amount of hair in your fist at the base of the scalp (it's a straightforward and simple maneuver, so don't overthink it). And voila! You have grabbed their hair and can now pull it. More like, hold onto it fiercely.

There are other ways, of course; this isn't the only way to grab hair. There is the ponytail method, where you make a ponytail out of a bunch of her hair, grab as much of it in your hand as possible, as close to the scalp as possible, and bam! Hair is ready for holding or pulling. This can work with braids as well.

What is important to remember is that "pulling" a woman's hair isn't about actually yanking and tugging on it with the purpose of pulling it out of her head. Remember, we are not here to hurt or harm anyone. It is more about controlling your lover's head through the hair in order to achieve certain positioning, a position of control, or in-the-moment dominance. This can be very exciting to a woman who's into that, as more of her body is now under your control for sex and pleasure.

It's very important to distinguish between being dominant through this act and coming off as an egotistical jerk (or a flamboyant dummy) and doing it in the heat of passion or during foreplay. Again, you must get to know the person's likes and dislikes in this. Timing is important, as is knowing if it's the right moment. Otherwise, you might just turn the person off or piss them off due to hurting their neck, hurting her head, pulling out hair, or pulling out her hair extensions. Not the intended goal.

What does this translate to? When in doubt, communicate! At its most basic, simply caressing a woman's hair can be a good enough start.

Hair play can be fun. For me personally, a woman's hair is an indispensable part of their allure. It is a part of their being that, like all their other parts, I strove to understand in order to enjoy. Now that's not to say that a woman with no hair is a deal breaker. I find bald women extremely attractive and even had a girlfriend with no hair once. But unless you plan on dating exclusively bald women, it might be better for you aspiring lovers to memorize the basics of a woman's hair and hair play.

The Epic Fail

This story is actually about what happened to me with my long, wavy/curly hair as opposed to me messing up while playing with a woman's hair.

I stood one day, at a friend's house, with a glorious mountain view in front of me, thinking about vaginas, when all of a sudden, the girl with me wanted to play with my hair. Mind you, my hair is not exactly the type that you can just easily play with. Since I decided to grow it out, it has turned into a curly, tangly, two-foot-long, black, head dress. My own thoughts and feelings about my hair are entirely based on its need for constant maintenance and attention, and how to keep it healthy, so that it isn't all knotted and frizzy all the time. To almost everyone else, my hair is the subject of attention to various degrees because of its curliness, length and desirability to women. Straight-haired women apparently all crave curls. No idea why. Anyway, back to the girl.

This particular girl who started to stroke my hair had her own set of hairs on her head that just so happened to be even more tightly curled than my own. In light of this fact, I didn't worry about her bringing her hand up to stroke my hair because I figured, and mistakenly so, that she a) knew how to stroke the curly hair on my head, and b) might also know how to play with it in such a way that I might be able to learn a thing or two. That turned out to be a big nope.

As her hand made its way about halfway down the length of my hair, her fingers snagged. Then she kept going, snapping that curl-turned-knot, then proceeded down towards the ends of my hair…yet again getting caught up in the curls. She was forced to bring in her other hand to rescue herself from my hair.

Meanwhile, I withheld some of the anger caused by the pain, as my head is still very sensitive when having hair yanked out of my head. I let out a significant "ouch!" Surprisingly, I was met with a look of 'don't look at me, it isn't my fault, it's your curls' fault!' In the next moment, I was pretty clear about how I felt towards her look and remark. Then I followed that remark with an explanation as to how you can't just blindly stroke hair like mine, and that if she really does not know what she is doing to just refrain from doing it.

After some discussion, it became clear that she was also trying to be comforting to me, as well as show some affection. That I understood, so I couldn't be mad at her in any significant way – even though she tried an emotional reversal on me when her comfort attempt backfired. I guess she was butt-hurt that I was actually hurt at her unskilled attempt at soothing me by stroking/playing with my hair. Regardless, the whole brief experience served to teach me a big lesson about how to go about playing with different types of hair. Especially, with hair like mine.

I honestly wish that that was the only time she tried that move but, almost immediately after, she tried playing with my hair again while we were on the topic of it! And sure enough, this time it snagged on her ring and her nails. And my reaction was literally, "What the heck were you thinking? For real! Again?! We just went through this!"

She unsnagged herself from my hair quickly enough this time, so I very quickly revoked any and all unrequested hair play. I also made sure to show her the absolutely simplest way for her to touch my hair – without causing me physical harm.

It was because of this experience, and a few more afterwards, that I finally got a firsthand experiential perspective on what women have to deal with. I understood how they felt when men or boys or children, who do not know what they are doing, can do to someone to then make that person not want to let anyone touch their hair. It's in these little traumas or interludes, whatever you wanna call them, that can close someone up bit by bit. And it is all due to the fact that we are so uneducated about so many things! So, we blindly go into uncharted territory with another person, which often fails, and then, in turn, that transforms our good intentions into someone else's foreboding.

I know, I know, sometimes you just got to figure these things out through trial and error. From experience, all I'm saying is, when you go to play with or to touch someone else's hair, stopping for a moment and asking two simple questions, "May I touch it?" and "Is there any particular way you prefer?" can go a long way in preventing hair mishaps and making you a more considerate lover.

The Epic Success

As far as epic successes go, I've definitely had my share of those. Even if they didn't start out as successes, my acquired skills usually paid off in the end.

Here's one example....

I was part of a group tour for a single soldier program when I was in the military. I can't remember much about where we were or what it was that we were sightseeing, but I do remember that when I got onto the bus, the majority of the people on the bus were girls. To the delight of my eyeballs, practically all of them were very attractive. And to boot, they all had really nice hair. I mean all of them. Not sure if they all shared details about hair care back at the hotel, if they used the same stuff, or if there was something in the water, but let me tell ya…all the hairs were shining and shimmery and glistening and flowy. There was plenty of epic hair tossing too. You know, like those girls do in the movies.

I sat on an aisle seat on the bus. Can't remember if it was near the front, middle, or rear, but I do remember the laughter and all the talking that was going on. After a few minutes, the girl in the seat in front of me threw her hair over the headrest and right in front of my face. I literally felt the hair whoosh in front my face, stroking my nose, and filling the air right in front of me with the sweet scents that only women can exude.

No longer was I staring at the back of the seat in front of me; now I was staring at a thick bunch of brunette strands of what should be called hair, but I hesitated to do so because they all seemed to shimmer and shine. And with every jolt of her head from conversation with her friend, they waved and moved about, reflecting light and seemingly beckoning me like streamers in the wind.

I reached out with the back of my hand and gently touched the hair, because in this instant, it appeared to have a life of its own. Sure enough, it was soft. Like silk. Magical even. It was such a beautiful sight that I glanced around to make sure that this wasn't some sort of weird hair dream. Sure enough, so many hair varieties on board the bus and all demonstrating their unique shine and shimmer.

After thinking to myself for a few moments about the absurdity of what I was about to do and ask, I prepared a defense for what words might come.

I tapped the girl on the shoulder from between the seats, mildly interrupting their conversation in the process, and pointed out that her hair was practically in my face. Told her that I didn't mind it…that it was quite beautiful in fact…and wondered if she would mind if I played with her hair.

Well, because I had interrupted their conversation, somehow this stopped ALL other conversations on the bus between all the other girls. I noticed this, felt awkward, but maintained my courage and continued on.

I noticed and felt all the frowned foreheads and discerning looks about me, but I persisted and did not let that intimidate me. After a bit of casual back and forth, I eased her suspicions, and she leaned back more and sat up higher in order to give me access to more hair as well as to her scalp.

So, I began doing my thing. I ran my fingers through it gently at first, enjoying the sensations in between my fingers. All the while monitoring for knots and smoothness. I was super impressed with her hair care. Hardly any split ends, no knots. Just full, soft, shiny hair that was relatively straight – and kinda fluffy?!

I ran my fingers through it higher and higher until I reached her scalp. Then I changed techniques to use part of my fingertips and with a hint of nail as I went from the hairline into the scalp with gentle massaging scratches. I dragged my fingers and nails slowly and gently, all the while keeping bunches of hair separate from each other in between my fingers. Then I would run my hand down a length of hair till it felt about right, and then I would start again with the other and so on and so on.

Then I made a part in the middle, selected a small bunch of hair right at the hairline and gently but firmly, would tug on it and let it slip through my fingers with decreasing resistance until I reached halfway down the lock of hair or to the end. At that point, I would let it go completely. I continued repeating the process on other parts of her head.

During all this, I would catch the sweet scents of whatever it was that she used to wash her hair. It was delightful. At one point, one of her friends asked her how it was. Apparently, the amount of talking she was doing died down until she wasn't talking, just enjoying what I was doing with a pleasant look on her face. I do not recall her response, but after she gave it to her friend, I had a line of hands volunteering to let me play with their hair! It was a really funny scene now that I think about it in retrospect.

Turns out that the bus ride was only long enough for me to play with one other young woman's hair. I was asked at one point how I learned to play with hair like that. And, well, my life, being the fantastic adventure that it is, brought me to a point in my youth where I had a super tight-knit group of friends during my time in Louisiana. My best friend's brother loved it when people played with his hair. So much so that he would often sit on the floor in front of the couch so that we could all take turns playing with it while we watched TV. After observing how others did it, I established a basis for comparison in my mind, tried to replicate it and then improved upon it by asking for feedback whenever I did that to a current girlfriend.

In the end, I came up with my own way of doing it and got to practice on some female friends as well over time. And that was it.

What to take away from the hair chapter? Remember that it is ok to ask for permission and feedback when playing with a woman's hair. They are all different in sensitivity in their likes and dislikes. Remember, my advice here is just basic. If you genuinely tried everything I have suggested, and it hasn't worked, then communicate and try something new.

Also, remember that hair play for enjoyment is very different from hair play during foreplay and sex. And the effect it can have on a woman is also different from woman to woman. Don't assume every girl will respond the same way. That means that if you really like to pull a woman's hair during sex and you go for it with gusto without knowing whether she likes it or not, you might be butt-hurt if you get rejected for that. Conversely, a woman might really like that surprise approach and respond favorably. In either case, talking it through beforehand is ok and helps to create a space of caring about each other's likes and dislikes.

Chapter 5: Neck: Not Just a Vampire's Domain

The goldilocks zone for many. Oh yes, this is oh so true. A woman's neck has so much pleasure potential that it's kind of ridiculous. Seriously. One of my favorite foreplay memories of all time relates to how a woman reacted to me caressing her neck. Navigate this area correctly, and it could be a win-win for you both.

Highlights:

1. Yes, it is a Goldilocks zone for many, but NOT for all. Be sure to know for sure before you make any moves there.

2. Always start gently. Whatever you do, be gentle first, do not jump in with a grip of death, pokey, scratchy fingers or a vampire bite.

3. Your tools are your fingers, hands and lips. That means caresses, gentle holds, kisses, and even nibbles.

4. If you have facial hair, be mindful of whether it is soft, prickly or scruffy. Know the girl's likes and dislikes in this regard if you can.

5. If you decide to use your lips, do not leave a bunch of drool, spit, or slobber on her neck. Sound familiar?

6. Hickeys are a no-go, unless requested, so don't go trying to suck her neck skin clean off.

7. If you know for a fact that the girl likes the use of teeth or a little biting, test nibble before test bite.

8. Merely using the touch of your lips gently on her neck, while breathing in slowly, as you trace your lips from her collarbone towards her jaw, can have a great effect.

9. The back of the neck is also deserving of attention with gentle caresses. Mind the hair, though.

10. The neck is usually given attention before, after, or during kissing and most often when the female is clothed. Don't forget to pay attention to it during and after clothes come off.

The lines and composition of a woman's neck can be very alluring. There is great beauty as well as great sensitivity. For this area, gentleness is the watchword. So don't go getting all hyped up and rough and gruff around the neck. Be considerate, listen to her breath, body language, and reactions to your touches. It is typically safe to spend a little bit of time here, so don't rush, but don't linger either. And if in doubt, be sure to ask about preferences or her personal likes and dislikes because at that point, you can't go wrong (so long as you are able to execute well).

The basics in detail

1. Yes, it is the Goldilocks zone for many females, but not for all. Sometimes bad experiences make it so that women do not like their necks messed with in one, many, or all ways (till trust and confidence can be established, usually). So first and foremost, make sure that it is something the girl is into. And, as I have mentioned before, the safest and easiest way to know is usually just to ask. Talk about it. Please also remember that they don't need to justify why they do or don't like or want something. Just accept the no if she says no.

2. Always start gently. The neck has many different sensitive areas. It's not just full of major nerves; it is also the location of the vital airway, vital blood flow, and is easily affected by temperature changes. This means you don't wanna start off just strangling away, biting, or leaving big ole hickies, especially in a cold environment. Remember, you can always work your way up from gentleness, whether it is touches, kisses, or nibbles. But if you kick it off with too much right away, not only can you harm the girl, but you can also make it so that they never want you or anyone else near their neck again.

3. Your basic tools are your fingers, hands, and lips. With a little practice and through getting to know what the girl likes, nibbling with your teeth can feel really nice as well.

Caressing a lovely lady's neck with your hands and fingers is typically a more sensual touch and reserved for real connection and feelings. Intimately close moments free you up to use your hands and fingers in gentle strokes and in a caring fashion. It might sound strange to read this, but it's true. The neck is a really vulnerable and sensitive area for any human.

In the heat of passion, while gearing up for sex and during sex, more firm and strong holds can generally be more acceptable due to the obvious intensity that passionate sex can bring. I recommend that you focus more on the back of the neck if you go for a neck grab in order to bring her close, or to hold her tightly in that area. It allows you to support her head, it avoids the throat and arteries running through the front of her neck, and it places her hair close to your fingertips should you want to go for that instead. Once again, though, you have to take the girl into consideration. I got a little too intense with one female before I asked about her neck – and she quickly let me know what her boundaries were in that area. Not all women are so upfront. Some endure the mental discomfort or suffer through it mentally, and then either blow up on you or are put off completely afterwards. As aspiring lovers, we're not mind readers, but we can use our voices to communicate.

And as a warning note for when using your lips and tongue, women often use perfume in their neck area. Or they can even have some make-up there as well, depending on whether they stop at the jaw line or not. Placing your lips here can be hit or miss, by a lot. I say that because many perfumes that women wear do not feel good on the lips or tongue – and taste even worse! Same goes for makeup that might be there. If you keep this in mind and think ahead, you can visually scout out the area or have a good sniff or two to check if the area has been booby-trapped! Or, you could just ask.

Apart from being wary of things that taste bad and can rub off onto you, my suggestion here is to start with gentle but firm kisses in the neck area. Depending on your approach angle – from the collarbones up, from the cheeks down, or from the ears down – this will change where your hands are and what you should consider going for. If you're going from the collarbones up, for example, your nose and lips will be involved. You can use both gently to rub against the skin of her neck as you go up from either side, but don't lick. Let the gentle friction of your lips and nose be what she feels as you go up towards her jaw or as you go around towards the side or back of her neck. Wait till that natural pause point before planting a gentle but firm kiss on her neck.

If you're approaching from the cheeks, then back and down, or from the ears on down, your face might be straight or sideways. Most likely sideways a bit unless she's leaning back or on her side. Same thing though. Trace her skin with your lips and even a bit of your nose before planting the kiss. After doing that a bit, then you could focus on kisses and nibbles solely. But whatever you do, don't endure the taste of nasty perfume or make-up because when you kiss then she will taste it as well. Better to mention it when it happens so that she knows because some ladies just aren't aware of this happening.

If you go for the kisses option on her neck, don't just kiss all around. It usually helps to have a goal or destination in mind. For example, if you start kissing her neck where the neck meets the shoulder, you will typically go up from there if you are both completely dressed. So, the ear becomes the destination and the goal potentially. After the ear, you can move towards her jaw line, and by this point, she will either turn to kiss you or allow you to make it to her lips and then kiss. If you are undressing or she's topless already, then you can kiss her neck and work your way down. If you are already having sex and your face is buried in her neck, kissing it, nibbling, even firm bites while there are just fine. You don't have to go anywhere specific in that situation because all you are doing is adding extra sensation to her body apart from the intercourse. Now, most of that occurs instinctively to some degree, depending on you as the lover, but if not, that's why I'm sharing it here.

4. Mind the scruff. As a man, if you have facial hair, always be attentive to the fact that if you are trying to be gentle and sensual, a prickly beard, goatee, or mustache can foil your plans. Any move in that area can easily become something itchy or something to laugh about because it tickles. Or worse, a mild rash because of the sensitivity of the girl's skin.

I find that most women won't say anything about it because, since they are with a man, that is part of the package. Some women even love the scruffiness of facial stubble and how it feels, despite it leaving their skin rashy and pink-looking. Some don't like it, but it's not enough of a deterrent to keep you from being intimate with them. It is worth talking about facial hair, though, because some women like the look of a beard or mustache, but maybe not the feel of it in certain areas. Me personally, I don't like the feel of my own facial hair when doing certain things with women, despite it not bothering them at all. And I know I keep repeating this over and over, lover, and I will continue to, but the easiest way to cover these things is to casually talk about it. How do you feel about this? How do you feel about that? Do you like this or that? You can manage that.

5. Do not leave a line of spit or drool or slobber on the poor woman's neck! This should be self-explanatory, but in case it isn't, please believe me (or just ask the nearest female) that the circumstances, moments, and technique required to make saliva acceptable are not part of the basics. So, forget about it in the beginning.

I know that in porn, spit and slobber is a thing. But in real life, with a girl you just met or are just starting to do things with, that is a no-go. And look, let me confess here that when I am really turned on by a woman, or she is exactly my kinda hotness, or I'm just sex starved, my mouth actually will start to water more at the thought of tasting her lips, body, etc. So, when I start to get intimate with a girl, I have to swallow lots of extra saliva and spit just to keep a woman's neck dry. All of our mouths constantly produce spit and saliva, so I get it, it can be challenging. The easiest thing to do is to keep your tongue out of it and use only your lips. That way you minimize the chance of drooling on her.

6. Hickeys really are a middle school thing. And also hit or miss for adults. There are some women out there who like hickeys for one reason or another. Do not assume that the woman you are with, or are starting to date, does like them. I think the whole idea of a hickey is to leave your mark on the person. But let me tell ya, when the sex is good, or the foreplay is awesome, mark or no mark, it's ok. Only when you get to people that are into kink, S&M, or BDSM and stuff like that do you start to find people who like hickeys or visible markings to be left on them. So, unless the person you are about to get intimate with is into hickeys and such, don't go arbitrarily trying to leave a hickey on a woman's neck.

On the other hand, if you're into hickeys, by all means let her know where you want one and see what she's willing to do.

7. Test nibble before test bite. Again, not all women like teeth on their neck but, if you are going to do this, make sure you ask first. If you haven't asked, and are going for it, do so very carefully. You can even stop just after your first test nibble and ask, "How does that feel?" or "Is that ok?" Whatever you do, do not just chomp down and think it's all gonna be hunky dory because chances are, it's not.

Once you go for it and she says yes, or she clearly likes it or moans in pleasure, now you're in it. At this point, it's about considering how hard to bite and where to bite. From the front, you have the two neck muscles on either side of the throat. Those are pretty decent to start with, but they can be thin, so you must be gentle. The sides of the neck are a bit more robust, but if you start just above the shoulder joint on the trap muscle and work your way up, now you've got something. You can continue that right up until the back of the neck and head, which would then bring you up to her ear area. This is usually much easier if you're standing or sitting.

During sex, it all depends on the position you are in – and your capacity to multitask. I'm all for multiple points of stimulation when it comes to sex, so it's important not to forget the neck area when making love. Just be sure to remember that no matter what the circumstance of biting, don't leave a mark on the woman where it could compromise her job if she can't cover it up. That's why it's a bit better to bite on the back of the neck if it could affect her job. Most women have long hair, and that can easily cover something like that up.

One other thing to take into consideration is that you don't just simply bite skin when you bite. You can try this on yourself on your arm if you like. Where you bite on your arm will determine how much muscle tissue is underneath the skin. Pick a spot, like close to the wrist, where there is little muscle and mostly skin. If you bite into it, unless you take even the bone into your mouth, chances are you're only going to be able to take the skin into your mouth to bite onto. If you do it higher on the arm where there is muscle, then you have to adapt your bite. This is so that you don't just take in skin but also the muscle into your mouth. How you bite will change because now you are actually trying to affect the muscle tissue underneath, along with the skin, but with your mouth. A similar thing applies when going for a bite on a woman's neck.

While kissing on the neck produces one type of sensation, biting a girl's neck needs to take into consideration the skin and tissues underneath because this will produce a whole different sensation. That's why, for example, you don't bite or nibble directly on a woman's throat due to the Adam's apple, which is made up of hard tissue just underneath the skin. It's kissable but not biteable. By sensing the skin and muscle as you practice biting on your arm with different pressures, you can then feel with your teeth more accurately the makeup of the skin and muscle on a woman's neck, so that you don't bite down incorrectly. It can be fun to discover this about a girl if you just take it lightly and get some feedback. But if you can read her body signals and reactions well enough, that too will suffice.

8. Tracing your lips gently across the neck from the collarbone towards the jaw and in other directions is a very effective way to sensitize a woman to your touch before getting more into it. Don't get me wrong, there are moments when you and a woman may just jump right into it – or where even the foreplay starts off intensely. But that's not often the case. Creating some build-up with gentle touches can often go a long way. To that end, instead of licking and slobbering all over a girl, you can relax your lips, leave them a bit parted and then proceed to gently follow the lines of her exquisite form. You can start from the collarbone, her jawbone, cheeks, shoulders, or neck, just make sure that you continue with a destination in mind. Also, make sure that you plant a firm but gentle kiss at the end of your route. And you can do this more than once back-to-back.

9. The back of the neck is also worthy of attention. Usually with gentle caresses. Mind the hair, though.

A long time ago, when I was still a young soldier, I was riding in a truck with a retired older gentleman, and we got to talking about women and random things that we discovered about driving them crazy with pleasure. He mentioned that the back of the neck was an area that he had some success with and proceeded to tell me in detail what he did and how he felt that few people really did that. I mentioned a bit of it in the neck biting section.

When you approach a girl from the rear, whether it's to hug her from behind or to spoon her during sex with her back to your chest, her neck is fully made available to you. If you carefully gather her hair and move it to one side, you'll see it right there.

Unless you have a gargantuan mouth, my aspiring lover, you'll have to pick one side of the neck or the other to kiss and nibble on because that is where the muscles are. As you get halfway up the neck, continue your gentle nibbles and bites and gradually increase pressure until you reach the base of her skull, where the muscles attach. Usually, there is hair there as well, which can be tricky to navigate without biting and pulling hair with your teeth. But if you can manage it correctly, the sensation can truly be something else for the woman you are with. It might just be easier to stop at the hairline, though.

One side note to consider is that you can also have control of her head if you have one hand firmly holding her hair from the base of her head. In the previous chapter, I mentioned that if you grab a woman's hair correctly, you can control her head to a degree in order to enhance the situation by exerting sexual dominance for her pleasure. That means that you would dig in and take control of her head via her hair and then use that to position her head where you want it – so that you can have access to her neck all the way up. And as you take your final bite at the base of her skull, where the muscles end, the force of your grip should equal the force of your bite so that they register in intensity. Don't bite forever or super hard, just firmly enough and for a moment.

All of this is easier said than done, by the way. Chemistry plays a big role – and so does your ability to feel what she likes or to communicate what you're doing. Buuuuuuuut, if she's cool and you're both having fun, it shouldn't be a problem. She might even enjoy herself a little extra, and you too.

10. The neck is usually given attention before, after, or during kissing and most often when the female is clothed. Don't forget to pay attention to it after the clothing comes off. This is pretty self-explanatory, but I added it here because when a woman's clothing comes off, our attention tends to be immediately diverted to her previously covered parts. That's both fine and natural, but as you get more acclimated with multi-tasking when making love, I'm sure you'll be able tell some difference between giving attention to her neck vs not.

The neck area of a woman is truly a hot spot for pleasure and intensity. Some women out there are into way more kinky things when it comes to what they like done to their neck. I've had women start to choke themselves because I wouldn't. I've even had it where a woman wanted me to bite her so hard that she would bleed. I'm still not comfortable with that idea. I'm here to tell ya: when a woman asks you to do something that just isn't you, or you don't have the experience to do it, or it just makes you feel uncomfortable, it is perfectly ok to say no. And when you say no, say it confidently and own it. Just don't let that stop you from trying things that you are curious about.

The general idea to keep in mind with a woman's neck is that it is a very delicate and sensual area…in a way that is unlike any other area of her body. You can just as easily end up tickling her as you could make her swoon with pleasurable sensations. Mood has a lot to do with it, too. If you're in a fun, playful mood and try to do something in the neck area, chances are the woman will be extra sensitive and start to laugh, giggle or something. So don't go trying to push her buttons in that area, if she has any, while goofing around, because it can backfire. There's a chance the fun and giggling could ruin the sexy mood, and that's a wrap. But, if her neck is the key to getting her going and in the mood, then you'd better master that shit quick so you can both enjoy yourselves.

The Epic Fail

Once upon a time, in my barracks room, I was making out with this girl during a long and lovely night, and it was going great. When all of a sudden, I decided to play vampire with her neck…and it did not go so well. First of all, let me say that if you are kissing a girl and the experience is going great, the connection is awesome, and the passion is fierce without a need or want to do anything else, then keep kissing. On this occasion, I had the bright idea of kissing the skin on her neck and nibbling on it. Well, the urge was ever so mild in comparison to how much I was enjoying what we were already doing, but my curiosity got the better of me at the wrong moment, and I rolled with it. Bad idea.

She wasn't too thrilled that I stopped kissing her. This was obvious by the mildly confused look on her face. To her credit, she rolled with what I was moving to do. Maybe out of curiosity, who knows? All I know is that the moment I went for the win on her neck, I quickly realized I'd made an error. Once my lips made contact, I discovered she had some delicious-smelling – but absolutely awful-tasting, bitter as hell – perfume on her neck. My lips, tongue and mouth quickly became saturated with the god-awful taste. To make matters worse, the more I kissed and explored her neck, the worse it got in my mouth. And since I was committed to this act and to seeing it through, boy, did that make it way worse. And yet I endured.

The scent of her perfume and the warmth and feel of her skin were the only two saving graces.

Here's where the whole experience went sideways. As I continued to kiss, nibble and explore her neck, my mouth tasted terrible. (Remember, the only reason I continued was because I had already committed to the act, so I might as well see it through to the bitter end.

Literally). I could no longer be as passionate or serious about it, which changed the overall vibe, and she started to get ticklish. As a result, she began to withdraw her neck and giggle. Once I picked up on the gist that the moment was pretty much over for her, I moved away from her neck and went in for the kiss…which turned out to be a majorly terrible idea!

The moment our mouths made full contact, tongues included, the previous epic kissing was wiped clean from our memories by the new and traumatic sensation from the horrid taste I transferred into her mouth from her own perfume on her neck. Oh, it was so, so bad! And nothing we did after that salvaged the scenario because now we both couldn't get the horridly bitter taste out of our mouths. We even brushed our teeth, rinsed, and scrubbed our mouths.

In the end, what could have ended as an amazing and passionate night of love and sex was ruined by my weak-ass need to want to dive into her neck on a whim. The only saving grace for this whole disaster was that we were able to laugh about it at the time, though nothing further happened that night. Boy, did I miss out.

The Epic Success

Once upon a time, in a lovely beachside city, on an island far, far away, I was at a club with a girl who was so sexy that she utterly took my breath away. We were both soldiers at the time, and I had never seen her in civilian clothing, only in uniform. We had agreed to meet at a club to hang out and dance, and I was really looking forward to it. We chatted and drank a bit. She went to dance by herself, and then I followed shortly thereafter. I moved to be behind her while we danced, and as I did so, she moved her hair over to one side, thereby exposing her neck a bit. She leaned her back into me as we moved to the rhythm of the music, she tilted her head back, and I began to kiss her neck and to bite it a bit. Immediately after I stopped kissing her neck, she mentioned that I had no idea what that does to her.

If there is anything in life that I like, it's a surprise. Surprises, genuine surprises, of the type that you can't predict and are pleasant, are just the stuff that makes me love life all the more. Well, in that moment, on that dance floor, she told me to discreetly reach below her skirt and to feel her inner thigh, not too high above the knees. As I did so on that dance floor, my fingers felt a wetness that I knew to be all too familiar. When she noticed my reaction to her wetness slowly dripping down her leg, she laughed and said, see, that is what you playing with my neck does to me.

Granted, in this epic success, I was in no way truly responsible for her body's reaction to me, as it was a natural response when a man plays with her neck. That didn't matter to me because I found out later that it was such an intense reaction because it was indeed specifically me doing the kissing and touching. That just goes to show that one never knows how a woman's body will react when giving some love and attention to her neck. Hopefully for you, my aspiring lover, the reaction you get out of your desired loved one will be something that is equally pleasing to both of you as well.

Chapter 6: Spine & Back: Those With a Sexy Back Know Where It's At

The exposed back of a woman's body is quite possibly the most underrated part of their sexy being by far. I know we all love butts, but if you look just above that round nipple-less mass, you might notice something. It is a large sensual area with such vast potential for pleasure – and yet most men just look right past it. Gentle strokes, caresses, kisses, and nibbles can go a long way here, but so can a good, simple back rub. Often, the back rub is the best way to go. No mouth needed.

Highlights:

1. Pay attention to it. If you don't even notice that a woman's spine can be sensual and likes attention, you won't even realize that it's there.

2. Know that there are right and wrong ways to notice or pay attention to a woman's back. Be gentle and loving, not abusive, harsh, or rough.

3. The spine and back are full of "untapped" nerves with their own sensations. As a result of this, beginning with soft, gentle caresses is usually a good idea.

4. Your basic tools for giving attention to a woman's back are: your fingertips, your fingernails (filed and smooth), your lips, the breath, your face and cheeks, and if you have it, your long hair.

5. Remember that when being intimate, there are other things outside of your bodily tools that you can use. Feathers, light or soft materials/clothing, and even flowers.

6. You can mix it up with kisses and some nibbles. As always, though, be sure to inquire at some point if nibbles are ok. If you already nibbled, ask if it was enjoyable.

7. Caressing and giving attention to a woman's back is also great when cuddling clothed, naked, or post sex. Just remember that this does not need to lead to sex or anything sexual. Sometimes caresses of the back/spine are just nice. Just like when someone scratches your back.

8. If you decide to kiss or use your lips and tongue, be mindful of any saliva you leave behind. A little is usually ok, just no slobber or puddles.

If you ever doubt the beauty of the back of a woman, just take the time to look up some pictures of women with dresses that have no back to them. When a woman wears a dress like that or is completely topless, but you can only see her from the rear, and she looks back at you, forget it. That is classic feminine defining beauty at its highest.

During my formative years of intimate and sexual experiences with females, I always appreciated their backsides. While most men often think of a woman's butt when it comes to a woman's backside, I have always literally thought of their physical back and spine. An old buddy of mine was about the only person I know that felt the same way. We would sit and chat about the girls we knew and their necks, backs, postures and so on. Others thought we were weird, but we just had extra appreciation for a woman's back.

In this era of electronic devices, too many of us walk around hunched over while looking at screens. In young men and women, this is most tragic. But, before the age of portable screens, poor posture was and still can be connected to other factors, including shyness, insecurity, lack of confidence, feeling too tall, or having big ole boobs.

We must give ourselves a reason to stand up straight, be confident, proud, and taller. As a male, it can make you a better lover and more attractive to the opposite sex. Just like pretty much everyone can appreciate a nice butt on someone, good posture (aka a straight back) is something that we men can appreciate too. Whether your partner or person of interest has good posture or not, a curved spine, or a straight one, giving attention, affection, cuddles and love to said person's backside will always be soothing and pleasant when done right in those intimate moments.

The basics in detail

1. Pay attention to it. If you don't appreciate that a woman's spine and back can be sensual and respond well to attention, you won't even realize that it's there.

Most of us men are generally attracted to other features in women. In order to be a better lover, you must see beyond those. One body part that definitely requires more attention is a woman's back. Look at it. Notice that it is there. See the nuances: the curvature, the absence of obvious features, the empty canvas that embodies a true artist's limitless playground.

In your quest to become a better lover, it is your duty to discover what is hidden in this vast area of a woman's body. The epicenter of nerves that carries all signals to and from the brain is housed here. With branches just beneath the skin, a true lover will embark on first realizing the sensuality of a woman's spine – and that it will respond to attention and sensation. Don't believe me? Just look at a woman's face when you even mention the phrase "back massage" – then see for yourself.

2. Know that there are right and wrong ways to notice or pay attention to a woman's back. Be gentle and loving, not abusive, harsh, or rough. This might seem like a no-brainer to some, but not always for others. A horror story shared with me by a young woman made this point clear.

This woman had started to become intimate with a man and eventually they started having sex. At one point, he rolled her over onto her stomach and then immediately started to bite, beat and claw on her back. He left her bruised, abused, and feeling violated. That was a huge lesson to me that showed me that there is more than one wrong way to give attention to a woman's back – and that a woman's backside is not the place to vent your anger or frustrations. It's also not the place to amateurishly practice your poor and harmful attempts at S&M.

The key word to start with is gentleness. The intent and emotion to infuse her backside with is love, not abuse. This also means that your teeth can be kept inside your cake hole initially. We don't jump straight to using our teeth as beginners, and as someone who is working towards mastering the basics.

Keep your cake hole shut for the most part. Focus on being gentle and infusing your mind and touch with loving energy, admiration, and appreciation for this moment of intimacy. Be grateful that a woman has allowed herself to let down her guard for you. Consciously appreciate the fact that she has been vulnerable enough to trust that you won't cause any harm.

3. The spine and back are full of "untapped" nerves with their own sensations. As a result of this, soft, gentle caresses go a long way.

If you have ever taken a moment to look at an image of the human body's nervous system (ahem, web search!), you would see that the backside has a unique pattern of nerves. It has a unique symmetry and composition that you really can't find anywhere else in the body. Because of this anatomical design there is a ton of untapped potential here for exploration and new sensations.

Most men want to jump right in with touching. My basic advice is for you to go right in with almost touching. Hover your hand a touch above her and just barely touch her before you begin the caresses over the skin so that your touch can be known and keenly sensed without being fully felt. This manner of caressing creates anticipation and heightened awareness in the nerves and the body in a way that can sometimes be better than actually touching itself. Anticipation of something you want, or desire can create a heightened response when one fully delivers on what they teased. This is especially so with the ladies. Begin in this way before finally giving her the actual soft and gentle caress she's been anticipating.

Be aware that for some women, gentle touches can be very ticklish and cause giggling or laughter, albeit in a pleasant manner. If this happens, just go with it. Sensual pleasure is one thing, but fun, happy, laugh-filled intimacy can be its own joy. Being playful in these moments can often transform an intimate moment into something you didn't anticipate, which can, in turn, become a wonderful memory.

All that being said, not every situation will play into this being possible. Even so, with every new encounter, the opportunities reset themselves, so just stay open and flexible, lover.

4. Your basic tools for giving attention to a woman's back are: your fingertips, your fingernails (filed and smooth), your lips, the breath, your face and cheeks, and if you have it, your long hair.

Remember, we are keeping things basic here, so don't get ahead of yourself. (Just in case your mind went straight to toys or whatnot).

Your nails should be cut, filed, and smooth. Depending on you as an individual, you may or may not have enough nails to use in order to be able to make use of them.

Your nails have a different feel to them than anything else. They are a semi-hard surface that can make shivers go up a woman's spine. Not to mention everyone at some point likes the skin on their back scratched. But what we are going for here is much more subtle and gentle than that. We want to soothe and accentuate. So, when you drag them slowly across a woman's skin, be sure to keep your fingers relaxed with the absolute minimum of pressure.

If you have not been keeping up on your nail hygiene, well, don't risk it. Last thing you wanna do is scratch the girl. But all is well…all you have to do is swap to your fingertips!

Your fingertips should preferably be smooth and hydrated so as to maximize your chances of creating a good experience for your would-be-lover. I would definitely recommend that you start by barely touching her skin. Let the presence of your fingertips and the warmth of your hand be known but hardly felt. Now, all that presumes that you are dealing with a bare exposed back, so don't try this until you get to that point.

Your lips and breath will most likely be used together. It should be obvious to say that you don't want to mush or slam your face and lips into a woman's back as you go about pleasing her. Once again, subtlety, gentleness, and barely making your lips felt as you breathe is important. Ensure that you breathe as normally as possible, but in a controlled and smooth fashion, so that she can feel that too.

Your lips and the warmth of your breath combined will make for some really good sensations on her spine and back. It's important to be aware of hand and body placement during such a move, though. As the woman will be on her belly, sitting up, or maybe even standing up, be conscious of your body movements and where you place your hands. More on that later.

The side of your face can be used as well. Especially if you shave. Sometimes, merely running the side of your cheek and face down a woman's back, circumstances depending, can be extremely nice while also potentially sending a signal as to your future intent, depending on where your face ends up. And for you bearded folk, the softness or coarseness of your beard and hair will play a big factor in how it is received. Whether the girl gets tickled or enjoys it, the only way to find out is to go for it.

When you make movements of one direction or another on a woman's back, while stimulating her, that can create anticipation around the direction where you will end up as well. She won't be able to see you while lying on her belly, and you can use that to your advantage to play with her mind as she goes along for the stimulating ride.

5. Remember that while being intimate, there are other things outside of your bodily tools that you can use. Feathers, light and soft materials like clothing, and even flowers.

Once you reach the stage where you are actually in a relationship with a girl, you will only use your natural-born tools for so long before you might want to experiment and try other things to augment what you got going on. In this case, there are simple things that you can do in order to achieve similar effects.

Clothing. Any light clothing can be used to great effect here. Anything from a tie to the underwear the girl herself is wearing could be used to stroke her back gently and ever so lightly in various ways. Now, for those who truly just draw a blank or can't summon the imagination to figure out how to tantalize a woman's backside softly and gently, here are some basic tips.

Draw some shapes. Figure eights, wavy lines, and swirls are some ideas. Slowly. You could also go from side to side, top to bottom and then reverse. It's that simple. You can use your instincts as to how long you want to keep that up, read the mood, listen to the woman's body, and see at what point she is ready to move onto something else. But above all, do not linger there longer than necessary. No matter how soothing or pleasurable something is, there's usually a limit on how long that lasts. So just bear that in mind.

Feathers and flowers are also a nice touch because they tend to be soft in a way that is unique and universally likeable. The added bonus to using flowers is that the petals can all have different textures and resistances right alongside their nice smell. You can even pluck them one by one and let them fall from different heights onto her back and see how it feels to her.

6. You can mix it up with kisses and some nibbles. As usual, though, be sure to inquire at some point if nibbles are ok. If you already nibbled, ask if it was done how they like or if it was pleasurable.

Gentle touches are just fine, but for some, the lips and teeth are where it's really at. The basic idea here is that you want to keep your saliva in your mouth; this is especially true when she is lying down. You don't need your mouth open all the way, and you don't need your tongue out of your mouth like some little kid about to lick the world's most delicious ice cream cone. That definitely sounds funny, but I know that for some of you, that is oh so true!

The real challenge here is that you have to sustain your body weight agilely over the woman's body, ensuring no other part of you touches her, while keeping your lips and mouth suspended over her backside as you glide and gently allow your lips to ever so barely touch her skin. For some this maneuver might be too easy, but for others without the muscular strength or endurance, it might be better for you to have a plan in your mind as to the how you are going to execute this and then move onto other stuff without tiring yourself out. Supporting your own weight in a semi push-up position is one thing. Doing it slowly while moving in one direction – without shaking or breathing too hard, and also trying to be sensual with a woman – that can be hard. I've definitely had ideas and intentions that far outweighed my ability to support myself with my arms.

I recommend that you save the nibbles till you know for sure that it is ok to do so. You can ask casually in conversation. You can ask during the intimate moments as you softly whisper into her ear. Or if nibbles have already been shared, ask about how she likes them so you can do it more to her tastes or liking.

Here's the thing about nibbles, though, you have to get them right. For those of you who have fewer instincts than others, and that's perfectly ok, you might be thinking, "but there are different types of skin, skin thicknesses, sensitivities, skin to fat ratios, skin to muscle tightness, etc." Those are good points. So, here is how you go about it: first, nibble/bite different portions of your own skin. Your hand, arm, shoulder, knees, calves and feet. You will quickly see (if you are paying attention) that each area of skin on the body is slightly different. And sometimes, it is way different from other areas, and since you can't bite your own back, just know that it is also really different from any other area of the body. And for most people, it can be way more sensitive.

Your approach then should be to either ask for a few communicative and fun test nibbles with your person of choice, or just go for it, with the knowledge I've shared in mind. Start off gently and go from there. When I was practicing these things, I really practiced on myself a lot. Nibbling and then biting different portions of my skin to get a really good feel for what the different areas felt like between my teeth as well as the muscle and fat beneath them. That's when I realized that I needed to pay attention to the difference between nibbling and biting, and how that applies to just nibbling a smaller portion of the skin or doing it big enough to also get the muscle or fat underneath. The baseline it gave me really served me well when it came to doing these things to a woman's back. Sometimes I was spot on. Other times, I failed and needed feedback, or feedback was instantly provided because of how badly I did it. More on that later.

Either way, remain aware, communicate, and be ready to be told no or to change your approach. Don't be rigid.

7. Caressing and giving attention to the back of your woman is also great when cuddling clothed, naked, or post sex. Just remember that this does not need to lead to sex or anything sexual. Sometimes caresses of the back are just nice. So please get it into your head that having intimate moments with a woman should be enjoyed in the moment. Not with the intention of getting to the next stage. Just stay open to continuing or stopping. Don't invest yourself in any one outcome, just be happy to be where you are.

These types of caressing moments can happen at any time and almost at any place. I know how nice back scratches and caresses feel to me, so to my close friends whenever their back is exposed in a way that allows me to show them platonic affection, I gently caress their back. Or if I have nails, I gently scratch their back. I especially do it if I know they are stressed. If you are getting to know someone of interest, you have to weigh up whether or not this is an appropriate move to make. Either way, it's well known that simply having your back scratched or caressed can be very soothing.

I have been in a scenario where I was with a woman, and we were completely undressed, things were getting hot and heavy, but she no longer wanted to go any further. She paused; I looked at her, completely understanding that something had changed within her, and told her it was ok. I explained that there was no pressure from me whatsoever to continue, and it was ok to just stop if she wanted to. She breathed a sigh of relief, lay down and I just lay next to her. I gently stroked her back for a while, and we just talked. After I was done caressing her, I covered most of her body with a sheet so she wouldn't get cold, and our conversation continued. In this case, you can see how caressing someone's back can be for closeness and showing care, rather than just getting from point A to B and the ultimate goal of attaining something sexual. It can be used for moments of comfort, support, and soothing.

Right now, many of you are thinking, "yeah, duh, doesn't everyone know that?" I'm here to tell ya that no, not everyone knows. The sooner people know basic things like this, the better off everyone will be.

8. If you decide to kiss her back and to use your lips and tongue, be mindful of any saliva you leave behind. A little is usually ok, just no slobber or puddles.

I mentioned this before already, but suffice to say that you don't need to be drooling onto a woman's back! When you get to the point of intimacy where you are kissing on a woman's back, it is natural to leave a little bit of moisture from your tongue or lips. The goal is not to leave so much spit that it looks like a slug, or a snail slowly crawled all over her back.

And I get it, sometimes when things are getting intense, you can leave more than you intend to, in those moments, it is usually best to just wipe it off in a smooth and quick fashion. But, if the amount of saliva you left is small, try this: breathe deep and focus your exhaled breath onto the moist area to dry it up quicker. This creates a cooling effect that can be nice when done correctly. That means no blowing like you're trying to float a ping pong ball away from your mouth. Once again, though, remain open to being told no or to stop or anything of the like, as not all females like these types of things at all times. Sometimes in the mood, sometimes not, that is ok.

Overall, the most important thing to keep in mind when doing anything with a woman's back and spine is that it is an area of great sensuality and trust. It's my blind spot. It's your blind spot. It's their blind spot. That being the case, show that you can be trusted with this sensuous area. Display the communication and confidence necessary to make her crave your touch and attention there. Sure, you won't always

get it right, and yes, you will make mistakes, but be humble about it all
and take it in stride. You don't need to be perfect the first time at this or
even your hundredth.

The Epic Fail

Remember the Russian beauty from earlier? The one who was
ruthlessly critical of my kissing? One night, I was giving her back
some attention when all of a sudden, she said to me, 'You bite like a
fish!'

I didn't just jump in and try to bite this girl. No, it was my usual
approach of starting sensually and then gradually working up to what I
felt the girl might like by listening to her body. And with this girl, well,
I could tell somehow that she would like biting. What I didn't
anticipate was how much I underestimated her liking being bit!

Up until that point in my life, I thought that I had a pretty good
grasp on how to give proper attention in a variety of ways to a
woman's back. After all, I was literally one of only two guys that I
knew of at that time who even appreciated a woman's back for what it
was. And also, since this was not my first time pleasuring a woman's
back area, well, I was confident enough not to worry in the slightest
about what I was doing. That was until this Russian girl laughed – and
then mocked my bites and nibbles.

My mind was also really confused because I've actually been
bitten by several different types of fish over the years, and let me tell
ya, it can go from feeling nice and like someone is tickling you to a
serious ouch! In my head, I was thinking, "has this chick been bitten by
a shark and then mocked it for being a pussy?!" So many questions!

You see, there is a BIG difference between how someone's skin
feels in my teeth when I bite versus when I nibble. And this is a whole
different world sensation than what it feels like when I am trying to
take a chunk of flesh from another person. It was definitely a sensation
I wasn't familiar with – until this girl asked me to bite like I've never
bitten anyone before. And as it turns out, when I tried to bite as
requested, holy-chompy-bear-jaws-Batman, it literally felt like I was
going to puncture flesh and draw blood! This disturbed me to the point
where I did not want to bite any longer. In any way whatsoever. Period.

She laughed and mocked me a bit more. And I gotta admit, in the
way that she did it, with her Russian accent, it was pretty funny.

Frustrating, but funny nonetheless. I drew a hard boundary there to be sure. I might bite like a fish, but this man ain't no shark.

A moment ago, I told you that there's a difference between biting someone's skin and feeling like you're gonna bite a chunk of flesh off. Well, with this particular person, their skin-to-fat-to-muscle composition was such that it confused my mouth and teeth in such a way that I couldn't accurately tell how to execute my bite! (On her upper back between her shoulder and neck). This confusion led me to lose confidence because I didn't know how to roll from there, and her advice wasn't helping because following it – according to my mind and teeth – would lead to blood! And I don't know about you, but I don't want someone else's blood in my mouth unless it conveys supernatural nighttime powers of which flying through the skies like Superman is the incentive bonus.

Needless to say, further attempts over time also didn't bear much better fruit. Due to this, for a long time, my back game was shaken. I had lost confidence since I couldn't please this one person! I mean, when a woman required this high level of grit from me in order to bite her like a damn shark, I just wasn't ready at the time.

As all that played out, I pretty much lost my feel on how to continue on from there, and I had to ask her how she liked things, as well as making sure that I was doing some things "hard enough". Which was pretty funny at the time. Due to this whole experience, though, I learned one form of extremes that some women are into when it comes to sex. Biting really freaking hard may not be extreme to them, but to this guy, who focused solely on being a passionate lover during that time, it was almost scary.

Long story short, I pretty much didn't get anything else right on that occasion of back play. I think I even made her laugh at one point when I was trying to be all sensual. I laugh about it now, but I felt like a total failure as a lover back then.

Years later, and through a funny set of circumstances, I finally bit her how she liked it. Exactly how she liked. And sure enough, she damn near collapsed from the sensation, it pleased her so much. Even more shocking, no blood! It left a good mark, though. Who knew that her soft, supple skin was also as tough freakin' triple-stacked leather? Turns out she also liked the look of the mark on her skin to boot. That's a whole different thing, though. Women can be weird sometimes. Don't forget that. And then they look at us like, 'tee-hee, I didn't do anything.' Pfft.

When your epic fail (or fails) come along, just take it all in your stride. Learn from it and just move on because that's how funny stories are made.

The Epic Success

I had the honor and privilege of spending time with a girl who, unbeknownst to me, loved to be caressed above all else. Turns out that her skin was very keenly attuned to caresses and gentle gliding touches. This was fantastic in so many ways and in so many parts of her body, but once she was lying down on her belly with her back exposed, I was amazed at the amazing playground her back turned out to be.

Now that I think about it, it might not be too fair to share this story as an epic success because so long as I was gentle and creative in stroking the skin on her backside, she was in ecstasy. Being that such a case is genuinely rare, I would rather share details of an epic success with a woman who had more or less normal sensation to make a better example of.

Ahem, and so there I was, on my bed, after doing some things for some time, with this truly ethereal female and me: mostly dressed. Her: mostly naked, while surrounded by fairies and peanut butter. When, all of a sudden, after taking off her shirt, she rolls over on the bed, exposing her back in order for me to take off her bra. That's when I realized that the sight of her freshly tousled hair, the nape of her neck and the line that was created from there all the way down her back, was just more than I could bear. I was in total awe. This was so pleasantly unfair.

We were pretty hot and heavy as far as the pace and the action, and yet, at the sight of this heart-stopping beauty, which was her hair, neck and back in that moment, I knew I had to take my time and breathe it in before continuing.

I maneuvered myself so as to straddle her left leg and hike up her right leg towards her side. I leaned in slowly and undid the hooks of her bra with my right hand while I supported myself with my left elbow while simultaneously and firmly gripping her hair with my left hand in order to keep it from covering up her neck. After unhooking the bra, I slowly moved the straps from her shoulders one at a time. As I did this, I savored the softness of her skin, its scent and the combined apprehension and tension that I could feel and see from her.

After the bra was completely off, I touched her hairline with two fingers and took my time tracing the smooth lines from her neck down to each shoulder. I followed that up by tracing her spine down to the top of her jeans.

Once I had my fill of exploring her back with my hands and fingers, I changed my positioning a bit. I got my face really close to her skin so that I could breathe her in and so that she could barely feel my lips grazing her skin as I went up from the base of her spine back up towards her neck, with only a few detours along the way.

During all of this, she would squirm and grip the sheets of the bed extra tightly, which was really freakin' hot. Her breathing would change from heavy and hard to long sighs followed by sudden exhales. I recall at one point changing my supported positioning from where I was to placing my hands directly on top of hers so that we could intertwine our fingers. This was for her to be able to have something to squeeze and hold onto, aside from just the bedsheets.

After I had used my fingers, lips, a bit of tongue and kisses in all areas of her back that made her squirm, I ended with my chest. My chest has always more or less been muscular because of my commitment to exercise, so I rubbed it against her, going up her spine, while at the same time starting to press the rest of me against her, so that she could feel my weight, as I approached her neck with my lips. I did all this and a bit more as well in order to tactically build up the anticipation for the next thing I would do.

I did a pretty good job of following my own advice on this one. I'll never forget this particular memory either because I was in the zone. My mind and body were so open and in tune with her body that I could practically feel and see what to do and where I needed to go. In certain moments, I could have sworn that her body was speaking to me. Even so, I reminded myself in my head to always start gently and then go from there. What I did was pretty basic stuff, but it completely worked. Needless to say, the build-up of pleasure and sensations from spending a minute or two on her back made it so that when she rolled over and revealed her bare chest, it was on like Donkey Kong.

I truly adore the literal backside of women. There is just something about it that is unlike any other area of the body. The entire area beckons to be explored. There is an elegance to it and a sensuality that practically begs me to be creative in the discovery of how to stimulate it in order to bring the girl to life.

I'm not sure if you see things that way and maybe you could care less. Either way, the basic ideas are here for you to try when the opportunity arises. And if the whole chapter didn't really speak to you or sound like anything, just be sure to rub her back, give good back scratches, and kiss along the shoulders and neckline, and you'll be fine.

Chapter 7: Breasts, Nipples, and Areolas: Making Suckers Out of Men Since 69,069 BCE

Let's get two things clear. Firstly, breasts are not sex organs. To be attracted to them or desire them is actually considered a fetish. How's that for a twist for those of you lovers who did not know? And secondly, not all women like to have their breasts messed with, touched, or given attention by men in the ways you might be imagining. Especially not without asking first at least. So don't go thinking that just because she has a pair, that she wants you to play with them, or give them attention in the ways you think and imagine.

My philosophy is to only touch them after lots of kissing, pressing, and squeezing of each other have already happened more than once. Always gently at first and then firmer from there and over the clothing. When the bra and top come off, I take the time at that moment to give them attention with hands first, and then lips in combo gently and then firmer from there as things progress. I also make it a point to not ignore them as the sex ensues in order to constantly maintain multiple points of stimulation. And, if for whatever reason I am at a loss for what to do, or I'm just curious as to what she likes, I just ask and go from there.

Highlights:

1. Unless a girl puts them in your face, asks you to look at them, or you two are already hot and heavy, pay attention to a woman's face and eyes as much as you can. But I know it's hard to resist a good booby trap.

2. When going in for the first kiss, it is not ok to immediately go for a boob grab. Save it for a more hot and heavy, mutually grabby moment.

3. Don't assume that because a woman's breasts are larger, they are more sensitive or that because they are smaller, they aren't sensitive. Every girl and every pair are different.

4. Nipple sensitivity can vary greatly from girl to girl and sometimes even from left breast to right breast. So don't go biting, grabbing, or pinching blindly without knowing.

5. It is not ok to treat a woman's bosom like a chew toy just because you're all excited. Show some self-control and remember, intelligent human, not wild animal.

6. Do not slap around or flick a woman's breasts because you feel like it or because you find it fun, or porn showed you so. In particular, her nipples.

7. If you have no idea what to do, or no clue how she might like things, or you're stunned in awe of the breastacular beauty that is in front of you, ask her how she likes them touched or what she likes in general. It's perfectly ok to ask. And if she doesn't know, play together.

8. Treat breasts sort of like you would a puppy or a kitten when you first encounter them. Nice and gentle at first, until you know how to handle them properly, then you can get firmer, have more fun, etc.

9. Please be aware that a woman's breast sensitivity, as well as her nipple sensitivity, can vary greatly due to her menstrual cycle, mood, and after having children.

10. Be aware of breast deception: push-up bras, padded bras, and inserts.

11. Natural breasts, silicone breasts, and saline breasts look and feel considerably different and can be just as enjoyable.

12. Handling bras, as in taking them off, can be easy or an art form, in regard to its difficulty. There are essentially two approaches: using your hands, the one-handed or the two-handed approach. Or she can do it.

13. Handling breasts of different sizes may seem like a no-brainer, but there are simple ways of handling them without just grabbing them like some sort of fun bag.

14. Take your time giving a woman's breasts attention. Enjoy it, but be sure to pay attention to the girl to see if she's enjoying herself too or if she's bored out of her mind.

15. Nipples aren't the only part that is sensitive and can be stimulated. The rest of the skin on the breast is full of potential.

The first real thing that you need to know and realize is that a pair of breasts' natural purpose is not purely for our entertainment and pleasure. Breasts are literally meant to nurture and feed baby humans. Reading this and understanding it are two different things. A good example of what I mean is if you are turned on by breasts but turned off at the sight of a woman breastfeeding in public or anywhere, you don't truly understand. This is important because if you are to be a better lover, and you are a breast lover, you must accept the truth that breasts are not purely here for your sexual pleasure and visual exploits. They may one day inevitably be the sole source of life, nutrition, and comfort for your child, which is their primary purpose. That also means that whenever and wherever your baby is hungry, the mother of your child should be free to feed said child without issue from the rest of us. So don't get their purposes confused just because you uncontrollably sexualize them.

For those of you who get it, awesome.

It is of utmost importance that you learn and accept the differences between your sexual interest in them and their natural purpose. It is the difference between being a more balanced human and a debased one.

A more balanced human sees the greater purpose in things and reality, understands more than one side and is therefore more considerate towards others. In that way, as it pertains to breasts, you will be more in control of your sexual energy towards them. This means that when your partner finds her breasts are sore because she is about to start her period, or during certain stages of pregnancy, or if she develops any medical issues within them, you will be able to prioritize her wellbeing over your sexual desires. In the end, that not only makes you a better partner and human being but also a better lover.

The next thing we need to break down, for those that don't know, is the difference between the nipple and areola. The nipple is the centermost portion that tends to stick up and get firm. Anything from the cold to arousal can make anyone's nipple hard or erect, men and women alike.

The areola is the circular skin around the nipple. They can manifest in all sorts of proportions, colors, and hairiness. They also often change after birth. You can have some that have almost no nipple and a big areola or a huge nipple and virtually no areola. It just depends. If you have any doubts, just inspect your own or conduct a web search and see. But I'm pretty sure you have already.

And yes, of course, this is really basic stuff, don't feel bad. If you didn't know, and even if you did know, we need to spell these things out from time to time for reminders.

Not everyone out there is a breast person, and of those that are, the tastes vary greatly. When I was first getting intimate with girls, I had no preference whatsoever. To me, all boobies were amazing, all boobies were magical, and all boobies were a mystery until revealed! But over the years, I've had enough experience and variety that I hope that some of my advice proves useful to you. And remember, I'll keep reminding you throughout the book, these are only the basics and fundamentals. Once you get to more advanced things with your partner or end up with a partner with very specific desires, everything is up in the air and some or most of what I have for you here may not apply. Or the opposite could be true, your individual experience will tell.

The basics in detail

1. Unless a girl puts them in your face, asks you to look at them, or you two are already hot and heavy, pay attention to a woman's face and eyes as much as possible. I know it's hard to resist a good booby trap.

This tip is all about maintaining your focus and showing self-discipline as well as respect. The lifeblood of a woman lies in her personality, voice, lip articulation when she talks, the gleam in her eye, her hair, the curves of her face, her cute cheeks and jawline, and the divine light creating smile. You will likely miss all that, alongside the subtle nuances that make her who she is, if you just pay attention to her breasts. Not to mention this approach points out that you are mainly just horny. Like me when I was 13.

Listen, I've been lucky enough to have muscular pecs for most of my adult life, and I have talked with plenty of women who have told me that they not only like a nice chest on a guy but that they also like the look of it in tight shirts. Do you know how many girls I have caught staring at my chest over the years? Maybe two, in passing.

If there is anything I have both observed and learned is that most women exercise way more discipline in their attractions towards men than men do towards women. My point? Return the favor.

Now I'm not expecting everyone to master this or to be able to do it every time in every circumstance just after reading this book. That's clearly unrealistic (myself included because I do like me a good boobytrap). What I do realistically want you to do is to practice. When you catch yourself failing, or failing miserably, call yourself out. So that when you are talking with a girl and you catch yourself staring at her chest, or she catches you, just own up to it gently and call yourself out. Of course, include those words politely and respectfully in the conversation and see what happens. Especially since she was the one who made them stand out.

And yes, I get it, many women out there set up their cleavage booby traps to show off what they got intentionally. It's super hard to resist at times – and impossible to resist at the worst of times. Another way that I handle this is either to hardcore ignore it while thinking, "Oh no, you're trying to set me up, and I'm gonna show you that it won't work." Or I look directly at her cleavage, then into her eyes, and comment on the fact that it's going to be difficult to have a conversation while she's trying to distract me at the same time. So, either she takes away the distraction, or she's gonna have to put up with me looking. Because if it's on display, the eyes are going to have their way. Just like that, you set yourself up for success as well as to call her out. If she laughs and is cool with it and doesn't get attitude or claim innocence that it isn't her problem, then you can likely engage with said female, and everything is okay. If she's anything but cool about it and turns things into drama, walk and go talk to someone else.

2. When going in for the first kiss, or even the second, it is not ok to immediately go for a boob grab. Save it for when you're both being mutually grabby.

I've been there. The girl is pretty, we like each other, there's palpable electricity because of the anticipation of the first kiss. Then, out of sheer excitement and desire, as we begin to kiss, my hand moves up to feel and grab her chest. Each time I made that mistake, luckily, without breaking lip lock, the girl grabbed my hand and moved it to her waist or to her back (sometimes to her butt) if I was moving too fast. All the while, I was mentally berating myself for making such a stupid move and for not controlling myself better. And yet, those lovely patient ladies didn't get upset or say much at all and merely continued to kiss me.

All of those experiences happened when I was younger, and since then, I have learned my lesson. That doesn't mean it can't happen in adulthood because lord knows I've heard so many stories, regardless of what age you start out at, that this scenario is very possible and for some of you even highly probable. Just keep in mind that going for that first kiss or set of kisses usually has nothing to do with her boobs. Usually. Just focus your hands on her waist or around her back while holding her, or one around her waist and one gently on her upper back, or the classic two-handed gentle cheek hold.

When you both have properly acquainted yourselves with each other and the intimacy has reached that level where you know beyond doubt it's ok, cool. But till then, hands off the hooties. You're trying to be a better lover, not an over-eager one, remember?

3. Don't assume that because a breast is larger, it is more sensitive or because it is smaller, that it isn't. Every girl and every pair are different.

Women's breasts run the whole gamut of sensitivities. Voluptuous women in general have told me that their breasts are more sensitive, whereas women with smaller breasts have told me that their breasts are less sensitive overall. But this hasn't always been the case in practice. What they would say would oftentimes differ from how they would react to actually having their breasts played with. Make of that what you will…but what I got from it is that what they're into oftentimes depends on their chemistry with a man. Now that's just from my life experience that I draw from. It could be completely different from others and even more so for you (assuming that you've had more than one partner). What I want you to keep in mind is that how you imagine yourself playing with a woman's breasts sexually, or what you fantasize about doing, will often be met harshly with reality. So, whatever you have in mind, if anything, I hope that you aren't too attached to it. Because oftentimes a woman, when she digs you and you're getting hot and heavy, will let you do what you want with her breasts, and you may think you're doing great! In reality, though, she might just be letting you have some fun even if it isn't what turns her on or makes her feel good.

When a woman's breasts are really full or big, the temptation can be to squeeze and grab or to jiggle them, or even to pinch. I'm sure in your head you have your own ideas about what to do, but oftentimes the way a woman will visualize her breasts played with is different from what you had in mind. All I'm saying is that you should probably take a moment to ask about that to see what she says and go from there. While it is always a safe thing to do, the more experience you have with breasts, the easier it will be for you to talk about them without feeling weird about it. And if a girl feels like it kills the mood to talk about it or to ask, just remind her that men aren't telepathic, and neither are they. Intuitive feelings and notions are great, but they are no substitute for words.

The picture I am trying to paint for you here is that there is such variety out there in the breast world, when it comes to sensitivities, that you really must pay attention to what a girl tells you and how you approach her chest. Be cool, play it safe at first and roll with the assumption that she's more sensitive to start with, because you can always turn the intensity from there.

For those of you who end up with a girl in the beginning who is into more intense and rougher things, all I can tell you is that you need to stay flexible and be able to roll with it – unless you are completely uncomfortable with the intensity and roughness. In which case, please speak up, let how you feel be known at the discovery of this new boundary, and just go from there. I say that because I had a girl once tell me she wanted to try cutting. That was essentially where you do small cuts on the breast and suck on the cut. Well, I was not ok with that at all in any way. Fortunately, I convinced her to never do that for a whole list of reasons. Listen, it doesn't matter how amazing the woman or the breast, if a woman wants to do something you are not ok with, stop. If she insists, walk. Got that lover?

4. Nipple sensitivity can vary greatly from girl to girl and sometimes even from left breast to right breast. So don't go grabbing or pinching blindly without knowing.

Having just talked about breast sensitivity, and now nipple sensitivity, one of the best examples is mothers. Many women I've met say that after breastfeeding, their nipples and breasts overall just aren't very sensitive, so they require more attention and stimulation in order to get something out of it. On the flipside, I have also had some mothers tell me that even though breastfeeding hurt like heck at first, and that they lost sensitivity for a time therein, they regained the sensitivity they lost and are now even more sensitive.

I tell you this because you must be situationally aware of what a woman is going through, or has gone through, in order to really know how to give attention to this particular area. To gain this information, the woman might willingly divulge herself or you might have to ask. Or you may have to just discover through the process of playing and fun if she doesn't want to share that info, or just wants you to figure it out. In the end, the smartest move is to start gently and work your way up slowly from there while gauging her reactions.

How to do this, you ask? Well, start off with your fingers. Index and thumb ideally (or index and middle finger pressed against the thumb), with gentle presses, squeezes, tugs and holds. Each one is different, so if you have prior experience, don't go thinking that whatever worked before will work again. Always keep what you know in your pocket and start with a clean slate to make it easier to discover and experience. You can always bring out what you know later when the right moments present themselves.

Use the first joint on your index and middle finger, by pressing them together, to gently press and squeeze a woman's nipple while you are using the whole rest of the hand to hold the breast itself. A basic but useful move if you're all hot and heavy with each other and you want to continue to kiss and hold her in that way.

You can use all of the fingers on one hand to gently caress and stroke a woman's nipple when erect. Just open your hand, spread your fingers apart, starting with your pinky, and slowly wave your hand over her breast and nipple. Make sure that each finger runs into her nipple as you wave it all the way over, with your index finger being the final finger to nudge. Then you can repeat the process by waving your hand back over in the opposite direction.

Beyond your basic hand and finger stuff, biting without knowing if and or what she likes, pinching or careless squeezing or death gripping, is highly discouraged. I've known men to go right for the nipple only to immediately pinch it and roll it between their thumb and index finger like they owned it or something. That's not to say that some women don't like that or that they don't find it stimulating, that just shouldn't be your default go-to. If a girl likes it more intensely and harder, then you work up to that unless she tells you from the get-go that that is what she likes. Otherwise, you might come across the wrong way.

Take into account that one breast and its nipple can be more sensitive than the other as well. You could even ask the woman which is more sensitive, and she will likely tell you, with a bit of surprise, at you knowing that one is more so than the other. That might not always be the case, but any woman who really knows her body will most likely be able to tell the difference if there is any.

5. It is not ok to treat a woman's bosom like a chew toy just because you're all excited. Show some self-control, you're not an animal. Look, I know that for most of us men, the very next thing after our hands that we want to use on a woman's breast is our mouths. When the opportunity arises to do so, please, with sugar on top, do not try to immediately treat her breast and nipples like some piece of gum that you can chew on as hard as you want with all your teeth.

Ever bite your lip hard at some random moment unexpectedly? It surprises you and makes you jerk in pain, right? It can be kind of like that for some women. But overall, it's just rude and inconsiderate as not all women like their boobs chewed on by teeth. At least, not how you imagine or desire to.

On the off chance that you have your mouth and chompers on a divine bosom and the woman mentions that she likes teeth and nibbling and can take harder or likes it harder, don't use that as an excuse to go from whatever level of force you are using to maximum. I made that mistake, and it didn't go well. It can be that she wants you to go harder, or that she might be bragging a little bit, or both. Either way, go harder slowly as you use your teeth. That way, you can find that point without putting her off or turning her off and suddenly ending your access to the wonder that is her breasts.

6. Do not slap around or flick a woman's breasts because you feel like it or because you find it fun. I'm not sure why some of us think that it's ok to just randomly slap a woman's breast around. Maybe because it's new to you and you wanna see them jiggle? Maybe that's your thing with every pair of breasts you get access to just because you enjoy it. Just remember that they are a part of a woman's body. A person. Not some detached object that you can treat how you want. In porn, they do those types of things all the time, but don't forget that that is entertainment, and they are getting paid. It is not educational. I know that sounds obvious, but do try to remember that lover.

There are times when sex turns fun. Where you both are just naked and playing around, enjoying each other and laughing, and in those moments, things like that can happen. She might slap your dick around without hurting you, you might do the same to her boobs, whatever.

Just don't go for something like that upon your first intimate encounter with a woman. Or the second, for that matter.

7. If you have no idea what to do, or no clue how she might like things, or you're stunned and in awe of the breastacular beauty that is in front of you, ask her how she likes them touched or what she likes in general. It's perfectly ok to ask.

Not gonna lie, there have been some moments, even as an adult with experience, when the shirt and bra came off, and I was wowed by what I saw. As in taken aback by the impression of what my eyes were feasting on. For lack of words, and lack of action, all I could muster in those rare moments was something to the effect of, "May I touch them?" It makes me laugh at myself now looking back because you just never expect something like that to happen – and then it does. Because of the reverence that I had in those rare moments, and because my brain suddenly just forgot everything. I would also immediately ask what she likes or what is ok to do. Fortunately, every single time, the women were very kind, smiling and endearing as we continued.

It's noticeable to women when we are either wowed, stunned, or impressed by their bodies or parts. Our natural reactions can help to eliminate any insecurities in those moments and fill them with confidence by our approval of their looks, so don't worry too much about not knowing what to do and just communicate and enjoy.

8. Treat breasts sort of like you would a puppy or a kitten when you first encounter them. Nice and gentle at first, until you know how to handle them properly, then you can get firmer, have more fun, etc. This is pretty self-explanatory, and I sort of touched on this earlier. Another reason why I mention it here is that breasts do tend to be sensitive overall, and you need to become familiar with the sort of touch that women and their breasts prefer. Being nice and gentle at first, as you pay attention to her responses and reactions, is typically the wise thing to do. Then, as you get familiar with each other, you can grab, squeeze and stuff.

9. Please be aware that a woman's breast sensitivity, as well as her nipple sensitivity, can vary greatly due to her menstrual cycle and mood.

In case you have never given it any thought, a woman's vagina isn't the only part of her body that has to be treated with care during certain times. As a woman approaches her menstrual cycle, her breasts will usually begin to swell and or become sore to some degree. I've made the mistake many times of getting all handsy while forgetting that her cycle was approaching, only to then be quickly reminded to be extra careful. It's because of things like that that I make it a point to try to memorize my partner's menstrual cycle so that I can anticipate these types of things, so as not to be caught unawares.

If your woman is in a bad mood or going through something emotional, that too can affect the sensitivity. You need to be aware of this as well. Why? Because sometimes you can have an argument or some really emotional moments with each other, and then have make-up sex or comfort sex. These are things you will need to play by ear, of course. The main point is that you can't treat a woman's breasts as you wish every single time you have them to play with until you are versed in, let's say, their temperament.

10. Be aware of breast deception: push-up bras, padded bras, and inserts. Now I know that in some women these things are easily detectable, but in others, not so much.

Women love to deceive men about what they really look like, but it's so standard that they don't even give it a second thought. They typically just see it as enhancing their looks or looking good for themselves. They can 'self-modify' in a myriad of ways, but one of their favorite methods is the strategic use of padded bras. Part of the reason is that most women have one breast that is smaller than the other. The size can vary from barely detectable and very insignificant to a very noticeable amount, both visually and in your hands. The women who don't opt for corrective surgery usually just wear inserts, padding of various types (gel being a good one), or special bras.

Women who have mostly proportional breasts will use padding and inserts and special bras just to make their bust look bigger or fuller and perkier than what it is (depending on the outfit) and to try to create some cleavage when they may normally have none. I've seen, and you can too if you just walk around and pay attention, that it's mostly women with very small breasts or are mostly nipples, who use the bra and pad deception religiously. So, you need to have a keen eye in order to spot this type of thing if you are a breast man.

It's also important to note that much of their clothing – shirts and tops – come prebuilt with pads or with padding slots. So, while not all women may be into that, when the option is there by default, they just roll with it.

Apart from this being a basic thing you should be aware of, it's
deception in the name of looking more beautiful or curvy to attract you
initially – even though the truth of what they really look like will be
revealed eventually. It'd be like if we men wore padding under our
clothes to create the effect of muscles. If that type of thing doesn't
bother you, cool, but otherwise, keep your eyes peeled while trying not
to get caught checking to see if she's mostly padding or not.

11. Natural breasts, silicone breasts, and saline breasts look and
feel considerably different and can be just as enjoyable. Bras are still
used for some effect occasionally.

Natural breasts that are enough for a woman are usually in a sports
bra, a really thin bra, or a supportive bra. Some women with large
breasts will use thick bras in order to better keep them pressed against
their chest, or go with two sports bras so they can contain the jiggling
around. The thing is that not all women have full breasts. Some women
create the illusion of fullness when they have breasts that may sag by
nature, after birth and post-breastfeeding, or because they have lost a
lot of weight. But because there is a lot of breast tissue, they can use a
bra to place their whole breast into, thereby making their chest look
nice and full while having it tightly held into shape. I'm not calling this
good or bad, I'm simply pointing out that natural breasts can look and
feel drastically different for different reasons, and that bras are used for
different purposes to create an effect. The point is to prepare you for
the possibilities you might encounter when getting intimate with a
woman. That way, you don't get all surprised or attached to a certain
idea about how her breasts will look… only for it to be the opposite.

Breasts and their fullness are generally affected by the size of the
mammary gland, the amount of fat present, the thickness and tightness
of the skin, how they are mounted on the torso, and sometimes by the
shape of the rib cage. For many women, but not all, when they gain
weight in the form of fat, their breasts get bigger. When they lose
weight, most of the time, the breasts don't shrink back in the same way
they were before. In fact, they can retain the increased amount of skin
and just kind of hollow themselves out, which is when they might look
all saggy. Now that's not to say that women can't have big, full breasts
and still be saggy. I'm just pointing out some of the reasons that that
can happen, though not guaranteed.

The overall point? Even though all those types of breasts are
natural, they can all still feel and appear very different. There is no one

experience to know them all. I even had an experience once where a woman's breasts were so out of this world, I thought they were fake for a good two minutes until I realized that they were perfectly natural. A one-time occurrence so truly rare.

Silicone breasts tend to be like round balls underneath the breast tissue or under the muscle tissue of the chest. They can look nice, and even be decent to hold in your hands, but the biggest thing you might notice is that apart from being firmer/harder, they are also colder. Since there are no blood vessels in the implant, the temperature is lower. You can notice this through the skin. If not massaged or attended to regularly, they can get stiff and extra cold temperatures can have an effect on how they feel too. I had two great experiences with silicone breasts, so they can be pretty nice, but I still prefer all-natural. Whatever you prefer is up to you, just be sure to pay attention to the signs in a woman's chest that may give away whether they are natural or not – if you have a preference.

Saline breasts are like silicone except they aren't as stiff and are more fluid like natural breasts. They have the same issue of feeling cooler and like silicone, it can be easily noticeable under the skin if the skin is stretched too tight. Not to mention that both of those tend to be rather round like a ball as they get bigger. Smaller implants can be more easily shaped like the teardrop that most people like.

There are many variations when it comes to breasts out there. Breast cancer, reconstruction surgery, Gigantomastia (a condition that can cause breasts to grow extremely large), implants, and even breast reductions, can all add to the variety that you may encounter. Only when you experience these situations will you know how you feel about them and how that allows you to bond with a woman and what kind of lover you become.

12. Handling bras, as in taking them off, can be easy or an art form in terms of its difficulty. There are essentially two approaches: using your hands, one-handed or two-handed. Or she can do it herself.

It can be tricky, but it's simple enough. First, know that women can have snaps in the front as well. That is to say, between the cups. Those are the easiest to undo because you can look right at it with the breasts right there. The simplest way to handle the snaps on a bra that is on the back is to just have the girl turn around. But what fun is that?

Now, trying to undo the snaps while kissing or not looking, that's where skill comes in and where technique matters. The bras with the snaps on the back get harder the more snaps they have, but the same technique will work either way. Think of the motion like snapping your fingers: press your thumb and index finger together, then pull them apart. Your middle finger should be naturally curved under your index finger.

If you're kissing a girl and working one-handed with your dominant hand, place your thumb and index finger on either side of the bra clasp (not directly on the hook). Slip your middle finger under the bra band and under your index finger, so you have one finger underneath and one over, with your thumb on the opposite side of the clasp.

Press your thumb toward your index and ring finger to bend the clasp upward at the hooks. Then press firmly, push up slightly, and slide your thumb and index finger apart in the same motion you'd use to snap your fingers.

The squeezing together of the fingers and bra is the challenging part because bras can be tight, and you need the slack in the center in order for the snaps to be loose enough for them to come undone when you do the snap motion with your thumb and index finger. If done right, within two seconds you can have the bra snap undone and the breasts freed from their cages.

The simplest way to undo a girl's bra is to just gently help her remove her shirt and then have her turn in order to remove her bra. No complicated maneuver and no blind handling. I've done this a lot too, but the other approach is more fun and a personal test of skill – so I try to go in blind whenever I can.

13. Handling breasts of different sizes may seem like a no-brainer, but there are simple ways of handling them without just grabbing them like some sort of fun bag. Not only can breasts vary extremely in size, shape, and form, but your reaction to them can vary as well. And the very first time I had the honor and privilege of being entrusted with a pair of breasts larger than I had ever encountered before, I thought I knew what to do. I quickly realized I actually didn't. This part of the chapter is all about sharing my ideas for how to handle breasts of different sizes, because if it isn't obvious already, you can't handle them all the same way.

We will start with giant and larger breasts because they require a bit more intricacy. Then we will talk about smaller breasts, and lastly, completely flat-chested women.

The thing about giant and large breasts is that once you get to the point where one hand is not enough, how you go about giving them attention changes. This is the reason why many of you have the philosophy that anything more than a handful is a waste, or you dislike it. Well, that also can come from not knowing how to handle more than what your hand is capable of. So, pay attention, lover, because this is basic stuff.

For giant breasts or breasts that are larger than your hand, you need to use both hands per breast first of all. If she is lying down, you need to approach the breast from the base of her chest. That means scoop it up, with one hand and wrists to either side. One from the rib cage on the right (as women's breasts of the larger size tend to flow into the armpit area when lying down) and the other by the sternum (middle of her chest) with your left hand. Bring your hands and wrists together so that the breast gathers in the middle.

Once you have it gathered up, the more breast there is, the higher up it will go as you squeeze it together, so bear that in mind. At that point, you can do various things. You could nuzzle the skin around the breast below the nipple to create some anticipation before you get to the nipple. You can kiss the area with full pressed, moist lips, or nibble, or merely squeeze firmly with both hands and press your warm face against her skin and breathe in or grab and hold while kissing her. You can also, without leaving excessive amounts of slobber, lick for a short distance around her areola and then suckle where you stop. But not on the areola or nipple itself yet. That will help to sensitize the area and create a little bit of build-up before you turn your attention to the nipple itself. It may not have the same effect on every girl, but it will at least do something.

All of that work was just for one giant breast. In order to be able to attend to two breasts, and doubly so if they are huge, your forearms will have to come into play as you scoop them up with each forearm, assuming she's lying down and that you don't have giant hands yourself. If they are that big, it is likely that your hands will be involved in holding them while your forearms do the majority of it. At that point, your lips and mouth are your best bet to give those big breasts good attention. I highly recommend going for one at a time, though if they are massive, unless she's standing or sitting straight because then gravity is your ally, and you don't have to scoop them as much. Not to mention that if she's sitting or standing, and her nipples are in a forward-facing position, you might not have to do much at all aside from some holding and maneuvering with your hands.

If, for whatever reason, the girl has an areola (the circular area of skin around the nipple) that is bigger than you can fit into your mouth, don't try to fit it all in anyway. For whatever weird reason, the first time I encountered a large areola, I was super intimidated and blown away because I had it in my head that it was all supposed to fit into my mouth. I have no idea where I got that from; I probably just made it up in my head. So, if you have any other similar silly idea in your mind, lover, get it out of there. Whether big or little, you can give the nipple area sufficient attention with the mouth you have.

If she is standing in front of you or any other non-laying position, it then becomes much easier to handle her bosom because they are just right there for you to squeeze, nuzzle, and enjoy. Oh, and don't awkwardly bend over if she's topless in front of you and shorter than you. If there is a height disparity in any way, just wait for or create the right moment to give them attention. You want it to be fluid and natural, not forced and awkward, despite how anxious you might be to get at those boobies – whether it's the 1st or 100th time. Moments in which you are sitting or lying down are usually best. If she happens to be standing on something, that also works.

When breasts are big but manageable, depending on your hand size, or the breasts are smaller, then it becomes much easier to manage. Two hands on even a big to mid-size breast will still be good because you can encompass it all in your hands from the base to the areola for a good, firm hold, which can feel nice to certain women. Smaller breasts will allow you to do the same with one hand on each so that you can then take your time giving each one some attention with your lips, mouth, and teeth. And I know I keep repeating this, but start gentle and work your way up from there in intensity.

14. Take your time giving a woman's breasts attention. Enjoy it, but be sure to pay attention to the girl to see if she's enjoying herself too or if she's bored out of her mind. This here is another simple one that many of you lovers out there miss. Usually, because of the patience and the good graces of the women out there who don't want to embarrass you or say anything. It doesn't matter how many times you

have handled a woman's breasts, take your time in the beginning, unless you are both ripping each other's clothes off from anticipation and passion. Don't be a desperate, hungry animal. Keep your wits about you because it directly leads into the second point: don't get so carried away that you ignore the woman these breasts are attached to.

Some women will let you have fun with their breasts. They may sit back and enjoy watching, or they may enjoy the feeling as well. But you know what else they do sometimes? They can get bored out of their minds because you don't know what you're doing, they don't feel much out of the whole thing, and as a result, they will display a face of little to no enjoyment. All of which you can miss if you are too in your head and too lost in lust to pay attention to her.

Remember to come from a place of pleasure-based feedback in your head. As you go about enjoying yourself and trying to please the girl, look for signs that she is enjoying herself. Her eyes are rolling into the back of her head, she's moaning in pleasure, she grips your hair or arms and hands, her body spasms, she looks at you while biting her lip, and there are many other signs as well that you can keep an eye out for. But if she's just lying there and not reacting and looking at the ceiling bored, that is your cue to stop, ask, or do something different. Got that lover?

15. Nipples aren't the only part that is sensitive and can be stimulated. The rest of the skin on the breast is full of potential. The idea here is that just focusing on her nipples for your enjoyment and her pleasure, as opposed to the whole rest of the breast, is a waste of a perfectly good breast. You can also kiss, suckle, caress, and nibble on the rest of the skin around the areola.

Not all nipples will be as sensitive to pleasure as you might think. Some might be more, some less. The same thing applies to the regular skin on a woman's breast. Either way, said skin will respond nicely to stimulation and kisses, and as such should still feel nice. That way, you can bring some positive sensations to the whole breast and not just the nipple and areola.

Ultimately, take your time giving a woman's breasts attention. Enjoy it, but be sure to pay attention to the girl to see if she's enjoying herself too or if she's bored out of her mind. There's nothing worse than getting carried away, and she's just waiting for you to be done. Also, remember that nipples aren't the only part that is sensitive and can be stimulated. Importantly, don't forget that they aren't chew toys.

The rest of the skin on the breast is full of potential. So, touch, kiss, suckle and nibble on non-nipple areas as well and see how she reacts in contrast to nipple stimulation. In the end, as you make love to a woman, don't get so caught up in thrusting away that you forget that there are breasts there that you can stimulate simultaneously in order to make her feel as much pleasure as possible. That bit of extra multitasking and effort can make the difference between just an average lover and a good lover.

Lastly, it is worth noting that a woman's heart is right underneath her bosom. And whether the girl you are with will realize it or not, stimulating her breasts can stimulate her heart.

The Epic Fail

To be honest, I've had more than a few boob failures in my past. I'll detail a few of them so you can see how badly those situations went – for your own amusement!

Ok, there was this one time, not at band camp, when I went to see this one girl who happened to have huge breasts. I didn't know if we were going to mess around, and I didn't know exactly how large her breasts were, but I had a lot of hope in me that we would do something. Upon arrival at her location, we quickly caught up, chatted and laughed. Before I knew it, we were in her bedroom.

This girl always wore baggy shirts, and I hadn't seen her in a while, so when she took her shirt off, I finally got to see the real size of her breasts. And let me tell ya, they were enormous! When she took off her bra, I immediately noticed that one of her cups could fit my head in it easily. To prove my thought, I grabbed her bra and tried to put it on my head. Sure enough, I was right. She laughed at me, and then we continued on with getting naked. But then I suddenly realized that I had never played with boobs of such huge proportions and had little clue how to handle them properly.

I fumbled around trying to handle them both at the same time. That didn't work. I then tried one boob at a time… that was super difficult as well. It was a big, heavy, hard handle, and everything I thought I knew about how to handle boobies just didn't work. I felt like my hands were too small, like my mouth was too little, and like there was clearly more breast than I could handle. Visually, they looked amazing, but in reality, I was in over my head.

Being so disappointed with myself after that experience, I became doubly determined to never let that happen again, and so, it never did. I learned how to manage big ole boobies, but as fate would have it, I only ever got to handle breasts that large two other times in my life. That's just how it goes.

Another story, and a much shorter one, was when a wonderfully voluptuous woman and I spent a weekend together. Upon getting to the place we were staying, we immediately got undressed and started making out and exploring each other's bodies. When I got to her fantastically full bosom, she mentioned that her nipples were quite tough and that I could bite her nipples harder. Well, I took that to heart and bit down…needless to say, that was not received well at all and kind of soured the whole rest of the experience.

In my head, I just did what she said I could do because I had had women tell me that before, and it went well. This time, not so much. Either way, lesson learned. Don't chomp down – even if they say so. Work your way up, little by little, in pressure to play it safe and to find what her true limits are.

Another time, I was naked with this girl, going down on her, when all of a sudden, I decided to reach up and play with one of her breasts as I licked her pussy. For some reason, I only used my left hand and kept my eyes closed the whole time as I went down on her. Well, after about ten minutes of fondling her breast, I realized that I couldn't find the nipple anywhere on her breast, no matter how thoroughly I mentally mapped and explored her breast. After another minute passed, I gave up and just started to reach up higher in order to get to her arm when it happened: my hand unexpectedly ran into a big nipple and areola and a huge breast.

Turns out that what I was fondling the whole time was a fat roll. A cleverly shaped fat roll at that. Well, at least that's how my mind perceived it. So, I opened my eyes for confirmation, and sure enough, her fat roll below her breast was indeed not a breast at all. For over ten minutes, I was fondling that, and she said nothing! I wasn't mad, though, just impressed she didn't say anything and left me to my own devices with her body. Maybe she thought I was weird for liking to fondle her giant love handle? I never found out nor asked. But either way, after that experience, I learned two things. One, open your eyes to make sure you are touching what you mean to touch. And two, maybe don't go for a girl who is that overweight next time. Thinner girls tend

to have smaller boobs, which is fine because I love boobies either way.
But at least you won't have to worry about mistaking a fat roll for a
boob.

The Epic Success

While I was in the Army, I ran into a Cuban girl once. We took a
liking to each other, and we went out of our way to try to spend some
time together. When we finally met up, we did not have sex. We did,
however, make out intensely and take most of our clothes off.

When I got to play with her breasts finally, I noticed that they were
of a size, ratio, and proportion I had yet to encounter at that point in my
life. Not to mention that she had very large areolas. The bonus was that
her breasts were kind of perfect in proportion to my hands, which made
it much simpler to grab them both at the same time. As I did so, I
made sure to grab them at the base of each very firmly so that they
protruded towards my face more than normal. This allowed me to give
each of them attention in turn while maintaining a good grip. What
surprised me was that she really responded positively to my way of
gripping each and to how I handled them.

As she started to feel my lips, tongue and teeth a bit, her positive
response turned into moans of pleasure. Then, as I squeezed her breasts
as close to each other as I could, her nipples came into contact, and I
was able to suck on them both at the same time, which she really liked.
After that, I ignored her nipples and areolas and focused on the skin
underneath her breasts, which also drew more moans of approval. I got
to do all that to my heart's content before we started kissing again.
After we took a break, she mentioned how no one had handled her
breasts the way that I did and how much she liked it. I mentioned how
I had never handled a woman's breasts like that before either, and how
I had made it all up on the spot.

That whole interaction left a big impression on me as well because
had I just seen her breasts from afar or in a picture, I wouldn't have
thought much of them. But because they were there before me and I
could see them in person, smell them, and taste them, my body reacted,
and my impulses guided me on what to do and how. As a result of that,
I really enjoyed them, and she enjoyed what I did as well. Just goes to
show you that unless you're in person, you can't quite know for sure.

Boobies are great. They nurture human life in our early stages of development, and then later, they become the stuff of fun and pleasure. Whatever your tastes in breasts, respect and honor the boobs, treat them well, and call out well-made booby traps.

Chapter 8: The Abdomen and Belly Button: The Crossroads of Pleasure

A woman's abdomen and belly area can be really sensitive but also pleasurable. Sometimes, no matter how hard you try to be a good, sensuous lover, you won't be able to avoid tickling her. This is usually the transit area we pass as we go from one area of a woman's body to another, either from north to south or south to north, but there is some potential here. Some kisses, some touches, maybe a bit of licking on the way down. I always consider which way I am headed when in this zone because, in her mind, it can create anticipation each way for what follows next, so keep that in mind.

Highlights:

1. No two abdomens or belly buttons are alike.

2. Don't go in with the mindset that what you intend on doing will get you the result you want – as ticklishness can throw any sensual plan off track.

3. Expect the abdomen to move and actively react: possibly even to maybe, on the off chance, cause a fart due to laughter. Just sayin', be ready for anything!

4. The goal here is to stimulate her skin, not to massage her innards.

5. Your basic tools for this area are your hands, fingers, lips, tongue, and mouth, so be sure to read Book 1 and the part on personal hygiene first.

6. This might be challenging for some of you lovers out there, but do try to keep the saliva to a minimum.

7. If you do take a little time there, exploration with your fingers while tracing lines and gentle kisses usually is enough to build up the excitement and tension for whatever comes next. But remember about tickling.

8. Figure out which direction you want to go and then plan towards that direction. Are you going up or down? Towards her face or between her legs?

9. Last but not least, take the time to breathe her in. You're exploring an entire being, and this area is but a transition point to others. Some nice scents can be enjoyed here.

The basics in detail

1. The first thing I will share with you is that no two abdomens or belly buttons are alike. They are all different. I can hear you saying right now, "well duh". See, that's fine and dandy, but there are quite a few of you out there that are bridging the lack of experience with logic and reason, and you don't yet know that some abdomens and belly buttons may attract you, unusually enough, and others may turn you off.

You see, experience makes that knowledge real and keeps it forward in your mind as you go through your experiences. But being a logical brainiac without the experience of how to go about a woman's abdomen and belly button will cause you to make a girl giggle and laugh almost every time. Or worse, put her off with your fumbling around her abdomen. Especially if you neglected to ask and she forgot to tell you that she doesn't like her belly or belly button messed with.

I will remind you over and over of certain basic things in order to get you to remember them. Every woman is different, and every part of them is different. That's the underlying theme here. Keeping consciously aware of the differences and potentials out there will allow you to approach how you engage with this area of a woman without a fixed idea, apart from being aware of ticklishness.

By keeping your senses on point and open to receiving whatever the female is putting out feedback-wise, you can remain on point about what you do down there.

That area is so sensitive that no matter your best efforts, many times you will make the girl laugh or tickle her in some way. Now, don't get me wrong, that isn't a bad thing in and of itself. It's just that when that isn't the desired effect you were aiming for, it can put you off your game so to speak. Although some of the laughs that have ensued have been worth it.

2. Don't go in with the mindset that what you intend on doing will get you the result you want. The reason is that we are all sensitive to some degree in our abdomen area. Oftentimes, we can't help our own reaction to what someone is doing to us. One wrong, or right, move and laughter will ensue. So, stay flexible and wear your humor on your sleeve.

3. Expect the abdomen to move and actively react. Healthy breathing occurs through the use of your abdomen, and if the girl is excited or aroused, she will be breathing excitedly, which means that the abdominal area will be moving a lot. Keep that in mind before you make a move with your lip, tongue, fingers, or mouth so that you don't go thinking she's moving too much, or you offhandedly ask her to stay still.

4. Breasts have the ribcage immediately below them, which gives them support and something hard to press against. The abdomen is just one big cavity filled with squishy innards, so the whole thing is soft and squeezable (unless she a six pack of abs or something). The goal here is to stimulate her skin, not massage her innhas ards. Unless she has some rockin' abs, gentleness with your fingers and lips should be enough.

5. Your basic tools for this area are your hands, fingers, lips, tongue, and mouth. You are keeping things basic until you master them, so feathers and other additional materials, apart from your inborn tools, are a no-go at this point. Not to mention that the amount of time you spend will likely be so short that a few touches and some kisses will be about it.

6. Keep the saliva to a minimum. Licking is a thing (so long as it's soft and sensuous and not like a giant tongue lick, like that of a predator tasting its meal before it devours it whole). Girls are, for the most part, into this, but don't go leaving pools of your spit on her belly and or belly button. Not cool. So, if you can't manage that, leave the licking alone for the time being.

7. If you do take a little time there, exploration with your fingers while tracing lines and gentle kisses usually is enough to build up the excitement and tension for whatever comes next. You can also use your hands to hold her waist just above her hip bones, or on them, as some women like being held there as you kiss your way down or up.

8. Figure out which direction you want to go and then plan towards that direction. If you are making out with a girl lying down and decide to work your way down, then lift up her shirt to expose her belly. Your next step: do you go up or down? Well, figure out which way you are going and then apply kisses and touches accordingly as you go in the direction you desire.

9. Last but not least, take the time to breathe her in. Our skin may be our largest organ, but it doesn't mean that our skin is the same in every part of the body. The skin here is also different and has a different scent. I repeat, take the time to breathe her in. Feel her warmth and imagine you are breathing in the scent of a unique rose in full bloom, and let that fill your senses.

Girls can often do unexpected things when you get down to this area for some reason. So, be ready just in case, ok? Nothing bad though, so don't worry.

The abdomen and belly button area of women is a strange area in some ways. Some women like to hide theirs, others like to show it off. Some love to have it touched, others will tell you to stay away from it. Some will writhe and wriggle in pleasure and anticipation, while other women will start to laugh and giggle. Some of it has to do with mood, while some of it also has to do with chemistry.

Whether you choose to stay there briefly or to take your time, you will have to go either up towards the breasts or towards her groin. Regardless, this is a wonderful area to explore and to be well acquainted with. Just be aware that women who have given birth and have major stretch marks, may not like the attention in this area. Women who have had surgery and have those scars down there, or women with larger bellies, may not like that part of their bodies being touched. If that's the case, respect it, don't question it or try to convince her otherwise, just accept it and move on. Making her feel comfortable and enjoying the rest of the intimacy together should be the focus in those moments.

In my eyes, the waistline is one of the many alluring features of females in general. I'm sure that most of you agree. It is so simple, yet it draws your attention. It's in the middle of everything, and yet you can easily underappreciate it if you don't take the time to discover and explore it.

The Epic Fail

I don't remember the exact time and location, but I do remember that it was when I was in the military. There was a girl I liked who was energetic and lively. Turned out she was into me as well, and not too long after that, we ended up in my room.

After some playful banter, we started kissing. Clothes quickly started to come off, and as I was working my way down while kissing this girl on her belly, excited at the prospect of tasting her pussy and lost in the moment, the next thing I knew, I got a smack on the side of the head.

I was trying to go down on her slowly and smoothly when I got this sudden reflex knee-jerk to the side of my head. Turned out I had accidentally tickled her belly with my tongue. She was too sensitive after that, so even going down on her proved to be too much, and we just ended up having a big naked tickle fight instead. We eventually calmed down and restarted all the sexiness, but on the condition that I skipped her abdomen. And this time, my head received zero knee attacks, which was preferable.

A simple situation there. No big drama, and no real mistake either. Our energy was so jovial and peppy that she was too sensitized and the littlest thing would just make her laugh or convulse into jerky movements. Nowadays, I know that when things are fun and energetic like that certain things are automatically out the window. But back then, I still liked to do things a certain way because my situational awareness wasn't quite yet on point.

The Epic Success

Not so long ago, in a mysterious place called North America, on Earth, there was a girl who was interested in me. Naturally, at that young adult time in my life, if a girl liked me, there was a very high chance that I would like her. Why? Because back then, I really liked girls who really liked me (for the most part), but who also made it obvious that they liked me. And so, this girl and I decided to spend some time together. Eventually, we made it indoors to somewhere warm and with a bed. Namely, her place.

As we went into a full-blown make-out session and our clothes started to fly off, I noticed that she smelled really, really good.

Sometimes, when a lady sprays her perfume on her lady parts, it can be too much or too intense, but this time it was rather nice. We kissed, I made my way down to her chest, then down farther, and as I made it to her abdomen, I realized that her body was reacting especially positively to all the kissing, licking, and nibbling I was doing down there despite not reaching her pussy yet. Because she didn't appear to be tickled at all, but rather, more excited, I gave some attention to the left and right sides of her abdomen as well to make sure that I nibbled on her hip bones. This too seemed to be something that was causing her to writhe with pleasure, which of course, I loved.

After all the sex was over and we just chilled and talked, she opened up a bit and told me that she had never really had anyone go down on her. Or at least, not like I did. But more importantly, she was so excited and turned on by the time I reached her abdomen that everything I did felt amazing to her and felt really pleasurable. The side effect of that was that she got super wet. Drenched even. Which, of course, once I discovered this, I loved, although I did not know at the time that it was mostly due to the attention I gave to her abdomen. She said that she was surprised too, but in a great way.

Till that point in my adult life, I mostly gave attention to a woman's abdomen purely for my own gratification at the exploration and discovery of a woman's body, but after that, I decided to make sure to pay extra attention to see if that could enhance a woman's experience with me in bed. I mean, if the trigger to get her extra hot and wet is in this area, that just means I need to find it so I can reap the wet rewards! Mwahahaha! Anyway, lover, unless you have the same partner for life, and you know how she reacts to this area, keep an open mind because there could be a secret button there that can go undetected if you pass it up.

Chapter 9: The Fine Art of Butt Appreciation

Butts are awesome. For those butt men out there, a fine ass might be a necessity. But for the rest, it's just decoration that you may feel 'meh' about. Either way, they are necessary for locomotion and preferable to have to some degree to not have saggy skin back there. You can only do so many basic things with a girl's butt (apart from wanting to stare) when getting intimate. From squeezing and grabbing and holding to kissing, biting, and spanking. The key is timing and not overdoing it. I usually don't go for a butt touch or grab until we have made out pretty intensely at least twice. Also, situational awareness is key. You don't wanna grab ass where it isn't appropriate, like in front of a bunch of school kids. But in private and in bed, it's easiest to give it attention fluidly as you are doing other things at the same time. While kissing, during sex, during oral sex, or my favorite – during 69.

The Highlights:

1. Don't go playing grab ass right out the gate with a woman. Wait for the right moment.

2. When it is time for a butt grab, no half-ass pinching or slapping. Commit to a good firm grab and squeeze.

3. It's also a good idea to hold onto the woman around the waist with one arm as you use the other hand to grab onto her butt after consent is given or mutual grabbing has commenced.

4. Definitely take into account your height, as many of us men prefer shorter women, which could make her butt out of reach while standing up straight if your arms aren't long enough.

5. Bear in mind that women love to wear clothing that makes their butt look better than it would otherwise.

6. Once the clothes come off, while she is facing you, when she is bent over in doggy style position, or lying down on her belly, are the easiest ways to give some attention to her butt.

7. One good thing about spending some time playing sensually with a woman's ass is that it lets you get a closer look and smell at what she's got going on down there: because hygiene matters,

8. If sex of any kind isn't the goal and she's relaxed, and you've earned her trust, touching her butt as you so desire is usually ok. This means you'd better know how to give a good butt rub.

I've often talked with people about what features they most appreciate in their fellow humans, and the one that is always appreciated is the butt. Even those men who weren't into butts as part of what they looked for in a woman still appreciated a nice butt aesthetically. Sure, there are plenty of people who place limits on the size or dimensions of the posterior that they prefer. However, a well-shaped butt itself remains something most people want and appreciate in a partner. If for no other reason than it is preferable to the alternative – which is saggy skin where a butt should be.

And yes, I am well aware that the majority of you all take the time to look at a woman's butt when they are turned around or walking away. Who doesn't? Even women do that. For whatever reason, we men tend to neglect our glutes as a feature. In order to help remedy this, (because we want to be better lovers, don't we?) we men need to step up our butt game. Literally, take the steps, do some squats, leg lunges, iron mikes, run up some stairs and ride a bicycle in nature or the gym. Hike some good inclines or hills. Do whatever it takes. Apart from giving you something that the ladies can appreciate visually and physically, it may help with lower back problems and those loose jeans you wear with or without a belt.

Let's try to get ourselves out of the concave butt club and into the convex butt club, shall we?

Now, first things first, the only time it is acceptable to grab a girl's butt without asking is if that particular female gave you permission by explicitly telling you that you can grab her butt in the ways she is ok with. The exception to this is that this has already been established between you and said girl, or if, through nonverbal communication, she has made it clear that she wants you to touch or grab her ass. Girls have made this clear to me in a variety of ways. By grabbing my hands and putting them on their ass, by looking at me and insinuating that her ass needs grabbing, by pressing it up against me, by rubbing it against me, by grabbing their own ass and showing me or by coming up to me and parading it in my face or directly in front of my crotch.

If you don't know the girl and you want to grab her butt, if she hasn't given you permission in direct or indirect ways, the answer is no. Do not even try. If you know the girl and she hasn't ever said that you could, and the urge hits you, do not grab her ass. A girl walking by with a fine butt, and in your head, you think it's begging to be grabbed, just don't do it. Ass cheeks hangin' out as she walks by? Nope. She bends over (and it's not in your actual face or in front of your crotch) and there's a literal sign on her ass saying "touch me", hell no. Say no to booty traps. I know this is obvious to most of us out there and duh to the majority, but the reminders sometimes need to be spelt out and repeated. It's all part of the basics. And so many men fail at even that!

The basics in detail

1. Don't assume that because you are kissing a girl, holding her hand, or hugging her, that it is ok to grab her butt right away. Wait for the passion to rise and things to get more intense.

You need to realize that a woman's butt area can be rather in tune and sensitive at times because of her menstrual cycle, amongst other things. The feelings and sensations from something you do with her butt can reverberate and be felt between her legs if done right and if the girl is sensitive in that way. When a woman gets really turned on, if you wait to grab down there until she's in that mode, she will feel far more of what you do and react positively. Whereas if you grab a woman's butt prematurely, not only will you not get the added excitement stat bonus, it may have no effect or be found as a turn off.

When is a good or right moment? When you're kissing, and she's grabbing at you, or she grabs your butt, or your tongues are in each other's mouths, and the kissing is getting hot and heavy, and she's really pressing herself against you. It could also be less obvious, more subtle and sensual as often girls aren't that obvious. But mind you, this applies to girls you have just started to get close to. If you already have a girl, then the right moment is something the two of you should have worked out pretty easily. It can be done intuitively anytime.

2. When things get more intense and sensual/sexual, and you do grab her butt, for example, during a passionate kiss where she is also grabbing at you, don't do a half-assed pinch, grab or slap. Commit to a firm, not hard, full-handed grab and squeeze and then gently release before repeating again.

Also, notice that no permission was asked. Why? Because in this scenario, you have already made positive contact and gotten a go. You are already kissing, passion is flowing, perhaps she is even squeezing and grabbing at you as well. It's during this type of intense, passionate kissing that I usually find it ok to slide my hands down her hips to her butt. Because at this point, it is usually acceptable under two conditions. Firstly, it isn't in front of a bunch of people during the day in a public place. Secondly, there is enough privacy and sexual energy flowing back and forth that the grabbing of her butt feels like a natural extension of the very next moment. And if I happen to be wrong and she moves my hand back, then I don't attempt it again and just keep on kissing.

3. It's also a good idea to hold onto the woman around the waist with one arm as you use the other hand to grab onto her butt. Grabbing her butt with both hands is fine, but if you hold her close with one arm around her waist, which some women really love, then with the other you squeeze one cheek, which can turn up the intensity a bit in a good way. But remember, the right moment. Not just at any moment.

4. Definitely take into account your height as those of us men who prefer shorter women will likely end up with a girl whose butt is out of hand's reach. Why does that matter? Because you will look absolutely ridiculous hunching over all crooked just to grab at her butt. Wait till you are sitting or she is on a raised surface to do so because then it's more natural. So don't go getting overexcited or impatient, or it will look and feel forced.

5. Bear in mind that women love to wear clothing that makes their butts look better than when they're naked. This is something to keep in mind because of all these new leggings, yoga pants, and tights that are out there catering to the market of women who appreciate having their butts made to look perkier, tighter and rounder in clothing than without. I'm tellin ya, too many times I've seen women who have amazing butts until the clothes come off, and then it falls out. If you're into that or it doesn't matter, that's fine, but either way, be aware so that you aren't caught off guard by a butt that looks formidable until gravity reclaims it, and the clothing is no longer shaping it.

Not every woman out there has a genetically-gifted natural butt, nor do all women go out there and exercise in ways that make them have a great butt. Some women have no butt, just like some of us men, but unlike us men, some of those no butt women will wear special undies with butt pads or will just plain add butt pads under their clothing in order to look better. Honestly, I don't care either way because I can spot an unnatural butt easily enough, but for those of you out there with uncalibrated eyes, keep an eye out for unnatural movement. An all-natural butt that is mostly fat will move one way. An all-natural butt that is fit and mostly muscle will move another way. And a butt that isn't natural could move a few different ways in that it could be pads, could be implants, could be gel stuff, hard to say.

I will say that not all women wear pads and butt implants because they are trying to deceive or look better without working for it. Some women honestly have had accidents, medical issues, or just random life shit happen to where the musculature on their glutes is missing, doesn't function properly, or won't develop properly, etc. That's why it's important to look at the whole woman and see if that's the only thing that seems off. If so, still talk to her and maybe you'll find out what's the deal.

6. Once the clothes come off, while she is facing you, when she is bent over in doggy style position, or lying down on her belly, are the easiest ways to give some attention to her butt. You can use your hands on her butt if she's facing you and you're kissing her abdomen, but there's not much you can do apart from squeezing it a lot while her chest is in your face or on your head. And if her back is facing you while she's standing, and you're sitting, then her butt should be right there in your face. But again, in that position, there isn't much you can do apart from basic grabs and squeezes until she either bends over, gets on all fours, or lies down.

Depending on your tastes, a woman's butt may be a decoration around what you really desire (her pussy) if you aren't a butt man. It could also be a main feature right next to another main feature. Apart from a massage, there isn't much else to do with a woman's butt apart from squeezing it, kissing on it, nibbling, maybe some slaps or smacks if she's into that, and that's about it. Yes, there is more that you can do – but I don't consider that part of the basics of what you need to know in order to navigate that area. So, keep it simple there, lover.

If she is bent over or in doggy style, obviously her pussy and ass are completely exposed. If she arches her back, especially so. These two are typically starting points for either oral sex or sex, but I'll get into that in those particular chapters. Apart from those two things, you can also just grab, squeeze, kiss, and or nibble on her butt in these positions as well.

7. One good thing about spending some time playing sensually with a woman's ass is that it lets you get a closer look and smell at what she's got going on down there. Guys, let's be honest here, we know that not all women have the presence of mind to try to maintain excellent personal hygiene down there. And it can really vary as to what we men can, and most likely will, encounter at some point. So, if you can help it, inspect it before you regret it.

If a woman is up front and communicative, she will divulge anything that she has going on down there. It could be her period and that she's wearing a tampon or a pad. She could have an STI, not just in her vagina or on her vulva, but maybe on her butt cheek or butt crack. She could have been really sweaty and have swamp ass. Maybe she didn't quite clean herself well enough in the bathroom, and she's got a clinger, or maybe she just started her period and didn't realize it, so there are smears of blood down there that you get to discover. It's also possible that she looks impeccably clean – yet stinks to high heaven due to some inner hygiene problem or because she used too much body spray. She could even just have a really hairy ass and crack that is not well-kempt at all.

I've actually had experiences where a woman has a giant hairy bush all over down there – front and back – but was completely immaculate, clean, and even smelled fresh! Definitely a one-time experience, though, so don't count on that too much for yourself. Anyway, my point is that giving some attention to a woman's butt for your gratification and for her pleasure is also a low-key way to see that all is well in the direction that you are headed. If it isn't, then you're just in time to turn back.

8. If sex of any kind isn't the goal, or you've already had sex, and you're together lounging around, and she's relaxed and you've earned her trust, then touching her butt as you so desire is ok. Time to learn how to give a good butt rub.

There are a few basic positions that you can rub a woman's butt from as she lies down. You can rub it from either side of her body while she lies down, and you are standing or sitting/kneeling (depending on whether or not you have a massage table), or you can do it by straddling her legs. I recommend placing a pillow on her legs if you're going to straddle her legs. If you're heavy or bony, this will prevent you from hurting her legs.

If you are sitting on either side of her body, you can apply pushing pressure to the butt cheek closest to you with the palms of your hands, or with your fingers, with the focus on your thumbs to guide and exert pressure from. You would start between the pelvis and hip bone and then slide your way up and over to the left in an arching left-leaning angle. That will follow the deep contours of that area. From that same vantage point, you also have the possibility to reach both hands over and across to the other butt cheek. But this time, using both hands, one on top of the other, you can apply pressure to the same spot between the pelvis and the hip bone. Then apply pressure through your fingers by pulling towards yourself and sliding your hands in the same arch as before. You can repeat the motion while making smaller circles along the way as well.

From the straddling position, you can lean forward a bit and place both palms face down, one on each butt cheek, and then place alternating pressure by pushing down with your torso instead of creating force with your arms and triceps. If you take the time to sense the bone structure underneath, you will feel where it is best to place pressure. Essentially, you want to focus on the deep tissue areas of her butt, not on the bony parts. You can do this process lightly at first and then apply more pressure as you repeat. You can also change it up and use the tips of your fingers and thumb. You even have the option to ball up your hand into a fist and use your knuckles to create a different effect with the same basic technique. Just no punching the butt! Ok?

That all may have sounded more complicated than it really is, but it really is simple to execute. And with more practice comes instinct! That's about it for knowing what to do and not to do with a girl's butt. The beginning is the hardest part. Once you two become an item, then it all sorts itself out with how you two set boundaries and comfort levels with each other. I had a girlfriend who wanted me to touch her butt all the time. Anytime, anywhere, anyplace was her policy, so long as it was me. Others were way more reserved and preferred everything at home in private.

Easy chapter, easy stuff. If you're lucky, you'll end up with a girl who really enjoys having her butt played with or squeezed. Because then the urges you have will be satiated everyday.

The Epic Fail

And so, there I was, in my room, harnessing the power of the force into my hands while also trying to rub a girl's butt, when I noticed that she was really getting into it. Her hips were gyrating gently and rhythmically. She kept arching her back and poking her butt towards me in obvious but subtle ways. She was also gripping the sheets tighter and tighter and burying her face into the bed as she did so. I squeezed each cheek at the same time in various ways just to make sure that my hands got their fill. I thought things were definitely going to go the way that I wanted, so I got my face really close to her butt. I could smell how wet she was, how fresh she was, and her ass and pussy were just centimeters away from my face. Then, all of a sudden, just as I'm rubbing both cheeks at once in a nice spread open fashion so I can see all the yumminess in between…and as my tongue starts touching her butt…she farts. Not once, but twice, in rapid succession. And that wasn't even the worst part. The worst part was that she caught me with my mouth literally wide open. Not only did I smell that fart in its entirety, but I also tasted it and practically swallowed it too. For real. To add insult to injury, the fart was such an intense spurt of gas that it puffed out my cheeks into full-on hamster mode!

She was immediately embarrassed, super apologetic, but also kinda laughing. I mean, it was funny. She proceeded to simultaneously explain that she felt so good and relaxed that it just came out. She claimed she didn't even feel the need to fart – which meant that it surprised her too! Now, me being who I am, I shook that shit off. I breathed it all out, inhaled some new fresh air, and laughed a lot because the more I replayed it in my head, the funnier it got. I reassured her it was all good and that it was no big deal because she had an amazing butt, and I was just getting started. Fortunately, nothing else came out apart from the gas (which was already undetectable and couldn't be smelled since I inhaled it all!)

I wasn't anywhere near done with her butt. She reassumed the position that I had her in, on her belly with a pillow underneath her hips to prop up her butt. This meant that I could resume what I was doing – while simultaneously praying that no more surprises would appear from her butt. And thank goodness, nothing else did.

I definitely got too close to her butt with my face as I rubbed her. I also rubbed her ass and spread it in such a way that caused her butt hole to open up and the fart to come out. Big fail. But you know what?

Sometimes you gotta take the good with the bad and just keep goin'
like a soldier.

The Epic Success

Once upon a time, in a country far, far away, I had a secret plan.
There was this girl that I really liked that I was visiting, and I had
concocted an idea to give her a bit of a body rub, with the prime
feature actually being the butt massage. Why the butt massage?
Because she had an amazing ass, and no one had ever given it attention
before me – in accordance with my standards. I told her that I wanted
her to shower and not to worry about lotioning up because I would
lotion her whole body for her and then give her a special massage.

After she showered, I had her lie down on her cushy yoga mat
since she didn't have a massage table. After I took my time lotioning
the whole back side of her body, I then focused exclusively on her butt.
I straddled her legs so that I could knead her butt cheeks
simultaneously and then one at a time. I moved to one side and
massaged one cheek, then the other. I swapped sides and repeated the
same thing in order to make sure her butt was completely massaged
properly.

Did I mention already that this woman had an amazing ass? As in,
genetically gifted with little to no exercise. And if she did do any
exercise, her butt was immediately further augmented, which was
crazy. Add to that her fantastic skin, and in some ways, I was enjoying
the massage more than she was. Anyway, I straddled her legs again and
began to massage her a bit more intimately. More passionate squeezing
and rubbing, and then barely grazing her between her legs with my
fingers. As I continued to rub and squeeze and knead, there was always
a little bit more touching than before. Well, needless to say, my whole
plan worked, and she was super worked up.

We had sex in that position on the floor, and we both loved it. So
much so in fact, that for a long time after, she wanted another special
massage. She would randomly ask me, "When can we do that again?"
Unfortunately for us both, the second time never happened, but boy
was that one time a success! Not only did I do everything right, I also
managed to give plenty of attention to an amazing butt while taking my
sweet time…and she loved every minute of it. That was a win-win all
around.

Chapter 10: Legs – There's Something in a Stride

There's a lot in a stride. When a woman walks, we men usually pay attention if those legs speak to us with their movements. They can be alluring, seductive, defining, and amazing. They are the gatekeepers, the pillars, and one third of the embrace we men receive when we are welcome and invited into a woman's being. There is some potential for stimulation here, however, so don't go skipping leg day in bed. Generally, the best times to pay attention to a lovely lady's legs are when you massaging them, as you make your way from her feet to her pussy or vice versa, and also when you are having sex, and her legs are by your arms, face, or general torso area. Squeezes, holds, kisses, nibbles, bites…these are all nice additions during moments of intimacy.

Highlights:

1. From the ankle to the hip, there are some major points of potential stimulation for pleasure: the ankle area, behind the knee, and the inner thigh.

2. Remember that not all women are naturally flexible. Don't go forcing a woman's legs clear behind her head if she isn't able to or if it hurts her.

3. Take your proportions and hers into account when thinking of doing things in bed with a woman.

4. Learn to accept that some women have naturally almost hairless legs and that some, no matter how often they shave, can have prickly legs.

5. I know it's obvious, but remember that you can have more creative positions and fun in sex the more flexible your legs are, not just hers.

6. Putting lotion on your woman's legs can be great foreplay.

7. Beware of the leg lock.

8. There are more or less five basic scenarios where you can attend to a lady's legs: while sitting, lying down, in massage, you're sitting and she's standing, and in sex.

9. Hairy legs, although less common nowadays, can still be encountered.

The legs of our fellow ladies are marvelous things, aren't they? Long, short, stocky, thick, muscular, thin, lanky, bowed, straight, bony, smooth, hairy, every shade and color from white to pitch dark brown. Those legs carry them everywhere, propel them forward and yet, somehow, when a woman shows off her legs, it can be something to marvel.

The ideas for learning how to love and give attention to a woman's legs aren't complicated or even that numerous. Of utmost importance, though, is to keep in mind that there is always a place and time for that. A woman's lower appendages aren't something you can just touch or grab and feel on a whim. Moreover, if you stop or pause to stare and look at them while in conversation with a woman, you will most likely get noticed right away because of how obvious it is that you are looking at them.

While this isn't an intentionally made booby trap (or leggy trap?) by women, they can be very ignorant of the very real effect their revealed shapely legs can have on a man. Which means that if you are talking with a woman who is ignorant of what she is showing off, do your best to stay focused on the conversation. The styles of women's dress can be varied, but many think nothing of wearing shorts that literally come up to their pussy and the effect that exposing that much leg around some of us men can have…while at the same time expecting us not to look or admire what they are clearly displaying. There can be some catch-22s there.

Don't forget that most of what is written below for you to consider only applies when your lovely legged lady is bare-legged.

The basics in detail

1. From the ankle to the hip, there are some points of potential stimulation for pleasure. This can vary (or not apply at all if she's not stimulated by leg touches) with the lovely lady you are with. But, overall, I have found that the inner thigh, behind the knee, all around the ankle, the inner calf muscle, and even behind the knee, all of these

can have a decent chance of producing nice sensations. Quite simply, you can produce nice sensations on a woman's skin with your fingertips as you caress upwards through what I call the leg line, by gently stroking or rubbing with your fingers or with your lips. Behind the knee, around the ankle, and the inner thigh can be stimulated more effectively with your lips overall.

The only downside is that if the lovely lady you are with is ticklish or really sensitive to the point of being ticklish or squirmy, stimulating these areas at the wrong moment may feel nice, but instead make her laugh rather than create heightened anticipation towards the direction of her yoni/pussy. Which means my dear lover, that if her legs start thrashing about from you tickling her, watch out. You might catch a foot to the face.

If the lovely lady you are with gets goosebumps/chicken skin from you touching her legs and she is cleanly shaven, there is a small chance that her legs will go from smooth to prickly in an instant. Not a bad thing in any way, just something to take note of.

2. Remember that not all women are naturally flexible. Don't go forcing a woman's legs clear behind her head if she isn't able to. In sex we men can get carried away trying to get into all sorts of positions with women. Or at least moving a woman's legs as far back as they can go in missionary. Try to keep yourself in check enough to notice whether you are spreading her legs super wide this way or that is causing her any discomfort. At the very least, if your attention capacity is minimal due to your hormones raging, take a moment to ask if it hurts her or if she's comfortable in that position(s).

I've been with women who were so nimble they spread and hugged their own legs to the point where I was very impressed because I never would have pushed their flexibility that far unknowingly. The opposite has also been true where I was just normally maneuvering a woman's legs, and she complained of pain due to her inflexibility. In both cases, I just adjusted to the new limits set by the current lover and continued on. The key point here is not to get hung up on the number of limitations due to a lack of flexibility once they are discovered. Instead, adjust with that new knowledge and continue on like a boss. Why? Because you are now instinctually aware of the possibilities of positions based on those limitations and can guide the sex accordingly.

3. Take your proportions and hers into account when thinking of doing things in bed with a woman. I say this because I know a lot of

women love tall men, and a lot of tall men love short women. I, for one, have been with women taller than me and women much shorter than me. From a personal standpoint, there were obvious pluses and minuses to each when it came to the effects of how long a woman's legs are due to height. But not always. I also discovered that proportions in ratio from ankle to hip and from hip to shoulder matter greatly, as I've seen women about my height with shorter legs than me because they had a longer torso and vice versa. That's the reason why I say take into account proportions instead of height.

A woman with shorter legs, if you are taller, won't have her hips in the same range as you for standing sex or even doggy style. In missionary, a woman with shorter legs, depending on your arm length and torso length, may or may not have a tricky time keeping her legs naturally supported by your arms.

A woman with longer legs, or longer, thicker proportions, may also be a bit too cumbersome or challenging to maneuver around if you're used to shorter, lighter legs. The upside is that in certain positions, if the legs are longer or as long as yours, you'll have an easier time in certain positions, and if she goes with your flow, you won't have to do much work moving her legs around in any way. The downside is that in other positions, they might be too heavy. This is an issue if you have a lazy lover who has little to no instinct on how to move her legs – or doesn't know how to go with your flow as you go from one position to another. This can tire you out if you have no fitness in your arms and body. Got that?

4. Learn to accept that some women have naturally almost hairless legs and that some, no matter how often they shave, can have prickly legs. I'm sure you'll have no time accepting that there are women out there who can have pretty hairless legs and that you might favor those or think nothing of it. Many of my fellow men will, however, take note when a lady's legs go from smooth to prickly. It takes time and effort for women to make their legs all smooth for themselves and for you, so appreciate it when they are how you like or prefer. Just remember that kissing or doing other slick things on a prickly leg may not work as well as on a smooth leg.

5. I know it's obvious, but remember that you can have more creative positions and fun in sex the more flexible both your legs are. What does that mean? Stretch, stretch, and stretch.

Women overall are more naturally flexible than men, to varying degrees. In order to be a better lover, or to at least improve your sexual game, becoming more flexible will benefit you as well, not just her. And you just might impress her with your flexibility.

6. Putting lotion on your woman's legs can be great foreplay. This is pretty simple. I enjoy putting lotion on whatever lady I'm with if she lets me. There is something special about starting at the ankles and then lotioning a lovely lady's legs all the way up to where they meet together; that can often lead to more than what you started out doing. Which is fine by me.

7. Beware of the leg lock. For those uninitiated lovers out there, the leg lock is applicable in two scenarios: oral sex and regular sex. Whether it's your face that is down there, or your hips, a lovely lady with long enough legs can wrap them around you and then lock ankles, squeeze, and keep you there if you are weak enough and she is strong enough. I personally love it when a woman wraps her legs around me, but not when she tries to lock me in.

There have been times, and I mean more than once, in which I was going down on a lovely lady with long, strong legs. Right before she had an orgasm, she wrapped her legs and thighs tight around my head, grabbed my hair, flexed as hard as she could and had her orgasm – while I was locked in place and unable to breathe. Sometimes fun. Most of the time, not so much. What's worse, and again, this has happened to me more than once, is when a woman leg locks me tight around the waist, either as she cums or as she senses me about to cum in order to force me to cum inside her. Beware of these women. Whatever you do, do not let yourself get caught in that trap. (Pussy trap? Leg trap?) If you're on the weak side strength-wise and lack the inner will in order to resist both the urge and the pleasure of it, she will most likely succeed.

That's yet another reason to stay fit and strong enough to at least resist a woman forcibly impregnating herself with your seed. The rich men have more to worry about this than the poor men, but when a woman is in love or is determined to have your child, any man can fall victim to this technique if the circumstances are right. I've gotten out of it each time, and unfortunately, due to my naivety and complete ignorance of these red flags in my youth, I remained with the ladies who tried that till the relationship ended for different reasons despite their best efforts. If anyone tried that shit now, forget it, she can go take a hike.

8. There are five basic scenarios where you can touch a lady's legs: when you are sitting next to each other or on each other, lying next to each other, during a massage, when you are sitting, and she is standing in front of you, and of course, during sex. Sure, your lovely lady can just straight up ask you to touch her legs for any number of reasons, but barring those types of situations, organically, those four or five circumstances are the usual and most common from what I've gathered.

If she has pants, jeans, or even yoga pants, caressing and resting your hand on her lap or giving gentle caresses is good enough.

As you lie next to each other and you can reach her legs, it's then possible to do more with touches and caresses. And if you approach her from her feet towards her hips, that gives you the opportunity to then caress and kiss her legs on your way up to lie next to her. That is assuming you don't make other pit stops along the way.

If you're sitting and she's standing in front of you, you can remove whatever is covering her legs, smoothly remove her panties, or touch and kiss her legs at whatever points you have accessible before moving on from there. And that is the biggest key to remember here: whatever attention you give to a lovely lady's long legs is only momentary on your way to her main pleasure center. Do not linger for too long here unless you can clearly see that she is enjoying herself. But even then, don't linger.

During a massage is the only time you can truly pay all the attention you want to your lady's legs. I will give you two simple ways to give some massage attention to those legs you have access to. The first is simple pressure. Start from the top of the ankle or base of the shin if she is facing up at you. Use your palms to apply pressure on the leg firmly with your body weight and not with the brute strength of your arms. You lean into your palms as you press and be sure to ask if the pressure is ok as you go up the leg/shins with one hand in front of the other as you go up. Skip the knee and then use both palms side by side on the thigh if she has significant thighs; otherwise, one hand in front of the other, like with the shins. You can even do both legs at the same time with one palm on each leg if her legs are slim enough. You can repeat this on the other side of her legs as well when she faces down, but once again, remember to skip the knees.

The second way is to firmly but gently rub and squeeze from her shin upwards towards the heart. This is best done with some oil or lotion. Continue rubbing and squeezing, skipping the knee till you get to her thighs. At the thigh, you'll have the upper thigh and inner thigh to contend with, and you can do both this way unless she has really thin legs. Just remember not to get too close to her crotch unless she desires you to do so. And even then, if you create some anticipation by not doing so, it will help to enhance sensations. You can also do this on the other side of her body, on her calves and hamstrings.

During sex, her legs are only accessible to give additional sensation and pleasure and not as the primary focus. Kissing, grabbing, nibbling, or gentle biting might work depending on the position you are in and where her legs are. In missionary, while leaning back, you can have both of them on your torso/chest to hold and kiss. If you straddle one leg and hug the other, then you have another opportunity there to give her more pleasurable sensations. It all depends on how aware you can be and your sense of awareness. Some ladies will care and light up if you do things to their legs that feel great on top of the sex, while others may be so immersed in the sex that they won't even register that you did something with their legs. In that sense, it might be more for your enjoyment than hers, but in either case, I will encourage you to do something because it makes the whole experience more immersive and fun for both of you.

9. Hairy legs, although less common nowadays, can still be encountered. How you like your legs hair wise is up to you. And although most women shave them and keep them smooth, some ladies like to go all natural. To what severity of the hairity you will encounter can depend on the girls genes or where she's from. I've seen Russian girls that didn't shave and had almost no hair on their legs anyway. I've also seen women who didn't shave and the hair was longer than mine. For me that was a turn off and a no go but I didn't hate, I just didn't engage. Whatever you prefer, that's what I recommend, pass up on what you aren't into, just don't hate.

One of my favorite things to see is to witness women walking as they do on any normal day. To me, their legs are like the lovely stems of flowers traversing the earth. They each have their step, flow and moves, but all are just amazing to behold. While there are things we can do with a lovely lady's legs in mutual passion, it's mostly in transition from one point to another or as the build-up towards the actual final destination that we end up giving them attention. Not to mention the obvious holding and maneuvering of their legs as you have sex. All I want to ensure is that even if you only stop briefly along the way, that you appreciate them and give them some attention because women might appreciate having more of their body loved on and noticed apart from their ass, pussy/yoni, and breasts.

The Epic Success

One day, I was munching on a burger, wondering if the trailer to the newest movie coming out would end up being better than the actual movie, when all of a sudden, as I chatted away with a girl's parents, I got the idea to touch their daughter's leg that sat next to me to see how she would react. The girl I happened to be sitting next to was a girl I really liked. I had come over to meet her parents and have dinner together. And since she really liked me too, she ensured that we sat next to each other.

The table was just big enough for her and me to sit next to each other, for her two brothers to sit across from us, and for her mom and dad at each end of the table. Dinner was burgers and fries, and some vegetables. This girl and I had been seeing each other when we could, but hadn't really done much apart from kissing. But for some reason, on this day. I decided to see how she would react to me touching her leg underneath the table. I should also mention that I was actively engaged in conversation with her mom and dad. They were asking me all sorts of questions, and we made jokes while conversing. Throughout this, I was also eating my burger and fries with only one hand. Her brothers were mainly harassing each other, but I would engage with them randomly as well.

Not long after we started eating and conversing, I decided to leave my right hand in my lap and to only use my left hand for eating. Once we were all actively talking and laughing, I started to gently caress the outside of her leg with the back of my hand. I felt the initial shock/ startle, but in the very next moment, her leg leaned into my touch. Seeing this as a good sign, I started to touch her leg from her knees on up with gentle caresses up and down. Then I would gently but firmly squeeze her thigh and then go right back to caressing her leg. Well, not long after doing that, she spread her legs even more. This was all unnoticeable underneath the table because of all the laughter and conversation, and eating going on. Not to mention that her spreading her legs a bit from their original relaxed state didn't mean they were suddenly wide open. It only meant that they were a bit more open than before, which I took to mean that I could now touch and squeeze and stroke her inner thigh, which I of course did.

The part that actually caught me by surprise, and that I by some miracle managed to suppress, was when her hand suddenly went underneath the table momentarily. In that moment, she grabbed my hand…and placed it directly on her pussy. Apparently, that wasn't enough because she then proceeded to move my hand, move her shorts and panties to the side and then to shove my fingers directly into her pussy. The next moment after, her hand came back up to the table, and all the conversation and laughter continued as if nothing was going on. Meanwhile, I nearly lost my mind – and almost spat up my burger.

To say she was wet was an understatement. And being the little devil I can be sometimes, I decided to take the risk to play with her until she had an orgasm. Yes. You read that right. Somehow, some way, I managed to finger her to the point of orgasm, and she miraculously managed to suppress it enough so as not to make it noticeable to her whole family. I noticed it in how she bit her burger extra passionately, slurped her drink while taking deep rhythmic breaths, and how she faked having digestive issues or trouble with the food, by biting her hand with a mouth full of food, in order to cover up the pleasure and orgasm.

At some point, she excused herself to use the bathroom, which I found out later was actually to clean up all her wetness. Anyway, that went really well! The simple attention I gave to her leg in those circumstances was risky to be sure, but because the girl and I had already kissed a lot and messed around a bit before this, I felt confident it would be ok even if she removed my hand from her leg. This shows how touching a girl's leg in a gentle but suggestive manner can immediately give you signals on which way to go next. Then there's the obvious part where she grabbed my hand and placed it where she wanted it. To me, that's ideal because it makes it obvious and clear what she wanted me to do. Of course, I could have pulled my hand away had I felt it was unsafe or didn't want to, but I went for it, and it all worked out!

The epic fail, on the other hand, placed me in a similar situation…but with a few key differences that resulted in a drastically different outcome.

The Epic Fail

In class one day, I was mentally wrangling with the idea of a threesome with two redheads while planning my next painting, when all of a sudden, I was pulled out of my head by the sudden feeling of a hand on my thigh. Under normal circumstances, I would have been overjoyed at the feeling of suddenly having a girl's hand grab my thigh underneath a table. But, since I was in a small military training classroom, almost shoulder to shoulder with other soldiers, I was unsure what to do. Add to that the fact that there were two instructors walking around that I didn't really know, and the girl and I had never done anything sexual together. I became really nervous but also excited at the thought of being able to get away with something like that under those circumstances.

The girl sitting right next to me was very attractive. She had short blonde hair, blue eyes, was relatively short and a little thick, and very voluptuous. I was very attracted to her and her body type, but I had got the feeling that she didn't really find me attractive, so I tried to pay her no mind from the day we met. So, we never really talked to one another, never mind touched each other.

It is necessary to emphasize that she was really, really, attractive to me because her body type was practically exactly my type at the time, and she exuded sexy deliciousness to me. That meant that it took extra discipline on my end to not pay her any attention and to ignore her as best I could. So, when she suddenly and slyly slid her hand under the desk and squeezed my thigh, I was not only a bit shocked but super surprised. Almost to the point where I couldn't hide my surprise from the others in the class. Her squeeze was strong too, and she glanced over at me when she squeezed me once again to make sure I got her meaning. At that moment, in my head, I thought it was on.

At some point during the same class, I decided to reciprocate. So, I also waited for a good moment and gave her leg some attention and a squeeze. Well, little did I know that it was noticed by more than just her and after the training class was over for the day, I got into trouble for sexually harassing a fellow soldier during training. Ugh. Even though I made it clear that I did not instigate it, I was merely reciprocating, the instructors didn't want to hear it.

The whole thing was innocent enough, so I didn't get into any real trouble over the whole thing. I just got my ass chewed a bit and was forced to sit elsewhere in the class for the duration of the training. Not only did I pick the wrong place at the wrong time, around the wrong people, to try to give some sexual attention and innuendo to that girl's leg, but I was also stigmatized after that for some time. It was as though I had gone out of my way to make unwanted advances to a girl who happened to be innocently sitting next to me. All that meant that the excitement I felt at taking that risk was not worth it in the end.

Needless to say, I found her way less attractive after that and stayed away from her. I didn't want to invite anything else from her, and never tried to do anything with her again – or in any other Army training environment for that matter.

The differences between these two situations should be evident. Not to mention the obvious signs and effects one can have on a girl, apart from getting caught, when touching her legs or thighs. Normal touches like resting your hand on her thigh while driving can be soothing and emotionally affirming. Doing the same thing under a table in the presence of others can have a whole different effect or feeling. And kissing, squeezing, and nibbling on her legs while making love can send a whole other set of signals and sensations. It's easy enough to recognize these things, but the point is to remember and practice them so that you can be a better lover to the woman who decides to share her legs with you. And to the girl you are getting to know, it's a good thing that you now know how to gently pace yourself so that you don't make a sudden move that completely turns her off.

Chapter 11: Feet (and Toes). Not the End & Not the Beginning

Not all women like their feet messed with or even touched. Fortunately, those ladies tend to be in the minority. For those ladies who don't mind or enjoy having their feet given some attention, there are several things that you can do that they would enjoy. I am aware that some of you stay away not only from your feet but from the ladies' feet as well, and that's fine. Just skip this chapter. But for all others, carry on, lovers, as you were.

My philosophy here is to generally give them some attention (if they aren't all sweaty and stinky) as soon as her shoes and socks come off, if we're on our way to sex. Some simple rubs, squeezes and then more during sex when we are in the missionary position. And when the moment is right, some kisses, suckles, and nibbles to the feet and toes for pleasure and fun.

Highlights

1. Find out whether or not the girl even likes her feet touched or messed with in any way.

2. There's a right place and a right time for touching or messing with a lady's feet. Personal hygiene, mood, location, and foreplay or during sex, are all factors. If she doesn't want to for whatever reason, don't push the issue. Just let it be. If she does, find out what her likes and dislikes are.

3. You may not be into touching or messing with feet, but who you end up with might be. Stay open-minded, but don't force yourself to do something you don't want to or dislike.

4. It's ok to have a foot fetish, but don't be creepy or weird about it.

5. Many ladies out there love foot massages. That doesn't mean that you assume that they all do and just try to start offering and rubbing random ladies. That's also kinda creepy.

6. Beyond foot massages for relaxation (as in for pleasure), nibbling, and even kissing her feet can create pleasurable sensations that she might enjoy.

7. If the girl likes the foot touch but rejects your attempt to kiss, nibble, or suckle on parts of it, don't press the issue and just stop; keep it at the level that makes her comfortable. (Remember that the whole point of doing these things is to increase pleasure and enjoyment, not to create displeasure and rejection.)

8. Don't over-ask for feedback. Just let her know that she can feel free to let you know how you're doing at any time.

9. Some women operate under the belief that women should have small feet in order to be feminine and pretty; do not feed into that.

Women's feet are definitely a critical component of completing the look of their legs. They go out of their way to show them off and to reveal their toes in sandals and flats. They also love to get them pampered by getting their toenails painted, hair shaved, calluses scraped, etc. At the same time, many women still wear heels and shoes that are bad for their feet. You've seen them. They cram their feet into tiny shoes that also squish their toes together in an unnatural way. They wear shoes that are too short so their toes might hang off the front edge, while their heel might overflow at the rear. They might have bunions, corns, calluses, hammer toe, ingrown toenails, or the most common one that I've observed, dry and ashy, cracked heels.

On the flip side, some women take great care of their feet! So much so that when they walk barefoot, wear flats, or walk in sandals, you might not only notice their pretty feet but also how they match their hands and nails. They can be painted or unpainted, but the point is that a man who pays attention will notice if a woman takes care of her feet or has nice feet or has nasty feet. Only the men who don't care about feet won't care about what a woman does with her feet. And since I pay attention to everything about women, we are definitely going to go over that here. In that sense, I hope that there is something useful to you in what is written below.

The Basics in Detail

1. Find out whether or not the girl even likes her feet touched or messed with in any way. This one is important and also rather obvious. You can ask directly or indirectly. I have had it on a rare occasion

where I was told not to touch her feet very early on when things started to get intimate. Just because she's willing to trust a masseuse with her feet doesn't mean she wants you to touch them.

2. There's a right place and a right time for touching or messing with a lady's feet. If she's getting home from work or a workout and she's all sweaty and dirty, maybe wait till she cleans her feet. If she's in a lousy mood for whatever reason, offering a foot rub may help if you let her vent while sitting on the couch, or it may make things worse. If you are at home, a public place, or at someone else's house, that might matter, so take that into consideration as well.

You could use a good foot rub to lead into some foreplay, or you could take it to an unexpected place and then rub her feet while you are making love to her in missionary style. She might like it, or she might ask what the heck you are doing because she loves it. Either way, take the time to learn what places and times messing with your woman's feet are good.

3. You may not be into touching or messing with feet, but who you end up with might be. Stay open-minded, but don't force yourself to do something you don't want to or dislike. I say that because some girls have some fetishes of their own that they will ask you to participate in them. For example, I was with one woman who was all about having her toes licked and sucked. She loved it. There was another who was all about having her feet rubbed at any time by anyone who was willing. Fortunately for her, she had nice feet.

There were a few more ladies that I encountered who had their own desires when it came to their feet, but I had to decline. Why? Because they had unattractive feet or what some of you might call, "nasty feet". To me, they weren't nasty because I don't get with girls who have what I consider to be nasty feet. But if their hygiene isn't up to par, or I just don't think their feet are that attractive in contrast to the rest of their body, I will take a hard pass at doing anything with them. And guess what? You should also practice saying no when you don't want to do something. It's ok. And definitely call out nasty feet if a girl is trying to get you to do something, should you encounter a nasty pair.

4. It's ok to have a foot fetish, but don't be creepy or weird about it. I have to underline this because there are some men out there who won't hesitate to try to touch a stranger's feet. Or worse, they don't even know a girl, have just met her, and then comment on her feet,

focus on them, and try to get the girl to let you do whatever it is that they desire with her feet.

Now some girls with hardcore foot fetishes might be all for letting you do what you want, but at least take the time to find that out before you start to try to talk to a woman about her feet. Jumping right into the foot topic for your own sake and selfish reasons without consideration for said owner of the feet is what makes it weird and creepy. This especially applies to you toe and foot suckers/lickers out there. I got my eye on you. To clarify what "creepy" often means from a woman's perspective: it usually refers to behavior or words that would only feel acceptable – or even welcome – if they came from someone she finds attractive or desirable. For example, if she feels uncomfortable with your foot-related advances but wouldn't feel that way if the same came from Brad Pitt, that contrast highlights the point. Even so, just because you may have the looks, the swag, or the rizz, doesn't protect you from being perceived as creepy. So, keep it consensual.

I've had women come up to me and ask me things right off the bat that were weird and creepy. I have also had women approach me with respect and then proceed to inquire about what I am into…before pitching to me what it is they want to do with me. The first method put me off and was an instant no. The latter was much more agreeable, kept me open-minded, and made me feel like considering her request (even if it was something that I had never thought about before). Same thing can apply to women when it comes to certain things like foot massages, rubs, fetishes etc. Be respectful and considerate, and her mind might be more open to whatever idea. Well, she will hear you out at the very least.

5. Many ladies out there love foot massages. And I mean LOVE. If you took my advice and jumped on the chance to take a massage course (as I suggested in Book 1), chances are you learned something about massaging feet. And while what you learn may not be all there is to learn about massaging feet, I highly recommend that after you pick up the basics of foot massaging, that you go online and search for more techniques that you can use. Trust me, if you have a woman who loves having her feet rubbed, she won't forget it or you. I've experienced certain women doing the whole rolling their eyes into the back of the head thing during a good foot massage. I've seen some become overjoyed with glee at the first rub of the foot. With one woman in particular that I remember, when I began rubbing her feet, she

practically pounced on me within minutes. Not a common reaction, but it can happen.

The only downside to this is if a woman asks you to rub her feet…when her feet just aren't feet you wanna rub. That can be a bit of a minefield if you have already declared your skills or abilities in that regard. With that in mind, what I suggest is that you keep your cake hole shut about what you can do or enjoy about a woman's body until you have determined that she has something you would enjoy touching. In that case, when the situation arises where her feet are revealed, if they weren't already due to sandals or whatever, depending on how you feel about them, that should determine what your next move is or what comes out of your cake hole.

6. Beyond massage for relaxation, as in for pleasure, using oil to rub her feet, nibbling, kissing her feet, and even toe sucking can be very pleasurable for certain females. If a girl has a foot fetish, then she will likely let you know just where and how often she likes what she likes. Otherwise, it is best to discover these things after good hygiene has been conducted, like after a shower or if she washes her feet. Just remember to ask in order to get consent and check in with her after she gives you the go-ahead to ensure she is still enjoying herself and not suffering through an unpleasant experience that she feels too guilty to say no to. Like when on a whim you decide to go full throttle on sucking her toes instead of giving her a gentle foot rub! Yeah, don't do that.

Using coconut oil usually works pretty well for a foot rub, but that also has a chance to turn more sensual if sexual energy and chemistry are in the air. Pinpoint techniques won't work well, so you'll have to apply pressure as you slide your digits (thumb and fingers) across her foot. Make sure your nails are cut, and try not to dig too much with your thumb alone. Distribute the pressure you apply in case her feet are sensitive because there is a lot of thin skin and many bony parts. To help with that, use both hands on either side of the foot (sort of like how you hold a sandwich). Rub with the thumbs and watch out for bony areas.

When a foot massage moves more towards sensual, or you're already naked and just having some foreplay, kissing and nibbling on her feet might be something she likes. Some girls are into you sucking their toes as well. Just mind your teeth. Again, remember hygiene and to make sure this is something that you want to do, not something that the woman is pressuring you into. Some girls think that their feet are all sexy and nice (when sometimes they aren't). It's really an individual preference thing. Still, if you enjoy it and she does as well, the methods you use with her toes won't be much different from what you would do with her hands.

Be sure to check in between the toes as well before you bring your mouth hole near them. Last thing you want is fuzzies, sweat gunk, or worse to end up in your mouth, even if she showered or washed her feet.

Nibbling can be pleasurable for a woman, but it can also tickle, so be ready for that. It can turn things into more fun and playfulness as well, so it isn't necessarily a bad thing. Ticklish spots vary, but the heel and Achilles tendon area tend to be a good spot for that, as well as the arches of the feet. Soft caresses will always tickle sooner or later, so bear that in mind if you wanna keep it fun and playful.

7. If the girl likes the foot touch but rejects your attempt to kiss, nibble, or suckle on parts of it, don't press the issue and just stop. Keep it at the level that makes her comfortable. Remember that the whole point of doing these things is to increase pleasure and enjoyment, not to create displeasure, tension, and rejection. That translates to don't let it bother you if you are enjoying and looking forward to doing foot stuff, and she shoots part of it down or completely. It happens.

The whole purpose of foreplay is to get warmed up for the main event anyway, which is typically the actual penetrative sex. Don't lose sight of what you both are into all this for. And if you haven't done anything with her feet and decide to during sex, it can be a gamble, but usually more acceptable during the doing of the deed.

One last tip: if she uses lotion or any other substance that isn't meant for the mouth, watch out. It can taste real nasty, and you might end up in a similar situation like in the neck area.

8. Don't over-ask for feedback. Just let her know that she can feel free to let you know how you're doing at any time. I say that because it can turn into a turn-off due to you showing your lack of confidence. If a woman starts to get turned off from you over asking when it comes to doing things with her body, or in this case, her feet, you could end up with a rejection. Women can be weird like that sometimes. Not guaranteed, but it is a possibility. Keep your asks brief and generic enough to allow them to answer as they please. Something simple you

can say while you are starting to do something is, "Let me know if it's good or if I hit a good spot." That way, you look for positive feedback instead of negative feedback. It feels good when you are told what is good to keep doing or to repeat, rather than being told what's not good all the time.

9. Some women operate under the belief that women should have small feet to be feminine and pretty. Do not feed into that. Some of you men also don't like women with big feet. Well, guess what? No one has a say in the size of their feet. Not you and not them. And yet some women have it in their heads that women should have small, pretty feet. I've never cared personally when it comes to foot size, even though I have my preferences, but I have never disparaged a woman I've been with for the size of her feet.

Some women are insecure about their feet. Other women don't care, and others are overconfident to the point that they think all men find their feet pretty or attractive. I always make it a goal to ensure that they feel as accepted for their natural looks as possible, and I would encourage you to do so as well. After all, I didn't get with them to reject them over something like that, stinky feet notwithstanding. But if her feet are a deal breaker or a turn off for whatever reason you have, it can't be helped.

Don't force it. Not all women are into having their feet touched, and many are all about the right moment, place and time. Going out of your way to create a situation where you can mess with her feet isn't organic. If she's into that, eventually the situation will present itself. Don't lose sight of the fact that legs and feet are temporary areas to spend time in order to create anticipation and excitement for the real goal of oral sex or a passionate love session. And remember, if you end up in bed together, you don't need to do everything on the first go. Her feet will still be there.

The Epic Success

Strangely enough, there I was half-dreaming, wondering why Netflix had such a small and crappy Anime selection while simultaneously having missionary-style sex with a girl, when all of a sudden, I realized that one of her feet was right next to my face. It snapped me out of my current thoughts and triggered a whole new idea. What if I sucked on her toes while I was sexing her? I'd never quite done that before, but it would give my mouth something to do – and a chance to evaluate if it is something this woman likes.

I freed my left hand from her breast, grabbed her foot, then slowly started to nibble and suck on a couple of her toes. As I did this, I just made sure not to mess with her nails with my tongue – to avoid scratching my mouth with her nails – and to involve my tongue to some degree with a little suction. It was weird and unusual to navigate, but not at all unpleasant to do. Focusing on that while having active sex in rhythm, while also using my other hand on her breast, took a little mental effort, but I got the hang of it after a minute or two.

I'm not sure how long I did that, but I do remember that eventually she did orgasm, then I came, and we both chilled afterwards and had a fun talk. She revealed that the moment I surprised her by sucking on her toes, she could feel nothing else. The surprise pleasure was so intense and amazing that she couldn't feel me inside her or the pleasure from sex. It even helped to make her cum in such a way that she felt sensations in her feet as she came! Pretty wild and also a one-time happening in my sexual life.

I wouldn't count on something happening like this for you, as this was definitely a one-off in how the toe sucking practically triggered an orgasm, but you never know.

The Epic Fail

I was trying to figure out why I had opened my big mouth about liking nice feet on a girl when this attractive woman in front of me revealed her feet. She was really cute. Great boobs, a little thick. Kinda sexy with nice legs. So, I figured, she's bound to have the kind of feet and toes that a lover like me would enjoy giving attention to during the right moments, right? Well, once she took off her shoes and they were up close to my face, my body had a different reaction.

Repulsion wasn't quite the right word to use at that moment. It was a complete absence of desire. She had calluses, bunions, and gangly nails. I could tell they were lotioned, but also not taken care of properly. She clearly operated under the belief that none of these detractors made her feet any less attractive to a man. Well, at least to this man, all of that mattered. And she had a bit of funk in between her toes to boot.

So as not to fully renege, I rubbed on her feet a bit (using that as an opportunity to clean her out between her toes) and then placed some strategic kisses on her feet combined with gentle touches that would hopefully turn into tickles. And sure enough, it worked. She got ticklish, started pulling her feet from my face and laughing, which then allowed me to make her even more ticklish with my touches. This meant that anything I did, even when I faked trying to put her toes into my mouth, caused her to yank her foot away in anticipation of the tickles.

We moved on to other things, didn't have sex, but I did give her an orgasm before we wrapped things up in order not to let her leave completely unsatisfied, and then she left. I had to admit to myself that ultimately, I am not a hardcore foot guy. I discovered that how into a girl's feet and toes I am is directly affected by a few factors. A woman has to maintain a certain care standard with her feet and toes in order for me to be attracted and not repelled. I also don't want to place most of my focus on any girl's feet unless it's foot rub time as a part of foreplay. I'm simply sharing this so that you have something to bounce your own likes or dislikes off of.

In either of these cases, I could have easily added stories about actual massage situations where a girl was blown away in a good way, or where I tried to massage another girl's feet at a completely inappropriate time when they were stinky and sweaty. Or the time a girl tried to rub my feet, only to hurt them – and then get mad at me for being hurt by her touch, which was crazy. Or even about the time I gave foot massages to a bunch of women with pretty feet simply because they were all hot and in bikinis and practically in line for me to give them a good foot rub. But because there is a clear line between rubbing a foot and placing any part of it in your mouth. It's easy to see how one is much easier to do than the other. And although I'm more prone to getting my hands on feet than into my mouth by far, it makes for slightly better stories to share the foot-in-mouth ones.

Chapter 12: The Vulva and the Vagina = The Yoni (E-oh-knee)

I think it was Betty White, God rest her beautiful soul, that once said, "Why does everyone say grow some balls. Balls are weak. Grow a vagina! Those things can take a pounding!" Vulvas and vaginas are truly marvelous things. I hope to share some details here that, to some, may seem a bit beyond basic information. But I assure you that all the info in this chapter is basic stuff you should download into your brain. A lot of other books have this info, though I may present it a tad differently.

All terms to describe girl and boy parts are scientifically named. Some of the terms they chose are fine. Others not so much. At least according to me, anyway. I know that we all have our preferences regardless of the official names in the biology texts or even when it comes to our own language. Other cultures of the world have their own names for these bits of ours. When it comes to pussy, my favorite word for it from other cultures is Yoni (e-oh-knee).

My philosophy when it comes to yonis is to know as much about them in general as possible. Then to learn as much as I can about my woman's vagina so that I can take as good care of it…without learning the scientific names of all the bits (because that only really matters when talking to doctors). My yoni curriculum involves learning lots of stuff that you may not care to know, but that is absolutely necessary if you ask me. Why? Because the education system, alongside many mothers out there, didn't do their jobs in educating their daughters (fortunately, many are working hard to do something about this) about their own body parts. There is also some sense of shyness, and even shame, when it comes to their own genitals. So, caring about ladies is, by extension, caring about their yonis if you ask me. And as such, it is part of this Casanova's Code.

Highlights:

1. Yoni/pussy can be more diverse in look and feel than our penises by far. (Age, body type, vulva structure, birth, diet, fitness, smoking, and use or lack thereof, can change it a lot)

2. The vulva is the official name of the outside of the pussy that is made up visually of the labia majora, labia minora, clitoris, vaginal opening, clitoral hood, urinary opening, and the mons pubis (the sometimes thicker mound of skin over the pubic bone).

3. The clit is the only organ in the human body with the sole purpose of pleasure.

4. Pubic hair is a normal thing, and women go to great lengths and even great pain to deal with it one way or another for themselves and for you. (Maintenance if they don't want any pubes, and maintenance if they want to retain them. Maintenance either way.)

5. We also use the term vagina interchangeably with the term pussy when talking about a woman's genitals, but vagina is the term for the inside of a pussy. The vagina is the interior portion that you feel and rub your dick against when you have sex. The word yoni encompasses the whole thing and more.

6. The smell, the look, the feel, and the taste of a pussy/yoni can tell you a lot about the compatibility of you and a woman. Not to mention it can also inform you of the level of hygiene or vaginal health a woman has going on down there, if you know what you're smellin'.

7. Does your dick size matter when it comes to pussy/yoni itself? No. And also yes.

8. Always start off gently when doing anything with a woman's pussy and work up in intensity from there.

9. Most pussy/yoni can be finicky and require particular things to stay in balance, so don't go muckin' it up with dirty fingers, dirty nails, dirty dick, dirty toys, or by shoving things into it or onto it that have no place there.

10. Pussies can look and feel extremely different from each other, and those who think that they all feel the same are not paying attention.

11. As a vagina goes through its monthly cycle, it can have discharge, change smell, feel different, be more wet, get less wet, or even be more sensitive.

12. Women actually have the ability to influence how tight their vagina can be. Whether or not they use that ability is a different story. All we can do for ourselves is to stretch.

13. Whether or not a woman is well hydrated can directly reflect her ability to get wet when horny or during sex. Regardless of that, some women are naturally wetter or drier than others.

14. Contrary to what some may believe, I know for a fact that smoking, smoking weed, and even drinking and eating certain things can change the taste and smell of a woman's pussy/yoni.

15. The cervix is at the end of the vaginal canal. It is very firm lover, so take note of this because it can hurt you or her if you hit it with your pulsating pole probe.

16. Although most women feel general pleasure when you place a finger, toy, or dick in their pussy/yoni, many women also have specific spots inside where it can feel especially good.

There is a lot to say here in this chapter about pussy. I prefer to use the term yoni, which I picked up in Hawai'i. Culturally, amongst us men, pussy is what we roll with when we talk about both the vulva and the vagina in combination, so that's what I will use throughout. But I'll still try to squeeze in yoni as much as I can. Why? Because there are times when you don't want to use the word pussy for whatever reason, and where another word that isn't western science-based, and is also all encompassing, like yoni, that means the same thing but doesn't sound so vulgar, can be equally understood and useful. Plus, it also sounds way better than the term vulva. I mean, it sounds like the female version of a Volvo vehicle and who wants to use that?

Pussy/yonis are amazing. They are also many things at the same time. The birth canal. The major pleasure center. It's wet, it's dry, it can take a beating, it's fragile, and it houses the only organ contained within humans that is solely built for pleasure. Plus, it can bleed once a month for decades and still be alive. This little fact alone explains all the stories I've heard over the years from women about the many unnoticeable and creative ways that they masturbated without anyone knowing.

As a man you think you masturbate a lot? Shit, there are tons of women out there that put you to shame, and you would never even know it, and they will never admit it. The main reason is that there are plenty of ladies out there who don't even need their hands to achieve the deed, and others who can do it merely by rubbing their thighs together. How unfair is that?!

As far as the details of this chapter, I'd love to cite sources here about all these details, but most of this I learned when I was very young. Other parts I just picked up along the way, so it'd be impossible to cite them all without arbitrarily looking up some biology textbook I've never seen before or some scientific website. Instead, how about you just check for yourself and see if any of this is valid and or accurate? You have a cell phone, and a search is only seconds away if you wanna check stuff. Anyway, let's get on with the details.

The basics in detail

1. Pussy can be more diverse in look and feel than penises by far. Just think about age, body type, vulva structure, labia sizes, labia colors, proportions, clit proportions, clitoral hoods, vaginal openings, diet, fitness, smoking, pre-birth, post-birth, and use or lack of use. The only things that can be different about us men are our balls, our length, our girth, color, veins, circumcision or not, and the shape of our head. Some dicks can curve this way or that, and some can get harder than others. But generally, that's about it. As we men get older, about the only things that can change are our ability to get an erection, maintain an erection, maybe a loss of some length, skin appearance, and a loss of some sensitivity. But overall, unless you become obese, or get circumcised, it will be about the same, minus some skin color differences and just older and less functional over time.

Yoni's/pussies, on the other hand, can have their labia in all manner of proportions. From fully present to almost unnoticeable, and even to where they are completely uneven on either side. Clits can vary in size and length, as well as their hoods. The clit can be so miniscule you can't even really see them and can also be so large as to appear like a micro penis. The hoods can be almost missing to completely covering the clit. The vaginal opening can be very small, even with a woman's legs spread wide open, or it can be cavernous and allow you to look right in. Then, after a woman gives birth, her pussy/yoni can completely change in look and feel and even in color. And this can happen after every birth. Not guaranteed, but I've seen it both ways. If a woman gains weight, it will change the look of her pussy. The appearance will be different if she loses a bunch of weight as well. Add to the mix how her skin changes depending on whether she smokes or what she smokes, and that too can change the look and feel. Lastly, a woman's age and usage affect everything, but even more so if a woman is constantly stuffing her pussy/yoni with bigger toys, her fists, or other objects for years on end.

If you have raised yourself on porn or have just your own made-up mental image from textbooks about what a pussy can be like, or if you think that having children won't affect it, you are leaving a lot of room for reality to surprise you.

Between men and women, women by far undergo the most bodily changes as they grow, age, and give birth to a family. These changes can be difficult to accept for those men who want a family but don't want their woman, or her parts, to change. I've even met men who were completely disappointed with how their woman's pussy changed after birth to the point where it affected the marriage. Now the opposite is also true, which is important to keep in mind. Sometimes the pussy/yoni stays the same, and in some rarer circumstances, it gets even better.

2. The vulva is the official name of the outside of the pussy that is made up visually of the labia majora, labia minora, clitoris, vaginal opening, clitoral hood, urinary opening, and the mons pubis. The mons pubis is the part of the pussy/yoni that is generally over the pubic bone. It can be a bit fatty and cushy, but not always. In the Army, we used to call this the FUPA – Fat Upper Pussy Area.

The labia majora are the thicker outer lips. Sometimes they are there, and fully out, other times they can be almost nonexistent. The labia minora, or the smaller inner lips, don't tend to be thicker at all, but they can go from almost not existent to completely protruding and thereby dominating the look of the vulva/yoni. Now we all may have our own preferences about this, or you may not have any, but whatever you do, accept what your woman has.

The clit is actually a much bigger organ than what you can see, as the majority of it is inside the female body. So, all you see is the tip of the clit-berg. The clitoral hood is supposed to cover the clit, but it isn't always, nor is it always fully present. And if you go down on a girl and just see a clit and no hood, it's fine.

The hole you can't miss is the opening of the vagina, and usually on the upper part of that hole is the pee hole. That pee hole is reason number one for being careful with a pussy/yoni. That little pee hole has little protection and is very short in length between her urinary bladder and the pee hole. For the ladies, this can make them more vulnerable to infections, obstructions, and irritations. That, amongst other reasons, is why women get urinary tract infections (UTIs) more than men.

I had a dear friend who got a UTI and went to two hospitals trying to get it treated, but they said she wasn't a priority. So she was forced to wait for hours, only for her infection to spread into her kidneys, then her bloodstream, and she died. She was 24. And this was in the US. If you care for your ladies and their private parts, my aspiring lovers, educate yourself further on what UTIs are like and make sure that if someone you care about has one, they get it treated post haste.

For us men, it is very important that you know this so that you are aware that your hygiene and what you try to do with a woman's genitals can have some serious consequences for the woman. It's also the main reason why, when you have a baby girl, and she needs to be cleaned because she pooped or peed, you need to wipe towards her back and not towards her front. Because if you wipe the wrong way, you will put all sorts of poop into her little sensitive areas and get her sick, as any good father knows.

A woman's vulva can be really intimidating to a lot of boys and men. I know for a fact that some of you think it's kinda nasty and don't want your face near it, much less put your mouth on it. And yet, you want your dick all up in it all the time. With that same mouth that you don't want to put on her pussy/yoni, you will articulate to her that you want her mouth to go down on you.

Look lover, pussy/yonis can take a while to get used to, just like a woman can take a long while to get used to your sperm. But the only way you are going to get used to being down there is to be down there and learn to love it, not just from a dick standpoint. Dicks and pussies/yonis are totally different in what one or another has to deal with or get used to, they get smegma and sweaty balls, and as a lover, this is our half.

For those of you men who already like it or are used to it, help your buddy out with encouragement if they get disgusted. In case that isn't enough, and even though I mention this again later, I'll tell you how to get used to a woman's pussy/yoni. The secret is simple: spend as much time with it, close to it (as in your face) as possible.

If you have any issues, you will have to communicate to your girl how you currently feel about pussy/yoni and how you want to change that. Assuming she's cool with it, that means that at every opportunity, you will need to have your face near her pussy. Rest your head on her lap while you watch things on your phone. Have her sit on your chest near your face as you relax. Whatever method you choose, the more time you spend near it and getting accustomed to how it smells, looks, and even tastes, eventually you will like or even love it. It took me two years. And even then, it was a constant thing with one girl for six months before I just woke up one day and it didn't bother me.

There's no guarantee, of course, that you will learn to like it this way or even to love it. But…it's important that you learn to get used to it at the very minimum enough to please your partner as much as possible.

3. The clit is the only organ in the human body with the sole purpose of pleasure. Listen here, lover, even though this is true, there are still plenty of women out there who don't masturbate much, even though they may like sex and have sensitive clits. There are plenty of women who, despite their pleasurable clit, don't often have clitoral orgasms very easily. There are plenty of women who have rubbed their clits from such a young age in such specific ways that those ways are now the only ways that they can cum, which puts you/us at a disadvantage in pleasing them because only they know the nuances of getting themselves off.

I'm sure that for you long-time masturbators out there, who have a certain way that works for you, you can relate to what I'm saying here.

After a woman orgasms from clitoral stimulation, she usually becomes hypersensitive on her clit and can't stand any further stimulation until at least a little time goes by. Remember that, so you don't push that button too far. There are lots of nerve endings in there, and women can react kind of like we do after we cum in the sense that more stimulation is either too much or unpleasant.

4. Pubic hair is a normal thing, and women go to great lengths and even great pain to deal with it one way or another. It is perfectly natural for human females to have pubic hair down there. It is neither good nor bad. It just is.

When I was a teenager growing up, I thought it looked really weird when an adult woman would shave her pussy in any way or style in porno mags. At the time, my logic was, 'I just got my pubes, so why would I want to shave them off?' Why would anyone else want to shave them off? Didn't they feel the same? It was a sign of maturity from boyhood to manhood for me. It was confusing, and I didn't particularly understand the need or logic.

When I got older and started to have sex, it became rather obvious as to why trimming or shaving your pubes might be practical and why women did it as well. One of my favorite jokes is, "How do you get rid of unwanted pubic hair? By spitting it out and flossing it from your teeth." Then I learned the great lengths and time that women spend just to get rid of body hair in general, and what they can go through just to have a smooth vulva/yoni. And aesthetically, I had to admit to myself that I prefer it that way. But it is just my preference.

Some women talk about waxing like it's no big deal. I'm here to tell ya that I've witnessed the after effects on some ladies to where it was a big freaking deal. Extreme pain, bruising, bleeding, and completely out of sexual commission for about a week, not to mention short-term traumatized. Some women are lucky and just don't feel it as extremely down there when it comes to getting their hairs yanked out, but it is no joke. So, if you have a girl who has her yoni waxed, you better appreciate what she is doing! Because that, lover, is the opposite of pleasure.

Women will also go get lasered or plucked. Neither of which feels good at all either. But no matter what method they choose, it takes money and lots of maintenance to keep hair in check, so the skin can be exposed and smooth. When women have a smooth vulva/yoni, it is usually more visually appealing to us men, and it also allows us to see how well their hygiene is or if she has some funk going on down there. Pay attention to that because a freshly shaved or smooth pussy/yoni is an easily inspectable one, especially for any type of obvious infection, whether it be fungal or viral. And to me, that is the biggest reason to favor a well-trimmed or shaven vulva/yoni. In the era of STIs, anything that makes it even a little bit easier to see if she's clean is a bonus.

Some women can be sneaky, devious liars, or just plain wanting to hide something they got going on, and they might do it by having a bush. The downside to a woman having pubes is that apart from making it harder to see if she has something going on down there that you might not wanna catch, is that unless she washes and cares for the hair appropriately, it can smell bad very easily.

Many of the women I have talked to, and a few I've been with that had pubes or a bush, when they insist that they're all clean and there are no smelly issues down below, it generally means that they do wash and clean that area – but that's it. Any smell that comes from that basic care is the smell they are used to, and therefore it isn't bad according to them. Unfortunately, some of them didn't realize that a smell they are used to doesn't equate to a smell we men will like. This, of course, directly influences whether we want to spend any time down there at all. And out of all those ladies I've encountered, only one understood this and made sure that not only was her bush clean, but that it smelled fresh.

Another thing to note is that with some women, shaving their pubes doesn't always produce a smooth surface area. Sometimes, due to unique skin, hair growth angles, and rigidity of the hair at the base, the skin can end up feeling like sandpaper or like little teeth are scraping your dick as you have sex. Not only will it rub you raw and bloody, but it will also take you out of commission for a while sex-wise as you heal from a raw dick.

Now, prickly hairs on the skin are normal as the hair starts to grow back. After waxing, it usually grows back softer, but on this particular type of hair and skin, the woman has to shave at the right angle, with the right cream, with the right razor, and with the right number of blades for her hair to not be like razor wire to your precious penile skin. That means you are going to have to speak up about the problem if you end up with that effect on your dick. And if she blows you off, doesn't care, laughs, or says it's your problem and not hers, you bounce and find a new girl. Got that lover? No need to run around with a bloody dick unless she is an amazing partner, the sex is amazing, she treats you like gold, and you are crazy in love. Then it might be worth it.

All pubes aren't the same. On some women, pubes don't even curl. This is more prevalent among Asian women by far. The textures can be different, the thickness, all of it. So don't be too surprised if one day you get with a woman and her pubes are of a completely different nature than you're used to. This happened to me once when one girl and I finally got some private time. Upon taking her panties off, it looked like the hair of a troll doll had somehow sprouted from her pubic area. I tried so hard not to laugh, but still chuckled a bit.

5. We also use the term vagina interchangeably with the term pussy when talking about a woman's genitals, but vagina is the term for the inside of a pussy. The vagina is the interior portion that you feel and rub your dick against when you have sex. The word yoni encompasses the whole thing and more. Not well known or too popular but maybe we can change that a bit. I love using the word pussy as much as the next guy who uses that word but Yoni just has a different ring to it that I like.

6. The smell, the look, the feel, and the taste of a pussy can tell you a lot about the compatibility of you and a woman or the level of hygiene and vaginal health a woman has. There are three things you will almost immediately notice about a woman's vulva. The first should become apparent the moment you take off her pants/shorts/dress/skirt/undies or whatever the girl is wearing, and that is: if there is any odor/scent. If there is a scent or smell, you will know even before you can look. If she is relatively clean and hygienic, there shouldn't be any significant scent at this point (barring some exceptions). If you unzip her and a strong, intense or deeply musky scent starts to emanate, that, my dear lover, is a red flag. If there isn't any right away, then that is a good sign. As you get your nose closer to it, there will be a scent of course, but more on that later.

When she is bottomless, and you have it bare in front of you, there should only be the scent of an aroused vulva if your nose works normally. It really is tough to describe, as there is a scent to each woman's groin and vagina just as there is to yours. Bottom line: if everything is in balance, the natural scent should not put you off. You don't have to like it, but it should not be off-putting to an extreme degree. If it does stink or put you off for whatever reason, that just might not be the vagina for you. We don't all like the same smells after all. Vulvas have a variety of odors/scents for a variety of reasons. So don't go thinking that just because you picked up a scent that something is immediately wrong. If nothing else, just remember that a woman will have a stronger scent when she is aroused or very turned on or when she's close to her period. And if it smells a little like pee, either you made her laugh really hard beforehand, or she just went to the bathroom and didn't splash fresh water down there to make sure that there isn't any pee there.

Compatibility is more than just getting along. When two bodies come together, there has to be a physical and biological compatibility too – and that especially applies to smells. You should be able to distinguish between smelling an odor that is repelling and probably unhygienic, or if it's simply a smell that doesn't attract you. It happens. It's happened to me a few times, and it can take a bit of time and experience to tell these two apart. At a minimum, if you love her smell, you're good. If you have never really liked the way pussy/yoni smells, but you really like the girl in all other aspects, then you might wanna invest some time in getting used to her scents.

As an example, I could tell from an early age that the smell of pussy/yoni was a bit pungent and strong. I didn't like it, but it didn't turn me off either. It took me two years from the moment I first performed oral sex before I finally learned to like it. And for me, it was literally an overnight thing. I just woke up one day, went to see my girl, we started to have sex, I went down on her, and I noticed that it didn't smell bad to me anymore. Just like that, the same scent I'd been smelling changed from bad to good. The same thing happened to me with Pop Tarts, mashed potatoes, pepperoni, mayonnaise, juicy juice, and even pickles. It might not be like that for you. It might be completely different, but stick with it; you never know.

The second is how it looks: Is there or isn't there a ton of hair? Is it visually clean? Does it have anything dangling from it? Does it have tissue paper attached to it? Or other observable things. This matters because, as much as some women will complain about men and their hygiene, plenty of women out there just don't have it fully together when it comes to their crotch. Due to the nature of the location of their genitalia, it is obviously very difficult to inspect without a mirror at the right angle. This means that some women haven't even really seen what they look like down there, much less inspect it on a regular basis. We're talking sweat moisture or drops from pee, crust from sweat or previous wetness they didn't attend to, fuzz from panties, sometimes dirt from not wearing panties and sitting in random locations without thinking. Even from having a hairy ass, but a clean pussy and having leftover pieces of whatever from not wiping properly. It's all possible and more.

Thirdly and lastly, how does it taste? Taste says a lot. Considering that pussy/yoni is not supposed to taste like vanilla or chocolate (although if it does, then your lady of choice has clearly sprayed something on there), the taste shouldn't be off-putting or revolting. On a healthy, balanced woman, it should taste rather neutral. Kind of like flavorless unsweetened jello, but not really, if that makes any sense. If you have ever tasted your own precum, a healthy wet pussy can taste like that. Diet, hydration, at what stage she might be in her cycle, and overall genetics, as well as age, can play into it as well. So just keep that in mind. That is my way of saying, if at first you don't like it, try, try again. Eventually, you get used to it, and if you're open enough and truly want to be a better lover, at some point things will turn, and you might just find that oral sex can be enjoyable, fun, and even delicious! Sort of like a non-chewable dessert that never runs out. For others, you might take a liking to it instantly.

Here's the kicker, though: almost all females smell slightly different, taste different, and look different down there. So, just because you got used to the flavors and scents of one, this will only carry you so far, if you are lucky enough to have repeat experiences with another lovely lady. On the flip side, you have many flavors to look forward to if you end up loving pussy/yoni.

Now this last bit might just blow your mind. Ready? Some vulvas/ vaginas will stink because they are too clean! You read that right. See, a woman's vagina has a very particular PH balance (Just think of a fish tank and how you have to check the water to make sure it isn't too acidic or too alkaline because if the PH isn't in the right range, it can then kill your fish). Your body has a PH balance, and a woman's vagina has its own individual balance. But don't take my word for it, go web search that stuff on your phone and read up on it. And if a girl cleans the inside of her vagina, via douching or other methods that are not good for it, she will inadvertently throw her vagina out of balance, causing it to smell or just plain not be right. Especially if she does this frequently. That means you can be staring at the most beautiful pussy/ yoni ever and yet have it stink to high heaven without any obvious indicators as to why. And how do I know this? Take a guess.

A vagina will naturally get rid of things inside it in its own way. Usually, gravity assists. If a girl goes digging around in there to "clean" it out, the balance inside can be messed up indefinitely if the girl does not know how to fix this, and it doesn't return to normal on its own.

The only thing a girl should lightly clean is the vulva (remember, that's the labia and stuff) itself. Now, if a girl has a huge bush or any amount of bush and it smells great and her vulva smells lovely, then chances are she takes the right kind of care down there to maintain that delicate balance. I tell you all these things because if the girl you are with doesn't even know the basics of her own genitals, then you knowing them and bringing this info up at the proper time might help her to take better care of herself. I know because I've run into this scenario more than once. This can be a delicate matter to approach though, so take care to have some tact about it.

Remember, we care about vulvas and vaginas and their health. Not just as the birth canal for new humans, or as the beholders of heavenly pleasures on earth or just for sex. Caring about them means caring about the woman it's a part of. And caring about a woman's health makes you a better lover, trust me.

7. Does your dick size matter when it comes to pussy itself? Yes. And also no. If you have never really thought about this one, strap yourself in while I break it down for ya.

Another common thing that is talked about often and in ways that are designed to create more debate and to obfuscate rather than logically answer the question is: does dick size matter in sex with vaginas? From everything I have learned, the answer is a contradictory yes and no. You'll see why it's just not as simple as yes OR no.

First of all, yes, your dick size matters for two reasons: there is a minimum distance and thickness required for penetration to be felt by a girl, and it can be different from girl to girl. All you have to do is research what a micro penis is to begin to get an answer. On the opposite side of that spectrum, there is an actual physical limit to the size of a penis that can fit into any one vagina before it tears or causes pain to the female. And yes, I am well aware that they can stretch and put out babies through that same canal. However, there is an entire framework of things that need to happen before that is possible and a complex bodily chemical sequence and endorphin release that occurs before you can push something like an elongated human watermelon out of a vagina and vulva.

My point is that just because a vagina is capable of taking something huge in theory doesn't mean it will work with every vagina in practice. (Not to mention that just as you can't instantly spread your legs and do a split on the ground as a man without proper repeated stretching and practice). So too must a vagina be given ample time and slow effort into having it stretch without pain or damage. There is also a minimum threshold that a penis must be in size and length in order to be felt by any individual woman. So, in that sense, yes, size matters.

Continuing along with the yes, there are also very real physical differences in the build of vaginas. I'm here to tell you that not all vaginas are built exactly alike. There are as many variations, no matter how similar, as there are women in the world.

For example, I had sex with one girl whose vagina wrapped around me like a form-fitting glove, and sex was very satisfying both for her and me. When I asked her about men of other sizes, she said that she stretched to fit almost every guy without pain and that she always went right back to her usual form and tightness right after. And when I say it form-fitted around my dick, it was like a surgical glove.

At another point in my life, I had sex with a girl whose vagina felt like an enormous cavern that I was entering into whose walls and depth were so vast I couldn't help but feel one tiny portion at a time. Like an earthworm in a large sewage pipe. And although we both felt pleasure, sex was not very satisfying for either of us, and the catch? She had never had sex with anyone before me, which meant that her vagina was built that way by default. Or she lied. But based on what I knew about her and what her best friend validated, I'm certain she did not lie. This pussy/yoni felt more like a large, fixed cavern where the form and shape didn't really change much, or just plain wouldn't unless you pushed down on the abdomen. That obviously meant that she was designed for much bigger dicks than what I am equipped with.

There was one particularly noteworthy experience with a female who had only ever had painful sex before she met me. I was the first guy she had sex with where it didn't hurt, and she felt only pleasure. We talked about it, and we concluded that her vagina was just not as elastic as others. She was smaller inside, so she couldn't really stretch to accommodate a larger penis. She wasn't the only girl that I ran into who was like this. I spoke with others who also described the same experience with us men.

Continuing on with the yes portion, there are those of you out there who have extremely thick, extremely long penises (or any combination or proportion of those two features). I, who happen to be very average, enjoy regular sex in the missionary position. With a normal stroke, I've managed to hit the cervix inside the girl with the head of my penis. And let me tell ya, she did not react very positively to that happening, nor did it feel good to me either. Because of that, I had to adjust and remember that even if my penis is just average in size and dimensions, one can still bottom out in a girl and cause pain. Those of you men who possess greater proportions, should you encounter a similar woman with a rather shallow vagina, you could really cause some damage or even hurt yourself if you are not careful. So, please be considerate.

I know this may be a bit frustrating to some of you because you can't completely insert yourself or get a full stroke, or she can't relax fully to allow you to sex her how you want. But you have to remember that it needs to be pleasurable for both of you. Not just us men. Her screaming and moaning as you smash it in and out of her, and her not telling you to stop, isn't a free pass to keep smashing without checking in with her to make sure that she is enjoying herself as well.

I know it's a thing in porn and a point of pride to a lot of men out there to have a big dick and to impress or pound a girl with it. What I want you to NEVER forget is that sex injuries are a real thing.

While stationed in South Korea, I knew a girl who had to get stitches because the man she had sex with was so large and rough that he literally tore her vagina at the opening. She was petite, mind you, so I couldn't imagine that it would take someone of extreme size to do this. I share this story because we can have serious and harmful effects on women. And if you want to be a better lover and care for vaginas more than you currently do, you need to be considerate and know these things. At least try to care for them more than you do about getting your nut off, at a minimum.

Another soldier whom I worked with somehow bruised the inside of his wife's vagina, as well as altering its position in her abdominal cavity, thereby causing her great pain and discomfort. She had to go see a doctor – all because he had a larger penis and they loved to have intense sex. He literally damaged his wife's insides; just think about that.

And on the flip side of that, I knew a guy who tore the skin of his dick off because he was too big, she was too tight, and everything was too dry. The skin on his dick literally tore off because she sat on him too hard and fast, while she was not wet enough. The key thing here was her ignorance. She was partially drunk, and after getting him hard, she thought she could just jump on it. He stupidly let it happen, thinking nothing serious would occur. Well, he knows better now. And don't forget, if you damage or break your dick, chances of it ever being the same as it was before are not high.

At the medical station I went to regularly in Camp Humphreys S. Korea, from 1999-2000, I once heard of a guy who had just been seen because a girl rode him so hard that it twisted one of his testicles and injured it so badly that he had to have it removed. You see, it isn't just penile injuries you can suffer; your balls are vulnerable too.

The last thing I will say is that some pussies/yonis out there just don't stretch very well. Some of them have very little give and are naturally very tight. With these vaginas, size always matters. I had sex with a girl whose vagina was so tight even my average dick was in shock. This girl also happened to masturbate with the smallest vibrating dildo I had seen at that time in my life. But my favorite story isn't even one of my own. When I was a young soldier, I was friends with a girl whom I lost touch with, but randomly ran into years later. We got talking, and when I asked her about love and relationships, she told me that she had a great guy for a brief minute, but when they went to have sex, his dick was so big that her reaction was like, "Where do you think that's goin? Oh, hell no!" We laughed at that pretty hard, but ultimately she had to let him go because she knew there was no way it was going to fit inside her. It was noticeably sad for her because I had never really heard her talk about a guy she liked so much in that way. But the reality is, there was just no way the sex was going to be enjoyable for her.

So, when you ask the question, "Does size matter in sex?", the answer is yes in this regard. Not everyone is physically compatible sexually, and if you force it, you can hurt yourself or the other person. I have known people who had the briefest of relationships because their bodies were just too physically different. Sex just wasn't possible in the ways they needed. And that's ok, don't force it. Sex compatibility can be a deal breaker due to physical limitations. That's okay.

On the flip side, when you answer no to that same question around whether or not penis size matters, there are some nuances and limitations. Due to the majority of us men being about average in size, it usually doesn't matter physically because the majority of men don't have boundary-pushing or boundary-breaking penises when it comes to getting inside a vagina/yoni.

The majority of women have vaginas that can usually accommodate average and below easily. At the same time, by design, vaginas can stretch a great deal! You have to get the woman to relax and get her turned on, but it usually stretches a good bit on the regular by design. And when you look at it from the birth perspective, compared to a baby, no penis compares. From this perspective, you could say that size does not matter.

Some women also have really tough vaginas. I have met women that have told me they have never felt pain, not once. One told me she loved it when a guy would hit her cervix because of how good it felt. The most surprising to me, though, were the women who loved the pain. To them, sex without some pain wasn't sex at all. To these women, size did not matter. All that mattered was how you used what you had to hit the spots they liked.

I have even met women who were hopelessly addicted to big or giant penises and would settle for nothing less. They would unabashedly ask men or tell men that if they weren't of that type, not to even talk to them. I know because I've been rejected more than a few times by such women.

Another way that size does not matter is in the simple acknowledgement that women can please themselves with a mere finger (or a fist), and we can please them with a finger as well. What does that say? Well, in all honesty, although more than a finger may be preferred, a finger or two's worth of length and girth will do.

Yes, your dick size matters if you are in the extremes of size, length, or girth, but it also doesn't if you find a girl who is a good fit for you. And no, your dick size doesn't matter if you are around the average size mark because most women can accommodate that easily, and the average represents the majority of us men. The only issue is if a girl has a particular preference when it comes to a penis. Essentially, just as personality compatibility is essential for a good relationship, to be a good lover you must also have a good base of physical genitalia compatibility where mutual pleasure and acceptance are effortless.

For the majority of us men, the answer is that our size does not matter. What matters is how you use what you got. It's the motion of your ocean lover. Just remember there's more to thrusting in and out, but I'll cover that in the sex chapter. What truly matters when you match well is that you warm her up first. Foreplay, turning her on, sensitizing her insides to crave you, and bringing out her desire to want you in her. Do all that and her vagina is likely to be very happy with you, regardless of your size and even if you're average or small.

It's like holding hands. Sometimes you link up great together, sometimes you don't. Sometimes there's the pussy/yoni for a night, and sometimes a pussy/yoni for forever.

8. Always start off gently when doing anything with a woman's pussy/yoni. There isn't much else to say about this. Pussies/yonis can take a pounding, but you have to start gently with any manner of touch before you work up to that. Granted, some women will tell you when they want to get outright fucked. Still, barring that, start off nice and gently, then work your way up lover. Don't start at the opposite end of the spectrum.

One more reason why this matters, apart from it helping you with auto lubrication through turning her on, is that if a woman is tense, anxious, not relaxed, or apprehensive, her vagina can actually stay rather firm and tighter than usual in a way that can make it uncomfortable for her and even painful. That can happen even if your penis isn't that big because she hasn't been sensitized for pleasure yet. Yet another reason to control your urges and be a considerate lover.

9. Most pussy can be finicky and require certain things to stay in balance, so don't go mucking it up with dirty fingers, dirty nails, dirty dick, dirty toys, or by shoving things into it or onto it that have no place there. Another self-explanatory one.

Are your hands clean? Is your dick clean? Even if it's clean, I hope you didn't put lotion or something else on it before sex (like I did once) because if you did, you might just ruin the night for both of you. Did you wash those toys first? And if you or she wants to shove random things in, be sure to clean those too.

Sex on the beach, on dirty surfaces, or when using food and many other things need to be thought of ahead of time. Some pussies/yonis are so resilient you could put dirt in them, and they will be fine (don't ask me how I know), but that is not the majority at all. Not even close. Default to care and hygiene, and you and she will be able to enjoy yourselves more without trips to the hospital or necessary long breaks to allow her to heal and recover.

10. Pussies can look and feel extremely different from each other, and those who think that they all feel the same are not paying attention. Women have different physical builds, and that is more present and obvious as you travel the world. That also affects how they look, the color, scent, and inner feel. They can feel and be like gloves, caverns,

waterfalls, stretchy walls, jello, slimy rubber, surgical gloves, satin tubes, or worse or even more magical.

To some men pussy is pussy, but I'm here to tell ya that that doesn't always apply. Add to that physical chemistry, and you are likely to run into one that might blow your mind. And on the opposite side of that spectrum, you might get with one that completely feels off or repulses you. That matters because even if there is a good personal chemistry between the two of you, if your bodies can't sync up well, in body-based relationships, it doesn't bode well for the relationship or its potential.

11. As a vagina goes through its monthly cycle, it can have discharge, change smell, feel different, be more wet, get less wet, or even be more sensitive. This is important to remember because pussy/yoni is nothing like a dick. Our dicks don't change in form or function due to the lunar cycle. But just because you had sex yesterday and she smelled great, felt great, and tasted great doesn't mean the same will also apply tomorrow. A woman's monthly cycle is exactly that, a cycle of changes and preparations for making babies every 28 days or so. What does that mean? It means that there might be times in your girl's cycle when you won't want to have sex due to discharge or a change in smell. Once again, this is why I am encouraging you to truly learn about and care for vaginas. The more you know, the better prepared you will be.

12. Women actually have the ability to manage how tight their vagina can be. Whether or not they use that ability is a different story. Women can flex their vagina in a similar way that you can when you flex or squeeze your dick to move. If they do this consistently, they can strengthen their vaginal muscles and increase the default tightness that it remains at. This ability can be developed to the point where they can make themselves cum just from the right squeezes and manipulations if they try hard enough. Although I'm sure not every woman would be able to do so.

It can also make sex more pleasurable for both of you. She could squeeze you more while you could fill and stretch her more. This is the complementary difference between us and women when it comes to sex. We love to feel the tightness and the squeeze, as that is really pleasurable for us. Women like to feel filled up inside and stretched to some degree. That is where the difference in pleasure and pain kicks in for some women. Some women can have their vagina stretched to its limit and still feel no pain, while others would be in excruciating pain from being stretched too much. Hopefully that gives you some idea.

Anyway, I've personally experienced women getting super relaxed in sex to where almost all control of their pussy is released and left loose. Having sex with a woman who just loosens herself up during sex like an empty plastic bag (an exaggeration) and having sex with a woman who actively participates and squeezes you and flexes as you have sex like a rubber surgical glove, is like night and day. After learning that difference, I began to call out women who did that in order to get them to engage actively in sex.

I tell you all that because if you're dick is hard and you are working hard as a lover and she's just laying there all relaxed enjoying you sexing her…and then you start getting soft because you aren't feeling much, it isn't your fault for losing your erection. Active participation makes for a better feeling vagina. So, if you don't call out a lazy lover, then at least don't have sex with her again. But if you have a receptive girl with you who didn't know this, have her look up some info online for women who can teach others how to make their vaginas stronger. It just might improve the satisfaction of both of your sex lives.

Keeping a tight vagina during sex can be challenging for some women in a similar way that it can be challenging for you as a man to stop from coming so fast when she feels really good. What I mean by that is that when you are having sex with a girl and the girl feels great from the sex, often, she will relax and give in to you. That relaxation causes her to release any tension she might have in her vagina, therefore making her feel looser than she would otherwise. Not every time, but it happens. This can be a challenging thing for women not to give in to because of the effect of the pleasure. It is similar to how we men, when we feel some great pussy/yoni that makes us want to cum right away, have to resist the urge to cum in order to have sex longer. Not exactly a one-for-one similarity, but close. We gotta resist the cum, they gotta resist the relax. Keep that in mind, lover.

13. Whether or not a woman is well hydrated can directly reflect her ability to get wet when horny or during sex. Either way, some women are naturally drier or wetter than others. I've run into this a lot with women, both in experience and just in conversation when probing for details.

The lube industry is huge and makes a ton of money from dry pussy/yoni. I'm here to tell ya that a lot of dry pussy would be fixed if those women just drank more water and maybe less alcohol, less carbonated beverages, less coffee, smoked less, and less sweet drinks. The women not affected by hydration (I know some of those as well) must have some sort of internal body prioritization mechanism that ensures that no matter what condition she's in, that her pussy/yoni gets wet. Some women just don't get very wet at all. Some, at the slightest touch, become soaked. I'm a fan of the wetness rather than the dryness, but that's just me.

Regardless of your situation, when you come upon it, just know that so long as you: (a) Make sure she's hydrated, and (b) Make sure she's genuinely turned on, chances are you won't have a dry pussy on your hands. If you do, then it's time for spit or lube.

14. Contrary to what some may believe, I know for a fact that smoking, smoking weed, and even drinking and eating certain things can change the taste of a woman's pussy. Yes, it is perceptible down there both in flavor and in how wet she can get. Weed can make a girl taste more bitter. Smoking can make a girl taste better or worse (which was weird to discover). Drinking more alcohol than water can change the viscosity of a woman's wetness, from clear and fluid to thick and kind of white, as well as give it a bit of a sour smell. Some women do naturally have a thicker and white-ish wetness to them, so keep that in mind as well. Interestingly, though, vegans tend to be a bit more flavorful than non-vegans (not guaranteed) when it comes to the taste of their pussy/yoni. (Don't ask me how I know.)

15. The cervix is at the end of the vaginal canal. It is very firm, so take note of this because it can hurt you or her if you hit it with your pulsating pole probe. I talked about it earlier, but it's worth mentioning here. If you stick your fingers all the way into a pussy/yoni, you will hit the back wall or end of it. That hard, round-ish part is called the cervix (web search it). To most women, it is not a pleasant thing to have it hit with a finger or a hard dick. There are some out there who do enjoy it being touched. But as it pertains to you, lover, be careful you don't ram your dick into it because if the head of your dick is sensitive, it can and will hurt.

16. Although most women feel general pleasure when you place a finger, toy or dick in their pussy, many women also have specific spots in which it can feel especially good. I'm sure that most of you guys

reading this have a way you like to rub one out or a spot on your dick that really feels good over the rest of the surface area. Maybe there's a grip or something that feels better when done in that way. With the ladies, both around the outside of the pussy (the vulva), which means the lips, clit hood, vaginal opening, as well as inside her vagina, there might be specific spots that really feel good or that can even be key in getting her off. That is why you should always take some time to explore and play down there, so that you can find these spots if they exist.

I'll list some examples from experience. One girl, as I ate her pussy/yoni, had a pleasure trigger point on the edge of her vaginal opening. So long as you really gently rubbed, in a circular fashion, the outer edge of her pussy hole, while licking her, she would explode into orgasm in short order. Another girl loved it when you licked her clit at the base of her clit instead of the tip. When done right, she too would come in short order. The final example was a girl who had a trigger point inside her pussy, up and to the left of her G-spot, in this little nook she had in her vagina. Had she never told me beforehand, I likely wouldn't have figured it out. But thank goodness that she did, as I was able to enjoy her and get her all riled up before pressing her favorite button in order to give her the release she craved.

There is a lot to learn about pussy/yonis in general. After that general knowledge I've just shared, you should learn all that you can about your particular woman's pussy/yoni as well. This study should include her menstrual cycle phases in order to be able to anticipate what's coming and why. It is my philosophy that you can't really say you care about or even love women – much less their pussy/yonis – until you get to a point where you can really tell when your partner's genitals are healthy, out of balance, or undergoing changes. If you don't care about it in this regard, you're totally slackin. And if you ever hope to have a real partner, it behoves you to learn this stuff now, as this knowledge is only basic at best.

The Epic Fail

I had to go way, way back for this story. All the way back to when I was still learning as a teen. Recalling this particular memory wasn't hard at all, surprisingly. In the early 90s, I had a girlfriend whose parents did not like Puerto Ricans at all. I remember her telling me that they were very prejudiced against Puerto Ricans…although I don't remember her ever telling me a reason. Because of this, we had to

sneak around, and they couldn't know that we were together –
otherwise her social life would likely end at the hands of her parents,
which we laughed about quite a lot.

At that point in my life, I was still trying to apply everything I had
taught myself about girls' bodies, so naturally I was nervous and
lacked experience. An opportunity came up for her to be out and about
unsupervised, so we used that chance to go into the woods somewhere
and sit on a log and make out. During that make-out session, her hand
made its way into my pants, and my hand made its way under her skirt.
Well, as fun as that was, I had little to no idea how to navigate her
yoni, and I was super afraid of accidentally touching her butthole, even
though mentally, I had all the parts and bits visually memorized.

Her pubes were kind of intertwined together, but she was really
wet, so I knew I was in the right area. As we kissed, I had to focus
really hard in order to part her pubes while still making out in a
coherent fashion. I remember it being kind of like touching a less wiry
and smoother bristle sponge that was also warm and damp.

Once I got the pubes separated with my furious four-finger
technique, I immediately made contact with something so warm, soft,
and wet that my initial reaction was "wow!"…and "eew!" at the same
time, which is hysterical to me now in retrospect. Either way, I went on
and tried to find her clit, which fortunately for me was not under a
hood and was nubby and hard enough that it made it easy to detect
from everything else she had going on down there. I had studied long
and hard in that library in Panama, as well as used my older brother's
Playboy magazines for reference, many times. So, I was confident that
I knew where the parts of a girl were located mentally. But when
actually touching the real thing without looking, while making out, and
while a girl's hand was on my dick, talk about a challenge! Not to
mention that she kept playing with my dick like it was some sort of
stick shift from a car.

Instead of rubbing it up and down or using my precum to lube up
my dick a bit for smoother strokes, which is something I can only say
now and not then, her idea of playing with a dick was to literally yank
it forward and back and left and right like a literal stick shift. And let
me tell ya, pleasure was not what I felt. That shit hurt a lot – and her
grip of death didn't help. But, a girl's warm and soft hand was on my
dick, which was rare at the time, so there was no way I was going to
complain, and so long as my hand was under her skirt.

While I was navigating her labia with my untrained fingers and their made-up dick-yoon-do technique, I finally managed to get in between them and get to the firm yet wet and soft space there that runs from under her clit down to the vaginal opening. Thing is, I felt like I was pretty far down there already. Like, so far down there that I may have somehow missed her vaginal hole and that at any moment I'd plunge my probing finger into her butt. My white belt in dick-yoon-do would not have been able to withstand such a mistake. I'd seen plenty of magazines and illustrations to know that the butthole was like right there next to the other hole. Knowing what comes out of that, and knowing that it was likely smelly and stinky, there was no way I was going anywhere near it if I could help it.

I was down there rubbing my finger up and down in between the space of her clit and hole, probing (or I should say "firmly poking") every minute point that I could while hoping to find her pussy hole. With each second, it felt like that space got longer and more mysterious. I dared to probe a little lower, but each time I would just panic and probe farther up before getting the courage to move back down again. And I gotta say, my probing was not getting gentler due to the pain I was feeling on my dick and yet, somehow, this girl was moaning up a storm while we kissed!

I mean, I was no expert, obviously, but I knew that I hadn't been playing with her clit, nor was I successful in fingering her. In retrospect, she was likely in discomfort or pain as well. But there was a chance that what I was doing wasn't painful but pleasurable and that she was genuinely moaning from the pleasure my explorations were giving her. Sigh, if only I could have said the same.

In the end, neither of us got off. Nor did we complain about each other. We were both quite happy and walked away smiling from that encounter, probably due to the sheer excitement of it all. If I recall, we had to stop because of the time limit, as she had to get back home. But boy, was that a big fail on my part. I couldn't tell this from that. I felt up in between her labia, not knowing where the vaginal opening was. I never did find it and completely ignored her clit. I poked and probed too hard and long and overestimated the location and proximity of her butt hole to her other hole. Not to mention, I didn't even show her or tell her how to play with my dick better than she was doing. C'est la vie.

The Epic Success

For this one, I shall share an encounter in my later teens that had some challenges. But, as a result of my previous experiences, I was prepared for the challenge. It was a warm sunny day, and a girl I hadn't seen in a while wanted to meet up with me. I came early in the morning, as that was the only time that worked for both of us, even though it was a short time window.

After I arrived at where she was staying, the sexual energy between us was super palpable, and it didn't take long before we were all over each other. As we started making out, my hands took their time exploring her body, but quickly made their way between her legs. While I had experienced a bush on a girl many times before, never had I had a bush of this magnitude to deal with. I mean, it was a freakin jungle! And there I was, a Puerto Rican without his machete to trim it all down.

As my hand slipped down between her legs, once again doing this blind as we make out, and as my other hand plays with her breasts, all of my remaining focus had to be expertly concentrated on the task of navigating her enormous bush. I was a blue belt in dick-yoon-do by then, so I wasn't too worried about how to handle this. Fortunately, there was a small wet spot in a deep portion of her bush that I was then able to home in on. I expertly started to part her pubes with my fingers because by this point, my dick-yoon-do was quite strong, they had had plenty of experience in developing the muscle memory necessary to confidently know how to accomplish the task at hand. I realized that parting her bush in order to get access to her pussy wasn't going to remain that way due to how full and springy her pubes were. Luckily for me, she was also really, really wet.

I coated my fingertip with her wetness and used it as a pseudo hair gel to make sure her pubes stayed on one side and then to repeatedly stroke said pubes to ensure they stayed that way. It totally worked. So, I quickly proceeded to do the same for the pubes on the other side of her labia. Next thing I knew, I had parted the seas! Give this guy some notches on his blue belt. I parted those pubes using her own wetness as gel and double checked the efficiency of my work with my fingers by stroking the now cleanly parted bush from side to side…as if I was combing it.

Now that the tropical jungle was conquered, I could proceed with the main quest of enjoying touching her and trying to make her cum. Once again, I used her wetness to my advantage and lubed up two fingers and gently rubbed them up and down her pussy while making sure to touch her clit each time. I went all the way up, ensuring I gently probed her hole when I made it all the way down. I ended up doing this solely with my middle finger while I used my index and ring fingers to gently touch her labia as I stroked her up and down. The method I chose to try to make her cum was simple: I would dip my middle finger in her pussy to make it wet, but never fully inserting it, then I would slide it up and play with her clit until the wetness started to dry up. Then I would slide my finger back down, re-dip it in her, slide it back up and play with her clit some more. I repeated this until she had a huge orgasm, and only after she came, did I insert my fingers inside of her to her delight.

Not once was I worried about her butt hole, nor did her pubes make me go "eww", and I was not only able to give her pleasure, but I was also able to make her cum.

In both of those situations, I was in my teens, yet I had the ability to reflect on what I did or messed up in order to do it better next time. But I think that's natural for those of us who always strive to do things better. As I got older, the whole not looking and doing everything blind thing went away, just as running into girls with bushes all but disappeared.

It is still very clear in my mind, though, that whole process of self-educating on what a girl's bits down there look like versus what it is actually like to touch them and navigate them. Nothing I ever read or saw, apart from real life, could have prepared me for the textures, smells, and feels of it all. So, if you take away anything from this chapter, it's that there is no substitute for the real thing. And even if you think you've seen it all or touched it all, inevitably there will come along a pussy or bush to surprise you.

Chapter 13: Foreplay & Fingering: The Dessert Before The Main Meal

Once upon a time, foreplay was all about the things that you and the girl did in person with each other before sex. You could also do some additional foreplay over the phone in order to get things warmed up in anticipation. Then, later, you could send emails with pictures to spice it up. Nowadays, you can use texts, video messages, and live video as foreplay before actually engaging physically. Whispers and sweet talk go a long way in foreplay, as well as kindness and consideration. But when it comes to actually physically touching the girl as part of foreplay, depending on the scenario, kissing, touching, and fingering are usually the main things we men end up doing as a prelude to sex.

My philosophy when it comes to foreplay is always to create the craving and anticipation with the girl for the next thing to come or the ultimate thing they desire. To that end, I will use whatever tools I have at my disposal during those moments of foreplay, whether they be long-distance or in person. From whispers to texts. The key lies in learning the girl well enough to know what works on her. This can make it tricky. But with some patience and playful back and forth, it's totally doable.

Highlights:

1. There are a lot of different types of things that different women can consider foreplay. Don't stay fixated on one idea. Whispers, glances, touches, kisses, dancing, laughing, story sharing, food, games, etc. It all depends on you and her.

2. Foreplay will usually be different depending on whether you and the woman have just met, have been together for a while, or are married, which is a notable distinction.

3. At a distance, foreplay can start with just looks and then conversation if the chemistry is right between you two.

4. Online or digital foreplay obviously involves cell phones and computers. Just don't jump straight to dick pics.

5. Don't forget that the main purpose of foreplay is to get each other all warmed up in order to build anticipation.

6. Many women don't know what they are doing when it comes to handling your dick when you reach the physical stage of foreplay. Though many think they do. Guide kindly.

7. Fingering a girl means that you know your fingers are clean and that your nails are not all gangly and are trimmed. Don't do it unless they are up to that standard. Go back to book 1 in the personal hygiene part if you haven't already.

 8. Most women shave nowadays, but bushes aren't uncommon. Either way, feel for the wetness, part the seas, lube your finger with her wetness, then gently stroke her pussy and clit before inserting. Got that, lover?

9. When you insert your fingers into a girl, save it for last and do it slowly…but go all the way in before you slowly move your finger, or two, in and out.

10. Kissing, touching, and rubbing of the breasts, ass, inner thighs, over the pussy/yoni, kissing and nibbling of the neck and ears, all of it is part of the delicious excitement that can be foreplay.

11. Foreplay ends when sex happens. Just to be clear, lover. So, foreplay your heart out until she jumps on you, or she rips your clothes off. Or both.

The basics in detail

1. There are a lot of different types of things that different women can consider foreplay. From spending money, to romance, to sexual teasing, massages, you doing manly things, being flirty, PDA (public displays of affection), sneaking around, laughter, playing games, kissing, touching, even doing the dishes, all sorts of stuff.

It can be really tricky as a man to figure out what it is exactly that a woman will like or not like when it comes to foreplay. That is, assuming she hasn't told you or insinuated anything. Because of that, I highly recommend that you keep it simple. When at a loss, talk about it.

Sweet whispers in the ear can work depending on the moment. Be sure not to yell or be loud, but it can be something simple like, "You truly look fabulous in that dress" to "Every time you touch my hand, my whole body comes to life". Right next to sweet whispers can be sweet kisses. It doesn't always have to be a kiss that is full of tongue and passion, or even on the mouth. It can be on the cheek, hand, or neck. It can be that you whisper into her ear something like, "Whatever you do, resist kissing me back." And then you gently kiss her cheeks, the side of her lips, each lip and then her lips, and see how long before she breaks down and kisses you back.

I found that kissing is usually the one part of foreplay that can tread the line of passion, clear sexual intent, and yet if done right, you can hold back and use it in foreplay to create even more anticipation and hunger. Which means that when done right, it can be one of the most potent forms of foreplay.

Foreplay can be in the form of just touching. Rubbing each other's inner thighs, touching the neck, wrapping your hands around her waistline and pressing her against you so that you can kiss her neck while simultaneously allowing her to feel you. It can also be giving each other looks as you go about some task at home, out and about, or even when around people or friends. That means you can be at a gathering, the movies, at dinner, and the whole time you could be teasing each other with touches here and there or in between each other's legs, kisses, rubs, nibbles, and squeezes.

You can literally turn it into play and leave little notes around for her to discover that will lead her from one thing to another and from one innuendo to another. With each find you can leave items or a note that will give both a clue for the next place to look and for what will happen when she reaches the end.

If you are already mostly naked, or completely naked, you can still have more foreplay before the sex. You can blindfold her and randomly touch her or kiss her so that she doesn't see or know what's coming.

You can send naughty text messages in the form of innuendos and then follow that up with teasing action. You can send short video clips that you filmed earlier while you and she are out and about with people. There are just so many things! Way more than I can list here so my overall recommendation is to either find a whole book (or many books) on foreplay and check them out and then try what feels right and good or, you can take the time to learn about the girl you like and see if you can learn enough to properly map out how to get her all worked up and hot and ready.

There is, of course, the option to just make it all up as you go along, but chances are that since you are reading this book, you're better off trying out what I said in the previous paragraphs. And since it's obvious, I can't tell you every basic detail about absolutely everything when it comes to foreplay, reading from others and your own experience is something you must do if you are committed to being a better lover.

2. Foreplay will usually be different depending on whether you and the woman have just met, have been together for a while or are married, which are all notable distinctions. And I know that might seem obvious now that you read that, but it's probably not something you consciously thought about, which is why it's worth bringing up.

For easy comparison's sake, just imagine what a woman you have been married to for some years might enjoy for foreplay versus a woman you just met. Then imagine a woman you have been married to and have children with, and what she might enjoy for foreplay, versus a girlfriend you've had for several months that is younger than you. Take the time to imagine it and let that sink in before reading on. Even if it's obvious at first, you need to play it out in your head and cover that thoroughly. If that is too much mental strain for you, then go and ask actual women in those situations what they enjoy for foreplay versus when they were single, younger, or not yet with child.

Making those obvious but simple observations can help when you have trouble coming up with things that might help to turn her on and get her in the mood. If for no other reason than we men can sometimes get caught up in what we think would be a great idea of foreplay versus what she might actually like and be excited by, that will put her in the mood for sex or playing more. If you're already in the mood, the foreplay is for fun. Making her excited to want to have more fun with you is a win-win. But at a minimum, foreplay can be a great way to get your partner in the mood when she isn't currently.

3. At a distance, foreplay can start with just looks if the chemistry is right between you two. Not all couples have the ability to play and be suggestive like that for whatever reason. But that doesn't mean you can't try anyway by either being spontaneous or by planning it out beforehand for more coordinated fun. So take the time to play with the idea of glances, specific looks, or subtle signals to see if they can work.

Just be careful not to try this on a stranger because your results will most likely not be favorable.

4. Online or digital foreplay obviously involves cell phones and computers. Sexts, pics, vids… consider that whatever game you are talking up, you can back up with actual action. And don't forget that just sending a girl, or your girl, a dick pic isn't foreplay. Yes, there are some women to whom that will do, but they are not the majority. Most women like words accompanied by great visualization that appeals to them. This means that you must have some knowledge about what they like or turns them on. Don't take my word on it, ask ladies you know or watch some online videos where women are interviewed and asked about these things, and you'll hear it for yourself.

I've met too many men who are great at talking a big game (via text, in person, etc) and then suck at the physical follow-through with women. Apparently, many of you aspiring lovers are also in that same boat of talking a big game and then failing miserably. If you can talk it up and get her going without going straight for dick pics, but your follow-through game is weak, then please rethink your idea of what being good at sex is. Because if you end up running into a girl you really want to be with, but she feels like she's been had/fooled because you talked a big game to get her, and then your follow-through sucked, you aren't going to be able to save it and keep her interested. In fact, she will be quite put off. So, if by chance you skipped the whole book and came straight here, or you got to this point and this describes you, reread the whole book front to back. I'd also advise finding other similar books to get enough knowledge so you don't suck at the follow-through and can turn that knowledge into experience.

It's ok to have shortcomings. We all have them. The worst thing you can do when it comes to digital foreplay with a girl is to fail to deliver or to intentionally deceive. I get it because I've done it in the past a few times. Thing is, I changed things up entirely and got even better results! Just own who you are and what you've got – and work with that.

Ok, now the other big thing is that immediately showing your dick to a woman is not foreplay. Either in the form of dick picks or in person. I mentioned this already, but some of you just don't get it yet. Remember, your dick is the big payoff at the end of the foreplay or the main feature that will transition foreplay into sex. That is to say, you being inside her in any way. Then that starts a whole set of other things, so don't go getting the two mixed up and thinking that foreplay is you sending her a dick pic and thinking it will get her all excited. Unless she specifically requests it, don't send the penis pic.

There is a huge but here, however. And that is, if she starts teasing you and hitting you up with all the foreplay body, breast, booty, and pussy pics. In person, to the point that she is grabbing at your dick, giving you a hand job or even a blow job. After those actions, the only thing left is for her to get it inside. Just make her crave it as much as possible in order to see and feel her ecstasy in that moment when it finally comes.

5. Don't forget that the main purpose of foreplay is to get each other all warmed up, hot and bothered. This is to make the sex you both want to have much more passionate, pleasurable, and intense. It is not a one-way street. Sometimes you initiate foreplay. Other times she does. Don't let it become one-sided. Make an effort. Regularly. Not only does foreplay do a great job of getting you and her all warmed up, it can really make sex more enjoyable and fun.

Once again, I'm repeating myself here a bit, lover, because women really do love some foreplay. For them, teasing and the mind game is where it's at or at least, where it starts. For us, it's in the visual stimulation. Knowing that difference will set you up for success.

Additionally, for those in long-term relationships, foreplay, in this case can mean knowing how to turn your partner on to get them in the mood for sex when they aren't in the mood. Not that they don't want to have sex in that current moment, that's different. But that there isn't a sexual atmosphere currently, and you're in the mood to turn it into one. Knowing your partner and using foreplay to get her turned on and in the mood for sex is a great key to having more sex and intimacy within your relationship. Sometimes work schedules and life are just ongoing, so if you don't make time for such things, then there won't be time. And if you want to continue to bond with your partner and stay close and grow together sexually, make the time for some good foreplay. The key is the word play, so make it playful.

6. Many women don't know what they are doing when it comes to handling your dick. What does this have to do with foreplay? Well, for us men, foreplay can usually be really easy and or simple. Something as simple as a woman laying her hands on our crotch or giving us a handjob without finishing can be great foreplay to get us all excited, sensitized, or up and ready. The point is that not all girls will be good

at this, so I want to give you some info on how to tell if she is good or bad at this.

Here's how to tell if she's average or bad: the girl might yank it, squeeze it super hard, be way too gentle, use only three fingers to grip it or maybe even just two (the classic ring finger and thumb circle jerk). They don't know where to focus on the dick; they squeeze the balls too hard or ignore the balls altogether. Her hands might be rougher than yours, maybe she hasn't learned about using spit yet, her hands might be soaked in sanitizing gel, her nails might be longer than a sabretooth tiger's teeth. She could be yanking it like it's a stick shift, she handles the same part of your dick the whole time and ignores the head, she doesn't use your pre-cum as lube, she uses the same method the whole time, or she has no clue how to get you hard and keep you hard apart from basic touching.

You can tell that she's good at a handjob if she uses both hands, uses your own pre-cum, spits into her own hand, knows how to work the head, includes your balls, figures out how to get you hard and keep you that way, grips you just right, includes all her finger in her grip, has a steady rhythm, and actually looks to you for feedback to see if she's doing a good job.

And don't get me wrong, a good handjob is great foreplay for us, but it goes from good to great when she knows what she's doing. So, when it comes to this portion of foreplay, don't be afraid to guide her. Many women act on what they think we like or act out of thinking that they know what to do from previous experiences. Very few, and I mean a tiny amount of the ladies, will actually look you in the eyes and ask you, as they start touching you, what do you like, how do you like it, or what part of your dick is the sensitive part. If she doesn't ask, don't be afraid to let her know. Speak up.

And yes, some girls might get offended, or butt-hurt or reply with, "I know what I'm doing". In those cases, your response needs to be something that makes it clear that she's never asked how you like it, and she's never had yours in her hands before, so what makes her think she knows what you like? If she humbles herself and then wants to know, cool. If more attitude ensues, I recommend foreplay over. Move on.

7. Fingering a girl means that first and foremost, you know your fingers are clean and that your nails are not all gangly and are trimmed. Don't do it unless they are up to that standard. Go back to Book 1 and

look in the personal hygiene part if you didn't already know or remember that. It's also worth noting that fingering a girl is the equivalent of a handjob for us.

When foreplay hits the fingering stage, that's when you know that your chances of things going all the way are almost solid. Typically, when foreplay gets really intimate, as it pertains to breasts, we still usually just rub them over her clothing. But when it comes to playing with a girl's pussy, we usually end up going underneath.

Consider rubbing outside of the clothes for a decent bit before going under to her panties. You can firmly rub your hand in between a bit. You can pause, if your hand is physically hot, and press your hand/fingers up against her clothing so that she can feel the heat of your hands and the pressure of your hands firmly underneath her clothing. But remember to always start off light before adding more pressure. The gentle rubbing and pressing is more teasing than going straight in for the firm rubs, although the amount of time in between each need only be moments.

If she is wearing panties, consider not going straight under the panties right away, even if the access is available. Having more direct contact with a barrier in between still keeps things in the foreplay teasing stage, and you want her as hot and wet as she can get before touching her with your clean hands. You can usually tell quite easily by how soaked she gets through her panties.

Additionally, at this point, I would stop. Let her be a bit disappointed that you didn't take it further and let her stay hot for a while before finding another opportunity to get her even hotter and bothered before yet again diving your hands underneath before finally touching her pussy. AND! Once again, be gentle. Savor each touch as you hold her close, your mouth and hers almost touching so that she can savor each moment and of course so that you can enjoy all the desire she has been holding back later in bed. It is possible, however, that she yanks your hand right back to her crotch or that she gets frustrated. Either way it can be fun.

Whether she has a bush or not, as you touch her labia and play with her pussy with one hand, you will most likely be tempted to put your fingers in her, if you didn't already go for it right away. I would say, don't. Feel the wetness, warmth, and softness first by tracing your finger, or fingers, gently down her labia so that you can create a mental map of how thick and long they are. Follow the lines to the side of each, in between each, and in between the hole and clit. Gently touch and explore the hole of her vagina without actually placing a finger inside. Doing that will get your finger wet so that you can then slide it upwards gently, once again feeling and tracing her folds and lines, until you get to the clit. This is how you earn your first belt in dick-yoon-do, my aspiring lover. Master that simple move.

If her clit is between the folds of her labia, you will have to spread them with your fingers a bit. Typically, you will use your index and ring finger to part her lips just enough for the middle finger to touch her clit. Once you begin rubbing the clit, don't use your nail. You want to use the fat, meaty portion of your finger and maybe close to the tip of your finger if your nails are far back enough from that point on your finger. That wetness of hers that you have on your finger should be enough to lubricate you for rubbing her clit. Be gentle. Once again, use your finger to discover its dimensions and trace its roundness; this is a momentary act and shouldn't take but a few seconds at most. Press gently and rub up and down a bit, then slide your finger back down to her hole, rewet your finger, slide it back to her clit, then rub either circularly or up and down again. Don't jump from the hole to the clit. Be sure to rub and touch as you go up. That simple method is pretty effective and should be enough to have her nicely tortured before removing your hand in order to continue the foreplay. Unless she tackles you to the floor. In which case, success and game on!

After fingering, your fingers will be wet and or moist. You have three choices at that point. One, you clean your fingers by sucking on them like barbecue sauce and letting her see. Two, you discreetly wipe it off on your jeans and continue on. Or three, you just let them air-dry. If the girl you just fingered is rare and awesome and wants to reverse the foreplay you just did to her by blowing your mind, she will take option four and hold your hand and suck your fingers dry to taste her own wetness. Some girls do this, but it's rare. However you clean your digits, just remember what your fingers touch if you are going to use them again…so that you don't dirty them up and then bring that to her pussy. This applies even after you wash your hands.

On the off chance that the girl has funk going on down there, you should detect it the moment you either get under her pants or as you are fingering or immediately after you pull your hand out. If it's super funky, go wash your hands. If it's mildly funky, dry off on the pants. In either funky case, do not lick and certainly don't let her do it either if you want to kiss her later.

8. Most women shave nowadays, but bushes aren't uncommon. Either way, feel for the wetness, part the seas, lube your finger with her wetness, and then gently stroke her pussy and clit before inserting. Got all that, lover?

Don't be surprised by a bush. Be surprised by a stinky and unkempt bush. So long as it's hygienic, no problem. Be sure to be adept with finger articulation so that you can use one hand to both make your way through the bush, spread the bush to get access to her pussy, then use the wetness to enjoy. If the bush is extra thick and it's difficult to find her vaginal hole, then feel for a wet spot and focus on that as you use your finger to spread the pubes to one side or the other, as I mentioned in the previous chapter.

If you get to a hole that is tightly shut and has little ridges, that's her butthole. You've gone too far. The vaginal hole is more loosely open and usually way more moist unless she's been wet and the wetness seeps south.

If you get your fingers into a bush and a smell immediately comes up that isn't flowers or fresh scented, abort. Let it be, and keep your touches limited to outside of her clothing for this portion of the foreplay. All dick-yoon-do practioners that are aspiring lovers must know when to retreat. And if a bush is a deal breaker for you, politely withdraw your hand from her crotch, apologize, say your peace as to why, and then make your exit in as kind and considerate a way as possible.

9. When you insert your fingers into a girl, save it for last after touching her in other ways. Always do it slowly, but go all the way before you slowly move your finger, or fingers, in and out. I mentioned that you should hold things back as long as possible while still not drawing things out for too long (don't rub her pussy endlessly hoping she'll cum or you could rub her raw). Well, actually fingering her should be the last step of playing with her pussy/yoni.

Here's how you do it. I've already covered how to go about getting down there and feeling your way and lubing your finger. Well, after your finger is covered in her wetness, you gently feel for her hole and trace a small circle or two around the edges of her hole in order to get another mental map of her contours. Slowly slip one finger in only, and as you do, keep it relaxed enough so that your finger follows the contours of her vagina inside. Once you insert it the whole way in, pause, hold gently but firmly, with the rest of your hand and fingers, the rest of her pussy/yoni. Let yourself, and her, savor that moment. Trust me, if done right, she'll love that moment of first insertion. Slipping your finger or fingers in and out slowly will suffice. You can mix it up with some clit rubbing as well, so that you aren't performing the same motion the whole time.

Once fingering becomes a more common thing and you get used to it, you can use the come here method to finger a woman. In the US, we use our open palm upwards and then curl our fingers towards us to signal for someone to come here. Well, when you finger a girl, you can do this with one or two fingers inside of her, usually the middle and ring fingers. After inserting them relaxed, ensuring they are properly wet for smooth insertion, you then gently but firmly make the same come here motion with your fingers while ensuring that you aren't scratching her vaginal walls with your nails. If you do this closer to the entrance of her vagina, you will touch the back side of her pubic bone and the inner wall of her vagina. This spot is commonly known as the G-spot. It can be very pleasurable depending on the girl, but since we're just talking foreplay here and only the basics, don't go trying to get her to do anything else apart from feeling pleasure towards an orgasm. Forget any ideas you might have about trying to get her to squirt.

While fingering, be cautious of jabbing your finger too far in as well. If you hit her cervix with your nail, or snag her insides with a nail, it will likely really hurt her and ruin both your nights.

10. Kissing, touching, and rubbing of the breasts, ass, inner thighs, over the pussy/yoni, kissing and nibbling of the neck and ears: all of it is part of the delicious excitement that can be foreplay. As with everything in life, timing is key.

Kissing and gentle touching can be done in front of most people, so it shouldn't be a problem. If the interest is high and or the chemistry is good, often, kissing can be enough for foreplay. Kissing gets the passion and blood going, and add to that the squeezing, grabbing, and touching that happens alongside it, and well, it can do the trick without needing much of anything else.

Grasping and touching her breasts, on the other hand, needs to be discreet, timed for when she is super warmed up sand horny. It also needs to be played well. Too soon, and you will likely get rejected. Time it right and it will be a nice addition to the excitement and stimulation of foreplay. You can't do it too late because you will eventually touch her breasts when you and she are naked, or she might grab your hands and make you touch them, which is always cool.

Rubbing of the inner thighs is best when seated, and people can't really tell or see. If you are kissing or have already gotten hot and heavy but haven't gone much farther yet, then touching her between her legs over her clothing can be very exciting and stimulating. Once again, though, you need to be sure that you are at that point of touching and that the timing is good. If she's not completely there yet or comfortable in the situation, you are likely not to be allowed or get rejected from that move. If you wait long enough, she'll hunger for it, and it should be fine. But don't forget that none of these are a given. You must pay attention to her to ensure that she is comfortable and gives consent to each of these things. And don't forget that consent isn't always with words, sometimes a look, a squeeze, her making room for you to make moves (like spreading her legs after you start to touch them), those can also be signs of consent. Don't get so caught up in your head that you ignore the true signals of her comfort and acceptance of you. Or that you ignore the do not pass go signal as she closes her thighs or subtly moves away from you, which is even more important.

Nibbling of the neck and ears – you can judge when it might seem like the right moment. But when you do it in public, time it so that a few people notice or are looking. It can be more exciting that way because you can get that feeling of being naughty and sneaky. But if it's all a private date between the two of you, then timing is all about going with the flow and learning to see the right moment for this or that.

11. Foreplay ends when sex happens. Just to be clear, lover. So, foreplay your heart out until she jumps on you or rips your clothes off. Or both. After that, any of the things mentioned above just become a part of sex and teasing a girl during sex can be very, very, fun as well. Nothing beats you teasing a girl during sex in just the right way so that she ends up pouncing on you like a starving cat.

Foreplay can be wildly different from anything I have written here. I tried to focus on certain things that I have witnessed or found out about over the decades that we men tend to be prone to, rather than an actual list of foreplay things that you can do (although I did mention some). Remember that foreplay evolves from when you first get together to where you have been together for a long while, and even more so after marriage and kids. Tastes and desires evolve as well, so don't stay too focused on the past or be too rigid. Strive to constantly learn and know what might be good or fun or enjoyable to the girl you're with so that it doesn't become too repetitive or boring over time. In the end, just remember to keep it playful! That's why it's called foreplay.

The Epic Fail

I was trying to break my record in Top Gear, while eating Twizzlers and scratching my butt, when all of a sudden, I remembered that I was supposed to meet up with a girl that particular evening. I quickly change gears and clothes before darting out of the house to meet up on time, all the while being super excited about this girl.

We met up at her place and started to hang out smoothly. As the movie we were watching went on, we started touching each other and then kissing. Not long after the kissing started, I tried to touch her neck and breasts when I noticed the vibe was changing. It seemed like she was recoiling and withdrawing at the same time. It was weird. I didn't know what to think about it, nor did I have the awareness to just stop and ask about it. Instead, I just tried changing tactics to see if she would respond to something else.

While the mutual kissing continued, I felt her lean back, and we ended up lying on the couch together with me on top. This is where things got really confusing. She was still kissing me, but she completely clammed up and became stiff. She didn't touch me apart from kissing me, and no matter where or how I touched her, she remained stiff as a board. It got to the point where I just stopped kissing her altogether and got up and asked what's wrong…because it had become plainly obvious that something was indeed off.

She slowly opened up and explained that she wanted to keep going, but also couldn't. We didn't do anything else after that. Initially, it felt like we would be having sex, so I came ready for that, but it went in the complete opposite direction. Apparently, she had bad experiences before with men, and even though she really wanted to continue with me, and led me to believe that is what she wanted as well, she had been triggered somehow and could no longer go on. Mentally, she wanted to, but her body just couldn't and would not move or relax. That somehow took a bunch of pressure off my shoulders, so we just chilled and watched the movie we intended to watch in the first place.

In this situation, I had no prior experience with frigid or rigid women or what could cause a woman to become frigid, cold, or rigid despite making plans to the opposite. There can be any number of reasons for that happening, from sexual trauma to just feeling overwhelmed. Even though everything started out fine with her, the vibe started to change quickly. I wasn't experienced nor aware enough to stop and ask about things the moment it became apparent that something was off about her and not right. She kept kissing me because she liked me and didn't want to reject me, but her somehow getting triggered due to previous trauma caused her to react in a way she could not help. I certainly didn't blame her at all and just tried to listen and adjust so that she could feel comfortable.

I consider this a failure in my part not because I messed up everything I tried to do, because believe me there were those situations in the past as well, but rather because in my haste and overwhelming desire I was listening more to myself and my own desires rather than paying attention to her properly in order to make sure she was cool with everything as things happened. Think of it this way, if a child wants to play a game with you and the game starts out fine, but then you notice the kid is scared or not having a good time, what do you do? Obviously, you stop and talk to the kid the moment you notice something is off, and if necessary, you change what you do together so the kid can feel comfy and happy. I'm not saying I treat women like little kids in that way, it's just that I adopted a similar attentive attitude towards them as a result of that particular experience. So don't forget to be attentive. Hold yourself back enough to see her clearly so that the foreplay you partake in together is pleasurable for you both, and you don't get so swept up in your own horniness that you can't see what's right in front of you.

The Epic Success

As I walked to the pre-selected café to meet my date, I had a lot of butterflies in my stomach. The girl I was going to meet up with was beautiful, had a unique charm about her, a full bright smile and a seductive quality that I found almost irresistible. Almost.

I arrived a little early, so I was already seated when she arrived. We exchanged looks the moment she came in, and the smiles hidden behind our lips became clearly evident for all to see. From the moment she sat down, there was palpable electricity in the air. We ordered some food and drink, and as we chatted, we sat a little closer. She leaned on me a little bit, and responding to her, I put my arm around her to make her more comfortable.

We talked and laughed, and I noticed that she was a bit chilly. I offered her my coat, and she gladly accepted as the hot drinks we ordered weren't quite enough to keep us warm entirely. She casually touched my thigh, and I placed my hand on hers, and just like that, we were holding hands. At one point, the conversation suddenly tapered off, and we were silent. She leaned into me, and I held her closer. Unfortunately, the couch wasn't as conducive to the cuddling we wanted to do, so I had her get up so that I could readjust my position, and she could then sit between my legs on the couch. That way, I could hold her properly, and she could just lean back.

She smelled so good, and her hair smelled so nice that I held and squeezed her extra tight, and she responded in kind. I kissed her neck softly, mostly just to feel the softness of her skin against my lips and to get a bit closer so as to breathe her in. But apparently, she liked the kisses and really let me know with her soft sounds and hand squeezes. At one point, we readjusted our positions, and we were face-to-face with the desire and gravity to kiss so present in the air that it was as if the room itself was lovingly pressuring us to come together. After a lot of touching of our cheeks and lips, we finally full-on kissed, and it was marvelous. The build-up to that moment from the previous hour of soft touching, holding, and squeezing made that kiss seem like the unexpected bonus of the night.

When the kissing started, the real touching, squeezing, and grabbing of each other began. At this point, the foreplay became more intense as it became crystal clear that we really wanted each other. She had somewhere to be, as did I, so we couldn't stay in that café kissing and touching as much as we wanted. I walked her to the tram stop, and we kissed and held each other for a bit longer before going our separate ways.

Not only was this an epic success in how I perceived and responded to her signals and body language, but I felt like I did things she really liked and was happy with. The final verification of this success was when she messaged me close to midnight, asking me if she could come over. Needless to say, the foreplay worked for us both better than I could have hoped, and all that build-up made for a great late night.

Chapter 14: Oral Sex: Yum Yum For Your Tum Tum

The Vulva and the Vagina chapter was just to familiarize you with pussy/yoni. This chapter is all about how to approach pussy/yoni with your mouth hole. Now I know for a fact that many of you aspiring lovers out there do not like to eat pussy/yoni for your own reasons. And of those that do eat pussy/yoni, some of you actually like it…but many of you do it only because you know she likes it. Some of you do it but don't enjoy it. Others don't like the experience and downright refuse. Then there are those who do enjoy it – and maybe even really like it. Lastly, there are those like me who absolutely love it and enjoy it even more when it's with someone you love. Like it or not, I've got all the basic stuff here to help you out one way or another.

My philosophy is start soft and gently in order to create more anticipation and desire, and then I work it up in intensity. I trace the lines and forms of her yoni with my lips and nose in order to become familiar with them. I play with her pussy a little bit to see how she reacts. But I don't just focus on the clit, and I keep an eye on her reactions. I also tend to ask what she likes, so that when I'm done playing, I can do what she likes to get her off. I sometimes also like to treat oral sex like eating ice cream, or like chewing gum, and eating jello all at the same time. In fact, I used to chew huge wads of gum all the time, back when I had multiple lovers at the same time because my jaw muscles would get tired from all the oral sex. All that extra daily chewing strengthened my jaw muscles (and tongue when the wad of gum gets huge) and made it so I could enjoy it even more. Which is awesome because to me, oral sex is like solving a puzzle with your eyes closed in order to get to the orgasmic prize.

The Highlights:

1. Pussy is an acquired taste both for your nose and for your mouth. So don't quit. Give it time.

2. Don't treat it as a chew toy.

3. Do use your tongue and lips. No need to rub your teeth or beard on it everywhere, though it happens.

4. Have a clean mouth. Bacteria in your stinky cake hole, along with anything else you have in there or on your beard, can affect the vagina. And if you get sores of any kind, don't go down.

5. If you have sores or get sores in your mouth of any type, wait till they are completely healed before engaging in oral (even if you don't have herpes and have tested negative, it's always safer and better to take the precaution for her sake).

6. Most women won't complain or say anything about us guys having a rough face. But a smooth face is generally better than a rough face down there if you love the slip and slide.

7. Do not just focus on the clit. Contrary to popular belief amongst many of us men, the clit is not the only way to make a girl feel pleasure and or cum.

8. Touching and stimulating only the clit and ignoring everything else down there is akin to a woman only sucking on the head of your dick and ignoring your shaft and balls completely.

9. Don't be scared or shy to ask a girl what she likes, or if she likes what you're doing or wants you to adjust anything. (Learning these things makes life easier, takes some pressure off of you, and makes it more fun).

10. Girls do like to be teased down there to an extent. The creation of anticipation of that next touch or lick is very powerful to women.

11. For those of you who are still adjusting to – or have yet to taste or enjoy the scent of a woman's pussy – the only way to adjust or learn to like it is to just keep doing it.

12. Her flavors and scents will change throughout her menstrual cycle. So don't expect her pussy to taste and smell the same every time you go down.

13. Vaginas have discharge. That is to say that fluidy things of various thicknesses, viscosities, and scents will and can come out of the vaginal hole at regular intervals. (That is all usually normal). So don't freak out, act in disgust, or let it repulse you. Acting this way while you are between a woman's legs can create huge

amounts of insecurity and angst over their vaginas, which may lead to confidence issues and maybe even sexual hang-ups.

14. Don't think all vaginas should be hairless. Pubes are a natural thing, so long as she is hygienic and clean, they shouldn't pose much of an issue. I say 'much' as opposed to no issue – because depending on the length and coarseness of the hair, it can be like sandpaper to your shaft.

15. Unless something is legitimately wrong, or you just aren't into it, don't go down on a girl for just a few seconds. If a girl did that to you, most of you would surely reply with, "that's it?" So, if you are going to do it, do it right. Don't half ass it.

16. Do include your fingers. But I would suggest that you don't start with them. Build up to it a bit. Fingers can add a lot and not just with inserting them, but in gentle touches on the labia as well as on the outer edge of her vaginal opening. Tease and tantalize that area first before inserting them inside. Then defer to my previous advice on fingering for all the details.

17. You can't go down on a girl whenever you want. For those that love it, she has every right to say no, and there might be more going on down there than she wants to tell you. So, if you get denied even when she's not on her period, accept it.

18. Women are very underserved in general when it comes to oral sex. Will you help change that?

19. Don't just flicker your tongue up and down. Be a little more creative than that. Try from left to right, circles clockwise and counterclockwise. Even little tugs on it through gentle but firm suction are welcome.

The basics in detail

1. Pussy is an acquired taste for both your nose and your mouth. So don't quit. Give it time. What do I mean by "don't quit"? Simple, keep at it. For the vast majority of you lovers out there, eating pussy/yoni wasn't the type of experience where, upon the first try, you thought to yourself, "Wow! Delicious!" I know because I didn't, and neither have the majority of men I've talked to in my life. And yet, somehow, we keep coming back to it.

All it really takes is to spend more time down there. Keep going down and keep going down until you get accustomed to the smells, tastes, wetness — all of it. It might seem to some of you that you will never get used to it, but trust me, you can. I'll admit that no one pussy/yoni is universally likeable, as we all have different tastes and smell preferences, but as long as you're compatible, if you keep at it, you'll learn to like it. But as far as loving it, that takes a unique girl, a unique pussy/yoni, or a rare connection for some of you. So, let's just focus on liking it. Save the loving it for your long-term girl.

2. Don't treat it as a chew toy. Now listen, some women do like a little nibble or bite here or there…but you have got to work your way up to that. You can't just go down there and think "chew toy!" for whatever reason, and then chomp down on the labia or the clit. Not cool. Not even a little. Not in the beginning, and especially not cool on the first time with someone. So, pretty please, for vulvas' sake, no biting. It can be painful, some women are hesitant to speak up or are shy when it hurts or is unpleasant, and some of you see that absence of 'no' as an ok to do whatever. Again, it's not. And if the urge is so strong that you really wanna do that, ask the girl first! IF – and only IF – she says yes, then little test nibbles first.

3. Techniques for oral sex should involve your tongue and lips. No need to rub your teeth or beard on it anywhere, though it happens. This brings up the issue of facial hair. For more on this, flip on over to Book 1, Part Two, Chapter 1, then find the section on facial hair. This advice is worthy of consideration when burying your face between a woman's legs.

There are a few basic ways to go about performing oral sex on a woman. For many of you, it should be pretty intuitive, but for those out there that literally have no clue or instinct as to the actual how, or no desire to do it but know that they will have to someday, well I will be as detailed as I can so you can visualize and then apply.

Before the methods, let's talk about angles. If a girl lies basically just flat on her back, legs spread, knees bent, feet flat on a surface, it places her pubic bone and pussy/yoni in a normal position. Typically. But if she raises her legs into the air to any capacity, it tilts her hips and raises the vulva to a more favorable and easier-to-access angle. It's usually a very intuitive thing, but just in case, I thought it was worth mentioning. So, if you are having difficulty accessing the vulva with your mouth and lips, try adjusting her hip angles a bit by asking her politely to raise her legs or by changing the placement of her legs yourself by moving the knees towards her head. The easiest way to do this is by pressing with your hands behind her knees. If your arms get tired, are too short, or not strong enough to hold them in that position, so that you can continue going down on her, then ask her to hold the legs for you. That will also free your hands so that you can use your fingers on her as well.

Now, let's talk about a few different basic techniques for those who require detail.

The tongue flicker! This method can be accomplished in three basic ways. The first method has you close enough to the girl's labia that you can reach the clit with your tongue as it sticks out from your lips, but your lips do not make contact with other parts of her vulva (labia, clit, etc.). For fun, let's call this the 'distant tongue flicker'. You can do it with your mouth completely open (but watch out for your saliva escaping through your bottom lip) or with your lips all pursed up, kind of like when you stick your tongue out at someone.

The basic way to use your tongue here is by moving it up and down. Just be sure to be close enough to the clit so that when you move it up and down, it makes contact with the clit both as it goes up and as it comes down. This isn't always necessary because you can also intentionally only touch the clit every time you flick/lick upwards. You can vary the speed at which you do it, but just be sure to try and judge what is most pleasant to the girl by her reactions. Don't forget that there is a human being attached to that clit, so how she reacts to what you do matters.

If a woman has a short clit, (yes, clits, very much like penises, come in different lengths, thicknesses, and sizes as mentioned in Chapter 12) while using the distant flick, keep in mind that the clitoral hood may be covering the clit. If that is the case, then you might need to move it back enough to fully expose it. With some women, the clitoral hood is barely present, if at all. If that's the case, then it's one less thing to worry about.

Some women get even more sensitive to clitoral stimulation when you move the hood back, which can be a great thing. In this case, starting gently is the key. And, if the stimulation is too much when you pull the hood back (as can happen), then it's not necessary to pull the hood back as it can serve as a type of buffer. You could simply stimulate her clit over/through the clitoral hood just like you would the clit itself.

I find that a simple way to pull back the clitoral hood is to use your thumb. Bring your hand/arm under, around, and over the girl's leg, or straight from in between. Then use your thumb to gently apply pressure on the clitoral hood and move it back just far enough. It might take a try or two to get the hang of it, but it's a fairly simple maneuver to get the hang of. Your other option is to use both hands, whether it's the thumbs or index fingers, either from in between the legs or under, over and around, to just spread the labia upwards a little. Doing that can also bring the hood back automatically, depending on the girl's anatomical composition down below. You'll see, it's way simpler than it sounds.

Understand that it is not always necessary to do this, as it can make little difference, if any, to a woman. In other circumstances, the girl might spread her labia or pull back her hood on her own in order to get more direct stimulation. So, play it by ear and communicate.

I digressed a bit there. Anyway, the next thing you can do is your standard lick. From below the clit to the clit and over. You can go as far as her pussy hole to start and then lick up. A bit slow and gentle but firm is good to start. Just be sure to press your tongue against her pussy with it spread wide. Then there is the full-on mouth and tongue move. You press your upper lip on and over the base/top of the clit and open your mouth to cover the whole pussy/vulva. While making sure you don't press your teeth against it, the lower lip of your open mouth should be covering the hole of the pussy/vulva or be close to the vaginal opening, complete with tongue out of your mouth. By doing this, you can taste and lick any tasty wetness that might be trying to escape via gravity. You then lick all the way up to the clit so that the clit is momentarily pressed up against your tongue and upper lip. You could also retract your tongue back into your mouth instinctively and press both your lips against the clit. Then, you open your mouth and do it again. In this sense, it becomes like a long lick technique that goes from hole to clit. As you do that whole motion, you can choose to go between the labia or on the labia as you lick. Both ways will provide different sensations for her to enjoy.

You can experiment with this a bit, as your head movement can enhance the motions in conjunction with your jaw. If you have a soft enough bottom lip, you can even just rub your lip up and down gently over her labia as you go from clit to hole. Just think of licking an ice cream cone tip and you'll get the gist, except that when your lower lips repeat what your tongue does, she can get back-to-back sensations.

Another way to use your lips and tongue is the closed-mouth tongue flicker. How do you accomplish this, you ask? This is another simple technique that you can do by taking the clit in between your lips, and while holding onto it with your lips, and sort of in your mouth, you can then flick it with your tongue in any which way or speed you want. Again, while paying close attention to the reactions of the girl you are with, all the while ensuring that you aren't using any teeth.

Also, you don't need a grip of death with your lips to do this. A nice, relaxed lippy grip with some suction should do. Unless you have thick lips, in which case, gripping it firmly with your lips should still be cool. Just don't rely on this completely in order to bring her to orgasm, ok? This is just a basic technique, not the go-to or the only one you do.

There are a variety of techniques. You can flick it up and down. Down then up. Only up. Only down…or even don't flick it at all, and instead do circles in either direction around the clit. And if you can manage it, you can even flick it sideways, left to right or right to left. Also, play with keeping your tongue thin and pointy, wide and flat, firm or soft. Though soft seems to be preferable from what I've learned.

All this, by the way, will definitely move you up in the rankings of dick-yoon-do with your girl.

If the clit is a bit short, or if you just wanna try it, you can apply a little bit of suction while it is between your lips in order to bring it a little farther into your mouth. Just be sure not to try to suck it clean off the woman you are with, like some vacuum cleaner, because then you can cause pain. Ensure you gauge the woman's reaction when applying suction to build confidence. And again, no teeth. That can be tricky, as you will tend to use your lips over your teeth to save the girl's privates from rubbing against them. This, in turn, can wear out the inner lining of your lips quickly, thereby causing pain or discomfort to you. Just keep in mind that that could be happening to her pussy/labia.

Part of the Casanova's Code means protecting your woman's pussy/yoni from harm whenever possible in order to ensure that it will be healthy for her – and available for you – in the next encounter should there be one.

The distant tongue flicker is the most used method in porn, from what I have seen. It is also the method primarily or singularly used by a lot of us men who will go down on a girl but are secretly not enjoying themselves. This is usually because many men like pussy for our dick and fingers, but don't care for it too much in our mouths. Or we are doing it just to reciprocate or because we feel obligated.

Another basic technique for oral sex is the basic lick. Typically, the basic lick is from the vaginal opening all the way to the clit, or just to the clit, consistently, in the same fashion that a dog drinks water or licks your face. If you have ever licked ice cream, whipped cream, or a popsicle, it's practically the same movement and technique. I can imagine some of you doing this and doing so with a very rigid tongue. And maybe even using the tip primarily. But as you get more into it and more relaxed doing it, you will more likely end up using the flat portion of your tongue, as opposed to the tip, when you lick with a more relaxed yet pressing technique. Just try not to be too mechanical about it.

The basic lick is highly adaptable and adjustable. You can incorporate keeping your tongue pointed or making it wide at any point. You can play with pressure and even change up what you do to the clit every time you get up to it. You can also lick in reverse by using the bottom of your tongue, if you can, to lick from the clit all the way down. In that motion, you lick on the way up and on the way down.

While you are down there, another thing you can do is to gently suckle the labia. If you do this with your head slightly turned to an angle, you can even suck along the length of the labia if they are long enough.

You can leave the labia alone while you perform oral sex, or you can use your fingers to gently spread them apart and hold them apart (if she has prominent enough labia). I personally recommend that you give them some attention via licking and suckling. You could also gently stroke and touch the labia as well as the vaginal opening without inserting any fingers as you pay attention to the clit.

It is important to note that all this is performed while in the traditional missionary position. It is the most basic and also the most convenient of positions to perform oral sex on a woman. So don't go trying to get all fancy in performing oral sex on a woman in doggy style, sideways, standing up, or 69 before getting the basics of the act right.

4. Having a clean mouth when you go down on a girl is really important. Bacteria in your stinky cake hole, along with anything else you have in there, can affect the vagina. I primarily mention this because you have a lot of bacteria in your mouth as it is. After you clean your mouth and scrub your tongue in the morning, this is usually the safest time that you can go down on a girl – assuming you don't clean your mouth throughout the day. After nighttime hygiene works as well. However, during the day, food and other types of bacteria can accumulate and have an impact. I'm not saying it's guaranteed, but it can happen to a degree where the woman's vagina can develop anything from itching and burning to an infection. Overall, so long as you clean your cake hole twice a day, you should be good.

I'm pretty sure that the majority of you men have not considered this issue, nor have you ever asked a girl how the health of her vagina was the next day after oral sex. And based on all the women I've talked to, this is something that the majority of them have not considered either. To many of them, vaginal issues after oral sex aren't fully recognized or acknowledged because the connection wasn't made between the oral sex and an unclean mouth.

This also means that you need to ensure that your mouth is clean before you use your saliva as lube on her vagina. If you do this first thing in the morning, for morning sex, without cleaning your mouth and tongue, you are definitely taking a chance of causing some funk to your girl…and maybe also to your dick. Got that lover?

5. If you have sores or get sores in your mouth of any type, wait till they are completely healed before engaging in oral. Even if you don't have herpes and have tested negative, it's always safer and better to take the precaution for her sake and protection.

I used to get canker sores in my mouth all the time, while not even knowing what they were until my 20s. Since then, I've done a lot of research and experimentation, and I can tell you that the majority of those types of sores happen as a result of your mouth being overly dry or overly acidic. I used to make them go away faster by applying peroxide. Then I discovered a mouthwash that actually kept my mouth from ever getting them, so long as I used it. It is called Glyco-Thymoline.

Protect your girl from yourself and take either preventative steps or proactive steps the moment you develop any sores in your mouth. If they are the contagious type and she gets something from you, chances are she will break out, and you'll maybe pass that back and forth, thereby delaying any sexual contact you can have with each other for quite a while. So even if you are only with each other, take precautions so you can enjoy each other without or at least with less frequent interruptions.

6. Most women won't complain or say anything about us guys having a rough face. But a smooth face is generally better than a rough face down there if you love the slip and slide. Otherwise leave it to the woman's feedback as to what you do with your facial hair – should you be flexible on shaving. Just remember to clean your facial hair after oral unless you want dried-sex-smelling-stickiness-turned-crud on your face as you walk around. (It doesn't always happen though…don't ask me how I know.) Lastly, be sure to actually use your lips and tongue more than your beard on her pussy. Some of you out there do more rubbing with your facial hair against a woman's privates than you do with your actual mouth tools. Unless she requests a pussy beard rub, or doesn't mind it all, stick to using your mouth tools.

7. Do not just focus on the clit. Contrary to popular belief amongst many of us men, the clit is not the only way to make a girl feel pleasure and or cum (it is the primary method, but not the only). You can suckle, lick, and nibble on the labia, which can actually do it for some women. You can also tongue and lick around the edges of the vaginal opening, as well as probe your tongue into her if it's long enough, or use your fingers. But don't just blindly jab into it. Start with the edges and familiarize yourself with her contours and shape before going in.

For some women, they need a finger or two inside as well as clitoral stimulation in order to really get off. Once again, I suggest that you start with one thing and then work your way up to more, including fingers. That said, some women will not be able to cum from clitoral stimulation at all, and they need either fingers inside or a dick. But since this is oral sex and you can't have regular sex and oral sex at the same time (unlike Plasticman or Mr Fantastic, lucky bastards), we'll just stick with fingers. So yeah, sometimes you really need to finger fuck a girl well to get her to climax. Either straight penetration or by trying for the G-spot (with a curved motion of the fingers while inside her in order to rub the semi-hard fleshy bit that's inside just above the vaginal opening).

When you do straight penetration, you can either keep your fingers relaxed or you can keep them mostly rigid. I have found that some women don't actually like rigid fingers jabbing in and out hard or fast in and out of their vaginas. There's usually a rhythm, speed, and sometimes even an angle that they prefer even if they don't vocalize it. So, if she says nothing, then take the time to experiment a bit and see how good it feels for her. She might like it all or not. Just be sure to check in with her to see.

8. Touching and stimulating only the clit and ignoring everything else down there is akin to a woman only sucking on the head of your dick and ignoring your shaft and balls completely. I really want you to think about this because for some of you it may seem counterintuitive. The reality is that women also enjoy stimulation down there in various ways, and it's up to you to enquire or to find out through exploration. I have even met women whose clits are so sensitive that they can't stand too much direct stimulation. This means sucking and licking is greatly limited amongst those women. Keep that in mind.

It is also worth noting that if you spend time licking, suckling, fingering, and paying attention to her pussy/yoni but not her clit, this can create a build-up of anticipation on her clit as it awaits being touched in some way. That means if you skillfully navigate her pussy/yoni, you can save the clitoral stimulation for last and see how she reacts after being teased for a while. Who knows, she might explode into orgasm. Or not, either way should be fun.

9. Don't be scared or shy to ask a girl what she likes or if what you're doing is something she likes or if she wants you to adjust anything. Learning these things makes things easier, takes some pressure off you, and makes it more enjoyable. Not to mention that you will later be able to use that knowledge to create anticipation and desire. By this, I mean that where she wants most to be touched can be what you avoid before you finally give it to her – in order to increase her payoff later as opposed to going straight for the orgasm (or that special spot she likes).

If the girl ridicules you, makes fun of you, talks shit, or expects you to be some sort of magical wizard that can speak to her body and then infer all knowledge necessary, then you need to get yourself a new girl. Not all women enjoy being asked about personal matters. Some even think that it takes away from the romanticism or the magic of the moment. Stupid standards and idiotic ways of demanding things from us men only make those types of women more delusional and demanding. Don't put up with that crap. Better to get your clothes on and leave than to subject yourself to a woman like that. If you are trying to learn what she likes and this is somehow a bad thing in her head, her head isn't wired right.

10. Girls do like to be teased down there to an extent. I've alluded to this a few times already. The creation of anticipation of that next touch or lick is very powerful to women. Remember that time a girl first brought her hand towards your dick? The anticipation, the hope, the knowing, and how that excited you until you finally felt her touch? Or the same build-up, but with her mouth instead? Or even that anticipation of that first kiss with a girl you really liked? That is what you want to do with a woman when it comes to oral sex. Create anticipation by making it clear where you are going and what you are going to do, but do not immediately fulfill her expectations. Make her wait just a bit longer than she thinks.

Touch and kiss all around the clit, but not on it. Touch first, gently with your fingers, all around it slowly. While you do so, have your lips near so that she can feel the warmth of your breath as you do so. Then follow that up with gentle (or firm-ish) kisses all around. On her inner thighs, around her labia, on her labia, around her clit…but not yet on it. Then firmer kisses. Then use your bottom lip to gently rub on her labia. Gently probe her vaginal hole with your tongue (as in gentle circles around its edges with a bit directly on it), and then when you are ready, and she's full of anticipation, you then take her clit into your mouth but hold it firmly so she can savor that moment before continuing on to any technique you prefer.

That is one basic method of teasing and creating anticipation for what is obviously coming. From that point on, it is up to you to innovate. So don't take what I'm saying here as the only way, or as sexual scripture; it's just an idea.

11. For those of you who are still adjusting to or have yet to taste or enjoy the scent of a woman's pussy, the only way to adjust or learn to like it, is to just keep doing it. Or at least spend more time in close proximity to it. At a minimum, you will get accustomed to it.

Many women still don't like the taste or even the smell of cum, but they still engage. And many, over time, do get accustomed to it even if they don't like it. And just like the many women who don't like it and testify to that, it is ok if you never do either. But, if you want to be a better lover, even if you don't like the taste and or smell of pussy/yoni, learning to enjoy it nonetheless is something your partner will appreciate regardless.

Let's be honest here, it's an acquired taste. As awesome as it was, and as overjoyed as I was the first time I ever touched pussy/yoni, I certainly didn't think to myself in that moment, "mmmm yum!" I instantly thought, "Wow, it smells, tastes blah, and has three layers of funk going with it!" But I kept at it because the thrill, enjoyment, and excitement were too much to contain (not to mention that I was irresistibly drawn to it as you likely are). Plus, I knew that girls liked oral sex. And if it had anything to do with a girl's body, I was determined to master and enjoy whatever act it was. Up to you how you approach it, but girls definitely have it a bit easier than men in the oral sex department.

Please remember: if you want to learn to like the various scents pussy comes with by design, then you gotta put your face right next to it at every opportunity…until it just becomes normal (assuming she's healthy and got no issues down there).

12. Her flavors and scents will change throughout her menstrual cycle. So don't expect her pussy to taste and smell the same every time you go down. This is something that you can actually learn to predict over time if the relationship is long enough.

The moon cycles directly influence a woman's menstrual cycle. And women who spend a lot of time together also tend to have their cycles become synced. Even if they started their period at different times normally, once any group of women spend enough time together, they will all menstruate at about the same time. Anyway, the cycles they go through can change how she gets wet on certain days, the type of discharge that may come out, the smells she exudes, the flavors she has, and more. So don't be surprised if one day your girl's pussy is nice and fresh, and the next day it seems off. It happens. That's how vaginas roll. It's also yet another reason women have it easier than men when it comes to giving oral sex (unless you got shitty hygiene).

13. Vaginas have discharge. I'm talking fluid of various thicknesses, viscosities, and scents will and can come out of the

vaginal hole at regular intervals. This is all usually normal. So don't freak out, act in disgust or let it repulse you. Doing so while you are between a woman's legs can create huge amounts of insecurity and angst over their vaginas, leading to confidence issues and maybe even sexual hang-ups. That means that you need to be prepared to handle it discreetly and swiftly without making a big fuss about it. If you are squeamish about these things, you'd better get used to it. It isn't guaranteed with every woman out there, but it's better to expect it and know about it for the sake of being prepared when it comes to oral sex.

If you go down on a girl and the smell is unusually strong and intense in a certain way that is off norm, you should not engage but rather talk to her about it and see how you wanna roll. If there is an unusually colored discharge that is thick but doesn't have much odor or anything, just mention it and ask if that's normal for her or if she's dehydrated. If you aren't sure, just ask. If the woman knows herself well enough, she should have an answer. Regardless, you don't need to stay down there if you aren't feeling it, and her vagina is unhealthy or just not appetizing. It happens. Just try again later and be cool about it. Either way, don't put her pussy in your mouth until that's resolved.

14. Don't think that all vaginas should be hairless. Pubes are a natural thing, so long as she is hygienic and clean, they shouldn't pose much of an issue. I say much of an issue as opposed to no issue because the length and coarseness of the hair can affect the difficulty level of pleasing a woman.

Some women have thick, coarse hair in their pubic area. Others, just stiff, poky hair. And yet others can have soft, tickly hair. The variety isn't a problem for most of us. The issue lies in your sensitivity to that hair and whether or not that hair of hers, assuming she hasn't shaved or just trims, is either rough or soft to your liking. There are times when you run into pubic hair that will feel like sandpaper and rub your dick raw as you have sex. But that can also happen when you are performing oral sex on a girl, as far as your lips are concerned. It's not common, but it can happen.

A woman shaving does make sex much smoother and easier, but it should be fine so long as she either trims or takes great care of it – so it doesn't look like you need a weed whacker to get access to the vagina. Worst case scenario, if a woman having a ton of pubes, hygienic or not, turns you off, just talk about it with her. Who knows, maybe she'll be cool about it, and you just have to shave it or trim it for her. That's happened to me more than once. I mentioned a couple of things, and the girl was like, "Cool, how about we go and shave my pussy then?" Naturally, now I'm a big fan of shaving my girl's pussy/yoni cos it can be fun!

Anyway, going down on a girl with a bush isn't bad so long as the hygiene is on point. Just part the bush if it's tangled, or if it's turned into a big curly cue, at the center of where the labia meet, hold it down with your fingers and lick away. But if it's messy, stinky, and unclean you need to tell her and leave it alone till it's right.

15. Unless something is legitimately wrong or you just aren't into it, don't go down on a girl for just a few seconds. If a girl did that to you, most of you would surely reply with, "That's it?" Do it properly. Don't half-ass it. Why? Because that's the only way you are going to learn to like it. If you're down there, might as well show her a good time.

Again, this advice doesn't apply if there is something legitimately wrong down below, like a strong funk, or colored ooze, or slime, sores, cuts, unusual growths (apart from moles or skin tags), bleeding, etc. If you see any of that when you get down there, do not pass go, do not collect $200, and call it out to her tactfully. Remember that moles and skin tags are nothing to worry about. If you have doubts, then web search images and descriptions so you can see the variety of their form and looks.

I will say, however, that they can be a bit of a turn off depending on the amount of them and the size or look of each. That is perfectly ok. If you go down on a girl and are turned off by the moles or skin tags she has, just mention something to the effect that nothing is wrong with her pussy, you just find the moles and skin tags to be a turn off aesthetically. We each have the right to speak up about these things, so exercise it – and remember to use tact.

16. Do include your fingers. But I would suggest that you don't start with them (as I mentioned earlier). Build up to it a bit. Fingers can add a lot, and not just by inserting them, but in gentle touches on the labia, and squeezes, as well as on the outer edge of her vaginal opening. Tease and tantalize that area first before inserting the fingers inside. Then defer to my advice on fingering for all the details. This follows on the tail of what I was saying earlier about teasing and creating anticipation.

Performing oral sex on a girl doesn't always make it possible to use your fingers simultaneously. The proportions of a woman's hips and pelvic bone have a lot to do with this. Sometimes a vulva is short in length from vaginal opening to clit, so you can only fit your mouth and face or fingers, but not at the same time. Other times it can be quite long, and then you have the chance to use both. In proportion to your head and mouth, that can sometimes make it impossible for you to insert any fingers into a woman's vagina as you enjoy tasting her. Please take these things into account. Don't go trying to force your fingers into a woman's vagina, knowing that she's petite and you have a giant mouth, as there really isn't much room for such a thing in that type of situation.

To many a woman, fingering them while licking or sucking on their clit is comparable to a man receiving oral sex, while the girl also uses a hand or hands on the shaft. The extra stimulation can feel great! The only difference is that we men must be careful about how forceful we are with fingers inside a vagina, what angles we finger from, and whether or not our nails will be scraping the vaginal walls in any way while doing so. Trust me, you do not want to scratch a woman in her insides. It can be very painful, cause a girl to bleed, possibly even get an infection, and maybe even get you rejected. Or at a minimum, result in the cessation of intimacy until she is healed.

When deciding to use your fingers on a girl while performing oral sex, make sure your hands are clean and washed and that your nails are also clean and trimmed so that there isn't any dirt underneath the nails nor any sharp edges on your nails. I talked about how to take care of your fingers and nails in the personal hygiene chapter of Book 1, and I've mentioned it multiple times in this book.

Always start with one finger at a time (unless she tells you to use more than one, or has a huge hole where it's clear one finger won't be enough). This helps to start with that initial sensation, which then allows you to build up to more fingers depending on how tight she is. Don't just shove it in there without lubrication either. At this point, if you have been performing oral sex, she should be wet at her vaginal opening. Use some of that to lube your finger before inserting, or some saliva. This process also serves to let her acclimate to the new sensation of your finger touching her and the anticipation of what comes next when you insert it. Worst case, you just lick your own finger to lube it up.

Some of you have skinny fingers, others have fat sausage fingers. Some girls are really tight down there, while some are really loose. All the more reason to always start with one finger and work your way from there. What's loose to me might be tight for you, and vice versa. Either way, when putting a finger in a girl, relax it. Let the contours of the woman's vaginal canal guide your finger at first. Let the act of penetration be the first pleasure they feel before you go probing about for a woman's G-spot or other pleasurable spots.

Nowadays, making a girl squirt seems to be the thing to try to do to a girl. Or at least see if she can squirt. Listen here, lover, that is not and should not be your primary goal in inserting a finger into a woman's vagina, whether you are performing oral sex or not. The primary purpose of inserting a finger into a woman's vagina while performing oral sex is to add extra stimulation in the form of pleasure. Never forget that or lose sight of it. Also, your goal shouldn't be to see how far you can stick your finger in there to try to feel her cervix. There is some nuance here, so pay close attention to her body language in all ways.

Do keep in mind that all the clitoral stimulation in the world is sometimes not enough to make some women cum. They may need some great finger work to get them to that point and over the edge to the climax. The finger work can be as simple as just thrusting it in and out of her pussy in rhythm while licking her. You could be thrusting straight in, at an upward angle or a downward angle. Take the time to figure out what works in order to get her over the edge.

One idea I want you to consider is the minimum effort required. If you start with the minimum stimulation necessary to get a girl going, you then see how long you can keep that up before nothing changes or she starts to climax. If nothing changes, then you add a bit more. You do that slowly until she eventually reaches a point where she hopefully explodes into an orgasm. Do all that you can orally before adding fingers, and even then, keep it simple with the fingers before trying any motions that are likely to hit a good spot or the G-spot in her. If you jump in with everything you've got going for that big G win, then it's hard to dial it back if she's become desensitized. If you ask me, start slow and simple and add from there.

17. You can't go down on a girl whenever you want. It's important to remember that for those who love it. She has every right to say no and there might be more going on down there than she wants to tell

you. If you get denied even when she's not on her period, accept it. It is quite possible that something might be going on, and that makes her uncomfortable enough to not want your face down there. When we're horny, we can be pushy with our women about sex and even oral sex (for those that love it), so just be patient and be considerate.

18. Women are very under-served in general when it comes to oral sex. I would be willing to wager that many of you taking the time and effort to not only orally pleasure your partner but to do so and enjoy it consistently, will make a big impact on the happiness and sexual gratification of your woman. And to me, that is what oral sex has the potential to do for a relationship. Let's keep each other happy and satisfied!

For those of my fellow men out there who just have a difficult time with it, or just plain don't like it, give it time and keep at it. It took me two years of constant attempts before I suddenly liked it one day. That doesn't mean I haven't met women whose taste or smell wasn't particularly to my liking. There were others that weren't great or tasty, but they still weren't that bad. And if you suspect that part of it might be a hygiene issue, then talk about it. Sometimes pussy stinks because a girl is cleaning it too much or cleaning it even though it doesn't need it. And that all comes down to education. If there are other issues, then visit a specialist together to explore solutions so that you can return to enjoying each other more.

In the end, if a basic blowjob is what does it for you on the regular, then chances are you are going to eat pussy/yoni in a basic way. If you are particular or like special attention or techniques from a girl when she goes down on you, don't be lazy and then give her basic shit if she too needs unique attention down there. If all else fails, just close your eyes and pretend you are eating the world's most delicious creamy ice cream or like when you just finished a delicious plate of food and you then lick the plate. Then I'm sure you can lick it with passion and gusto like a pro, and she'll be left wondering where all that licking passion awesomeness came from.

19. Don't just flicker your tongue up and down. Be a little more creative than that. Try from left to right, circles clockwise and counterclockwise. Even little tugs on it through gentle but firm suction are welcome.

Using your tongue slowly while licking from different angles can really feel amazing to women. Not to mention it can help you to find a licking angle that really does it for her in the moment. Try licking from her yoni hole, starting with dipping your tongue into her, then slowly licking up to her clit and slightly beyond. Try doing that from the top down. Then try combining it so you lick in continuous up and down strokes. Try licking from the side slightly. Try licking her in doggy style from just below the clit up to her ass. Try it slightly off angle. Try licking in ovals, not literal circles, while using the top of your tongue in one stroke and the underneath part of your tongue in the other. Practice placing your tongue flat on her clit and doing slow circles with your tongue whole barely moving it or by only moving your head ever so slightly in one circular direction and then the other.

Gently suck on it a little as you slowly lick or flick her clit. Or, try to suck on it gently while you slowly open your mouth and encompass more of her yoni into your mouth while maintaining suction. Try licking from the tip of her clit and over it towards the base of her fupa. You can even lick from either of her holes up to the underneath part of her clit and just to the tip of it before going back down and doing it again. If her labia are substantial, lick and suckle on them as well. Try to suckle on one from the bottom end, or the tip end of it, towards her clit all in one motion.

All the while you need to pay attention to her reactions and see if you hit a good spot or if she's just enjoying all your creativity. Don't forget that once you find that spot or technique that does it for her, you will most likely have to keep that up until she comes. Just try not to go faster or slower or to change much at all even as she cums. Women usually come better that way.

The last thing I'll say is this: if you ever have a sex partner that has a pussy/yoni that tastes, looks, feels, and smells as though it was created just for you, I hope you do your best and be at your best with that woman. I also hope that she is a good woman for you because those ladies tend to be one of a kind.

The Epic Success

On this occasion, there I was, playing Metroid again, having just slain a Mother Brain for the 369th time, when all of a sudden, I found myself in bed with this pretty blonde who had shown up at my door. After some quick clothing removal techniques that I learned from Ninjas, I made my way in between her gates of heaven and began to go down on her. Not knowing what she liked or what she's into, I decided to start slowly and omit any use of fingers until much later.

As I began with my lips only, I chose to keep things as dry as possible by resisting the urge to shove her entire vulva in my mouth, as well as resisting the urge to lick the slow, clear waterfall emanating from her heavenly gates. Soft kisses here and there. Rubbing my lips here and there. Then a little bit of nibbling with mostly my lips. After that, finally, some tongue from the bottom of her pussy to the top of her clit. Once on her clit, I held it firmly so that I could feel her squirm as she had been anticipating her clit being touched for a hot minute. Not only was she responding well, but her body couldn't hide the enjoyment either.

I went to work on her clit, slow at first and then quicker and with a couple of different techniques. Next thing I knew, she was beginning to tense up, her grip on me tightened, and she was having a major orgasm. I was kinda surprised but also happy about it. She later said that I was the only one to ever make her cum without using any fingers – but that she didn't want my head to get too big about it! In my mind, all I did was follow my own process when going down on someone for the first time. I was happy that it worked, but it didn't stroke my ego at all. It just boosted my confidence that I would be able to enjoy her body while giving her great pleasure.

Nothing fancy in that story, but I really did do everything as I've already explained in this book. I had clean hands and nails. My face was smooth. I took my time, starting with gentle light touches and progressively working towards more until she came. Later on, it wasn't always necessary to go through the whole process because I got to know her body, and it started to respond faster to my touches. In that sense, I just adjusted things, and it became easier to make her cum and to tease her with anticipation.

Things didn't go as well in my epic fail.

The Epic Fail

So, no shit there I was, wearing night vision goggles in a lightless room trying to subdue a giant anaconda, when all of a sudden, I found myself in bed with a sexy brunette. I don't mind doing things with a girl in the dark so long as things start with the lights on first. In this scenario, that's how it went, and I was having a great time.

We were having sex all over the room and going from position to position. At one point, I decided that I wanted to go down on her, and we did this in various positions as well. On one such change, I lay down, and she gently hovered her pussy over my face, just low enough so that I didn't really have to raise my head, but just high enough so that I wasn't suffocating. Well, I was a bit hungry and really into it, so after a few minutes I decided to get my fingers into the action as well.

It's worth noting that this girl got really wet. If you hit the right buttons and got her turned on, wetness was not an issue. This was one of the things that I enjoyed about her, since many women don't in fact get wet like that. Well, as she was on my face and I was doing my thing, fingers and all, I started to notice that she was way wetter than usual. Immediately, I got even hornier than I was already. But, after a minute, the wetness on my face took on a different feel and smell. I started to wonder what it was, and so…

I paused, tapped her ass with my free hand and told her to stop for a minute and go turn on the lights. She got up, flipped the switch, looked at me…I looked at her…and we both realized immediately that it wasn't wetness. It was blood. My face was literally covered in blood. We went to the bathroom, and I looked in the mirror. What stared back at me was what I would imagine I'd look like if I were a blood-sucking vampire, having just bathed in the blood of virgins. I couldn't help but laugh about it, and simultaneously I thought to myself, "If I don't handle this correctly, she could be traumatized by this". Not only would it ruin our night, but she could have issues for years when it came to oral sex or fingering.

Quickly washing my face, I engaged her in conversation in order to troubleshoot what happened and why she was bleeding so much. We figured out that it had to be one of my nails that scratched from the inside, as I had cut my nails shortly beforehand, and one of the corners was apparently still sharp. To our surprise, she stopped bleeding by the time I had my face and hands all clean.

We slowly re-engaged sexually to see if she would start bleeding again by me going down on her and just keeping a super close eye on things to see. Sure enough, no more bleeding. So, after that, no more fingers and back to regular sex.

Having talked about that moment with her years later, it turned out that she wasn't worried at all. She was more worried about me and slightly horrified because of the amount of blood all over my face. She thought I would have been both turned off and repulsed, and that I might never want to do anything with her ever again. I laughed because I'm a hard-core soldier lover – with a black belt in dick-yoon-do by that point in my life. I told her I was only concerned for her and that it didn't faze me. She was taken aback, but put at ease.

She didn't know that I'm a freakin' champ when it comes to sexual things. It took lots of experiences to make it so that things like that don't really faze me, but in the end, it was because I'm well aware that when engaging with women, random crazy shit can happen with their vaginas sometimes – and I need to be prepared for it.

In this epic fail, it's obvious what happened. The good thing is that she did not get an infection and that the bleeding stopped on its own. Both could have become major issues super-fast and thereby require a hospital visit pronto. It does go to show how getting super into things and neglecting even one little detail can go wrong and ruin, or almost ruin, what could be a fantastic sexual experience.

I made two mistakes there. One, I cut my nails too soon before sex. Obviously, they will be sharp and pointy. And the second mistake was that I did not take the time to file them or buff them smoothly to ensure this didn't happen. In fact, it is because of this one event that I then permanently started to file and or buff out my nails after cutting them. I in no way want to scratch a girl like that again. In the event that sex or anything sexual happens and my nails aren't properly maintained, I call myself out to the girl so that she knows, and I abstain from putting my finger on or in a vagina. That also makes it so that she doesn't wonder why I'm not using my hands in those moments.

Eating pussy/yoni is great! I love it. Didn't start out that way, though. Far from it. Nor did I know what I was doing for a long time as I learned. Even now, I am still learning things, which is kind of amazing. But it's cool since I love surprises. As for you lover, get yourself a clean, good-smelling, clean-tasting pussy/yoni and eat it till you love it.

Bonus: 69! The best thing ever invented was the 69 position. You can please and be pleased at the same time. The first time I saw this was in a book at the library at the age of nine. Not only was I blown away at the beauty of it, I was astounded that it was even possible to please and be pleased at the same time! Needless to say, that is the ultimate benefit of this position.

You can do it so that you are on top and she on the bottom or in reverse. Usually better for her to be on top though unless through experience with the girl you're with you realize that you being on top works best. Why is it generally better for her to be on top? Because it lets her decide how far to take you into her mouth. When you are on top the urge can be to just shove it into her mouth and thrust or hump away. In the off chance you do end up doing it that way, bear that in mind and stop yourself from doing that unless she requests it, ok lover?

The fun thing about 69 is that it puts her ass right in your face! And also that it lets you lick her in the reverse that you would normally. As in from the clit to towards her bum. You can squeeze and jiggle her butt or just hold it firmly as you devour her to your hearts content. Just don't be surprised if she stops going down on you if you're doin a really good job. It can be hard to focus and concentrate for and for her if you're both doin a great job at pleasing the other.

It is worth mentioning that if her personal hygiene down there isn't the greatest, you will have to endure it. Also, if she farts. Even worse, if you make her cum and she squirts or oozes all over your face. That can end up in your mouth, eyes, and even up your nose. Not fun. Funny. But not fun, don't ask me how I know.

Using your fingers in her can be challenging depending on yours and her proportions but it isn't impossible. While your down there don't forget to suckle and nibble on her labia, a bit on her thighs and even on her butt cheeks. Her bum hole should be accessible as well so you might even be able to tongue that a bit or give it some attention with long strokes of your tongue from her clit all the way to that part. Just apply some of the things already in this chapter and you should be fine. But remember, if she tenses up and stops sucking on you, you're probably on the right track to make her cum.

Chapter 15: Sex! The Main Course

Having sex with a woman can truly feel like a blessed act. I have considered myself extremely lucky any time a woman has given me the privilege of trusting me with her body. Even if I was shitty in bed, even if I was not in the mood or exhausted from a day's work, I still felt nothing but gratitude. And yet, too many of us men pursue the most beautiful women for sex as a trophy. The classic trophy fuck. When it comes to sex, please don't approach a woman like that, as something to conquer and brag about. Let it be mutual if anything because then you can brag about each other. Anyway, sex is awesome. Nothing like being skin on skin with a girl you love to enjoy some good sex with.

My philosophy when it comes to sex is simple: get her worked up as much as possible, make her cum with oral if possible first, then slow but firm for first insertion, maybe while maintaining eye contact. Then use the motion in my ocean to explore her seas. Keep her close at first, learn how flexible she is and limit positions to what she can handle. I resist the urge to just hump away and keep things to a certain rhythm to build up to something like that, rather than just going right to it. Lastly, I ask her where she wants it before I pull out when I'm about to cum and either finish on her or myself. I even pull out to cum when I'm wearing a condom. And if possible, I always recommend having her finish you off with her hands or mouth, or whatever combination she desires, because you can always finish yourself off when you're alone. Give her the opportunity to do it, and then make out with her furiously if you can – or look into her eyes as you cum.

Highlights:

1. Birds, dogs, cats, whales, rats, mice, and many more know how to thrust themselves in and out in order to mate. If that's all you're doing, then you're not doing anything special, so don't go thinking that you're all that.

2. Make sure there was enough foreplay to ensure she's warmed up, ready and relaxed…unless of course you're both actively just ripping each other's clothes off.

3. I do not recommend using period blood as lubricant during a woman's menstrual cycle in any way. Say no to period sex (if you can resist).

4. Don't just have sex indoors in cushioned square boxes.

5. To some women, sex equals 'we are now in a relationship'. Be aware of that before you do the deed.

6. Alcohol and sex are always a great recipe for something bad to happen. Marijuana and sex, on the other hand, can make things even more pleasurable.

7. How you have sex, what you can do in sex, and how long you can be physically active in sex is what I call sex fitness. Don't try anything fancy if you aren't sexually fit, or you'll hurt yourself.

8. It is ok to be dominant, submissive, or anything in between during sex. Just don't force anything and do it with someone who complements the sex you like.

9. Not pulling out before you cum is how you make babies when you don't wear a condom. The difference between pulling out as you cum vs well before you cum being key here.

10. Condoms are your friend. You have more custom options than ever, and it makes a difference.

11. Knowing how to use your dick during sex is actually more important than your dick size. And general knowledge of what different sex positions can do for you and her might be of use. And remember, for her and for you, the moment of initial entry can be the sweetest.

12. There is a real difference between making love, horny sex, just wanna fuck, passionate lovers, and electrifying chemistry.

13. Remember that there is an entire person there having sex with you, not just her pussy. Be considerate and pay attention to her and her body. Be in the moment as much as possible and remind yourself that you are with an actual woman, not making porn.

14. Do not try to get all BDSM-y or kinky or use toys right away. Especially with someone you just met or haven't been with long.

Kinky passions are better shared with someone you can actually explore that with over time.

15. Orgasms are not always possible for women through just sex. If you came, then get to work on finding out how you can let her have hers as well. But keep in mind that, as much as you may want to make her cum, you may not always be able to provide that.

The basics in detail

When it comes to sex, there is so much to say! I feel like I could have presented this chapter in so many different ways. It certainly took me a few attempts before I came up with something satisfactory. And so, the first thing I want to share with you about sex is: you are not anything special when it comes to how you perform sex. Why? Because I know for a fact that the basic movement in the act of sex is your thrust in and thrust out method, regardless of penis size or position. It is the fundamental thing that we do.

1. What does that mean? Frankly, it means that we are having sex with women in pretty much the same way lions, tigers, cats, dogs, horses, whales, mice, rats, birds, and an endless array of other animals do it. We hop on the girl, we hump in and out in straightforward ways, bust a nut, then we hop off – or are done when our dick is soft.

I'm not saying it's bad or good. I want you to take heed that if all you are doing when you have sex is humping on her and thrusting in and out in the most basic way possible (doesn't matter if she loves it and begs for more), other animals are doing the same thing with a lot less brain and intelligence. So, if you are doing basic animalistic shit, you aren't all that in bed. You have zero right to claim being awesome in bed. You're just normal. Animal-level basic. If she loves sex with you, it is your body, how you feel, and what you bring that makes it good (or awesome) for her. The thrust in and out…any one of us can do that.

It is in our inherent design that we feel pleasure from such a simple thrusting sexual act. But what can quantify you as a great lover, or being considered good in bed, is what you do beyond that to elevate the level of pleasure that a woman feels during the act. Now, connectivity – having great bodily and mental chemistry – can do a lot of the heavy lifting, as well as adding excitement. But, in the end, you must put in some effort because if you have all that connectivity but act in selfish ways, then it's a waste. Otherwise, if you brag that you're awesome in bed and that whoever you have sex with loves it, but all you do is hump in and out till you bust a nut, I'm not inclined to believe you. I'm more inclined to get the play-by-play from the ladies to know the truth of the experience. Which is what I usually do anyway.

One of the drawbacks of having an ego, based only on your ability to have sex on par with most of the animal kingdom, is that too many of you think you're a stallion because you fucked the shit out of a girl. Usually, that phrase "fucked the shit out of a girl," means that you fucked her hard and or fast. That's it. You pounded her pussy as if the harder you thrusted in there, the more it proved you're great in bed. You may even have convinced yourself of this because you heard moans or screams in either pleasure or pain (or a bit of both). Hate to tell you there, lover, but nope. That's not how it works. Some girls love to be pounded like that, and that's enough. Others not so much. Performing sex like this and having that be your claim to almightiness in bed? A one-trick pony? You're a no-go.

2. The most basic thing you need to know before you have sex with a girl is to make sure that there was enough build-up and foreplay to get her properly turned on, really wet, hungry, and nice and relaxed. About the only thing that can get in the way of sex when your dick is ready and she is ready, is a dry, unrelaxed pussy/yoni. Dry unrelaxed pussy/yoni can occur for about four reasons (likely more, but I'm only listing four): She's not turned on enough, or is nervous. She just isn't really into you, and somehow she's consensually allowed you to have sex with her. (I've done that. Let a girl have sex with me that I really didn't like or want…just to give her a chance to see if she could back up the shit she was talking). Thirdly, she's one of those girls who just have a hard time getting wet and or relaxed. Or she is dehydrated. Overall, just be sure to review Chapter 13, which covers foreplay and fingering. Then you'll at least know some basics of what to do before coitus.

Look, ensuring that there was good foreplay and that she is really turned on and hungry really works in your favor. When a woman gets all turned on, lots of blood rushes down between her legs. She will start to get wet, and her vaginal walls will also start to ache at some point. You know when your dick can get super hungry, sensitive and throbbing? It's like that for them, except they also crave being penetrated, whereas you crave the sensation of penetration. When a girl is at that point, the vast majority of the time, she doesn't care how big your dick is; she just wants you inside of her. So, if you are average or smaller, this plays to your advantage. After that, it's all about the motion in your ocean.

You can disregard everything that you just read if the chemistry is hot, you are helplessly all over each other, and are actively just ripping each other's clothes off. But hopefully not literally, because clothes can be expensive. If there is one thing that can bypass the need for any foreplay or warming up, it's that raw desire for each other. It can lead to one-night stands or more. But when it's there, instincts take over, and whether you know what to do or not at that point doesn't even really matter. So, if that happens to you, go with the flow.

3. I do not recommend using period blood as lubricant for sex during a woman's menstrual cycle in any way whatsoever. Even if the electricity and connection are on fire.

One of the things to keep in mind when learning this Casanova's code is not only to have standards but also boundaries. Many women out there will not be able to help themselves due to the hormones during their period and will crave sex intensely as a result. I've encountered this a lot. At some point, you are bound to get asked for sex despite the blood, and I'm tellin' you, in no way is using blood for lubricant a fun or cool idea. I don't care how hot she is. No one, in the history of humankind, has ever said: "Hey, your pussy is dry. How about we use blood as lube?"

I've heard it before. "Hey honey, I'm really horny. I know I'm on my period, but if we use a towel or do it in the shower, it'll be fine, please!" Somehow, my hormones would get the best of me, and on the rare occasion, I would cave and go for it. I wish I hadn't each and every time afterwards. So, you know I'm speaking from experience. Now, I do recognize that you may be different and that it might not faze you at all, but that's not why I want you to consider avoiding it. The real reason for avoiding having period sex is your girl's vaginal health. Most of the time, nothing may come of it, but the reality is that blood has never been meant to be used as a lubricant in sex. So, for her vagina's sake, be patient.

You never know how a vagina will react. That means keep that in mind as you get tempted or asked. All that being said, if the girl you are with uses that little silicone cup that latches on inside her to catch the blood in that, then it is possible to have sex. BUT! You have to be really careful and gentle so as not to dislodge it while it's inside. If you do, it will look like a small crime scene unfolded on the bed…couch…or wherever you did the deed. And someone is going to have to clean up all that blood, which is never fun.

Titty fucking. If your partner's breasts are big enough, this is a great alternative. The idea is simple: push boobs together, stick dick in the middle and carefully thrust away. With some lube, obviously.

And even though I'm not covering it in this book because it isn't a basic thing you need to master the basics of being a lover, anal sex is a great alternative, if your girl is already into it. If she isn't into it or has never done it – forget it. I won't talk about that here. Maybe in another book version of this book in the future…on second thought, I will cover that in another chapter solely because I know that in the past, anal is what I went for each time.

If your girl uses the diva cup or uses tampons, you can still use your fingers to play with her clit or use a toy on her clit to help her get some satisfaction and sexual relief till her period goes away. Only if she doesn't use a pad is direct clitoral stimulation possible. And of course, vibrators for her and a blowjob or a handjob for you, can tide you over till the blood has passed. Unless you happen to be a vampire, then just enjoy.

4. Don't just have sex indoors in cushioned square boxes. For those of you who like things outdoors, this might be obvious. But for those who are used to just doing the sex inside, listen up. All animals in nature, save humans and some flies, roaches, and dust mites, have sex outdoors in nature. We, for whatever reason, have decided that only inside, in private and on a bed, is where we should majorly conduct our sexual activities. Well, try it out outdoors. You don't have to do it in front of people, but you should try it outdoors in a safe environment. The feeling you get from that is completely different from indoors, and that is something I highly recommend you experience if you want to master the basics.

5. To some women, sex equals 'we are now in a relationship'. Be aware of this. This is a rather simple but very real idea. Some women don't really do the whole one-night stand or casual sex thing. To those women, if they have sex with you, that means they chose you. You are now in a relationship. Period. Whether it's talked about or not. And as a man, you may or may not have the same mentality or the intestinal fortitude to reject her. If you do, then fine. But for those that don't, be aware of this so that you can talk about it ahead of time, or even after

the fact, to be clear about your feelings on the issue. Don't get sucked into something you don't want, or seduce an innocent girl, just because you wanna fuck and then kick her to the curb.

Another reason why, to some women, sex equals we are now together or in a relationship, is if they discover that you are someone worth keeping. That means that it's possible that you sexed them so well that they don't want to lose that or that they feel such a strong connection, or so safe with you, that they know they want to be with you. That bond can be strong and instant, both biologically and mentally. Other times, it can be that even though you were both on the same page, she changes her mind because she has deemed you a keeper for one reason or another. Maybe you got money. It's easy to get sucked into a relationship when that happens, so again, be aware of this.

Learning how to handle these situations with clarity will make things much easier and way less of a headache. Better to have a girl upset and hurt because you want nothing more after sex than to let yourself get sucked into something that then drags out over time, only to end terribly for both of you. So, practice being honest and clear from the get-go.

All that being said, it is possible for you to genuinely like the girl – and her like you too – then you have sex and lose interest. Whether it was something with her body that turned you off, how she has sex, (maybe she said another guy's name during sex) or whether the moment of clarity after your orgasm made things crystal clear, if you lost interest, you have two choices: Honesty or a lie. I won't tell you how to roll here, but I will say this: know the difference between things not being to your taste/preferences and things just being plain bad or repulsive. Any comments or reasons you give for losing interest can truly affect a lady, so choose your words wisely. But if it's as simple as you lost interest or you aren't sexually compatible, that's ok. I would encourage you to tell the truth in that situation.

6. Alcohol and sex are always a great recipe for something bad to happen. Marijuana and sex, on the other hand, can make things even more pleasurable.

Drunk sex or even having sex with a girl who's drunk is something I never recommend, and it all comes down to a few key things. As a man who wants to master the basics of being a lover, improving the quality of your sex also comes with drawing certain boundaries.

Knowing when to say yes and when to say no is key. Drunk girl trying to get you in bed? No go. A sober girl trying to get you in bed? Could be a go. That way, you don't waste your time and energy on women and sex that isn't worth your time. No matter how horny you are or how long it's been, I encourage you to say no to drunk women. Just avoid sex with them at all costs. Seriously. All I need is to smell a drunk woman, and my body is immediately repulsed. Why? From experiences with drunk girls in the past, I learned my lesson. No thank you.

In case you haven't had that and are thinking something along the lines of, 'isn't that the whole point of going to bars and clubs? To hook up with a drunk girl?' Listen here, highspeed – a girl with alcohol in her system is different from a girl who is really drunk. One has her inhibitions loosened or relaxed, while the other may not remember who you are after the night is over. Drunk girls can vomit on you, lose bladder and bowel control, turn on you on a dime and accuse you of random shit. They can be violent, loud, steal your hat and stink of alcohol and cigarettes. Or even worse, after you hook up with one, they can claim that you took advantage of them because they were drunk. Please heed this advice and just skip the drunken women.

Married or have a partner, and you both like to get drunk at home and have fun with each other? No problem!

On the other hand, having sex while smoking weed…that can be awesome. It can enhance pleasure, sensation, etc. I'm fairly certain lots of you reading this already know that, but just as a reminder and for those that have yet to experience this, sex while high is better than drunk sex any day of the week. Don't believe me? Experiment and find out for yourself. Remember, it can also make you hungry, tired, give you dry mouth, and make you sleepy. So don't be surprised if you smoke weed for sex…only to pass out.

7. How you can have sex, what you can do in sex, and how long you can be physically active in sex is what I call sex fitness. And why does that matter? Because if you want to be a better lover, being able to have sex without getting winded, or tired quickly, or worn out from muscle failure, sex fitness is a prerequisite. I mentioned some of this in the first book when I talked about reasons why you should exercise.

Look, most of the missionary position itself is essentially just the push-up position on your knees. Kind of like a knee plank where you are constantly thrusting your hips up and down. Granted that during sex, you have both the pleasurable sensations and the woman as motivation to keep going. But in reality, you won't be able to do it nearly as much, or with as much control, as if you were in shape. Or at least in better shape than you might be in now. In that sense, doing push-ups and planks can help your missionary game.

There are also many other positions that require some degree of strength or endurance to be able to do them. I like picking a girl up completely and having sex standing up that way. That requires a lot of arm strength, back strength, and leg strength, not to mention stamina and endurance. For me personally, the reason I like that position is because of how it changes the pleasurable sensations I get. So even though you might not be into that, or into too many other positions, the reality is that if you increase your sex fitness, you'll be able to try other positions that will surely be accompanied by slightly different pleasure for you and for her. And if you are the monogamous, long-term relationship, or marriage type, then it will definitely serve you better in your relationship to increase your sex fitness to keep things interesting and fun.

Does that mean that you have to lift weights for this? No. There are plenty of other ways to get some fitness in that don't involve weightlifting. Yoga is actually very fit for this task. Any kind of consistent exercise that increases your fitness will do. Pull-ups, military style training, CrossFit, etc. Just be sure to stretch as well.

8. It's ok to be dominant, submissive, or anything else in between during sex (although most women do prefer a dominant man in bed). We aren't all the same. Some guys like to be in charge and on top when it comes to sex. Others of you prefer to be on the bottom and to let the woman do most of the work. Each for their own reasons. Don't let anyone tell you that how you like to be in sex is wrong or not manly or whatever. So long as it's communicated, consensual, and you both are into it, go for it.

If you happen to have a lover who isn't compatible or doesn't share your sexual tastes, then you move on. Don't try to convince them, reform them, or mold them (unless they are open to that). Since sex can be a critical component of a relationship, if you aren't sexually compatible, then it can be a deal breaker, and that's ok. Don't let a girl force you or guilt you into something that just doesn't feel right, and don't do that to her as well. She will either be open to new things or not.

Granted, there are extremes here when it comes to dominance and submissiveness, to say the least. But that's even more reason to find someone you are compatible with than to stay with a woman who isn't into what you are into, or not even willing to try.

9. Not pulling out before you cum is how you make babies. The difference between, as you cum vs well before, is key here. This matters because women do not magically become pregnant. 'Oh shit! She got pregnant!' That doesn't cut it. You get her pregnant. Your sperm, your responsibility. There is no debate about that, my dear lover. No sperm inside her, no pregnancy. Too easy.

Whether she is using contraception or not, even if you have a condom on, and she has the pill and a cervical cap, you still should pull out. Every time you don't, you are accepting that risk of fathering a child. There just isn't any other way about it. No sperm inside, no baby. Does that mean I have always pulled out? Nope. There have been certain circumstances where there was mutual trust between me and my sex partner at the time that neither of us wanted to be parents, so plenty of precautions were taken to ensure that didn't happen. But those ladies were in the minority whom I trusted enough to cum inside of.

Now, learning to pull out, especially for those who don't like to use condoms or just don't use them at all for whatever reason, is of utmost importance. We men know when we get that feeling that something is traveling down our tube, heading to our dick, and is about to release. For the extra sensitive out there, you can likely feel it all the way inside before your baby-making swimmer fluid even gets close to your pee exit hole. Either way, pull out before it gets to the base of your dick. Or, as soon as you even get the slightest sensation that you are about to start to cum or that your orgasm is close. Don't wait till the last second, even though that is always the urge. Come out earlier and have her help you to finish you off with her hands, mouth, or you do it yourself. This is the absolute best way to go – no matter who you are with or what position you are in. It's challenging and counterintuitive, but I know you can master this basic move. I believe in you.

10. Condoms are your friend. And even when you do use them, pulling out to come inside the condom is still the best option. I know that not all of you will do that, so I'm just emphasizing this for those who are more cautious and wish to be as careful as possible.

Fortunately, we live in an era that has tons of condom options. So, whatever the size of your dick, there is a condom size out there for you. There are even different materials. Your basic condom size might not work exactly for you in the way you like. Fortunately, if you look up condoms online, you will likely end up finding a website or two that has custom condom sizes available for order. From what I learned, it is as easy as taking your own measurements with a cloth tape measure and then matching that up with their available sizes.

One perspective I want you to consider when it comes to condoms is this: try to think of not wearing condoms as something both you and the girl can earn together. You don't want to risk getting a girl pregnant or getting (or giving) a sexually transmitted disease. Especially with someone you just met or recently met. You can earn her trust by showing that you can control your water at will while wearing condoms, and you can both earn each other's trust by getting thoroughly tested for sexually transmitted anything. If you both come out clean, then you can get rid of the condoms if you so mutually desire.

Is it always gonna be like that? Nah. Are things going to always be that easy to address and talk about? Nope. But you can try and see. If it doesn't go well, try again and again to keep up your boundaries. It's worth it. When you set rigid rules like that with yourself and a partner, you are setting up good boundaries for yourself. When it comes to ladies, sex, and relationships, setting up healthy boundaries can help you determine whether this person is someone worth investing in by how they react or respond to those boundaries.

11. Ok, now stop me if you've heard this one before, but knowing how to use your dick during sex is actually more important than your dick size. Yes, I can totally confirm that, and I'll give a simple example. Say you are with a girl who has had bigger, thicker dicks before you, and you have no clue since it's a random hookup. She doesn't know about vaginal fitness, and she gets stretched inside by bigger or thicker dicks – and remains more loose as a result. Now, she craves more of the same sensation while growing looser over time. Then you come along. You're average in length and girth, with nothing big to speak of. Can you get away with the average thrust in and out technique and expect her to feel much? Probably not. But what if you know how to angle your dick to rub in certain spots inside her while having her in certain positions? Then not only can you get her to feel something, but perhaps you can get her to feel something in a way she

hasn't felt before – regardless of whether she's loose, stretched out, or has a high body count. So you see, general knowledge of what different sex positions can do for you and her might be of use to you as well. Got that, lover? You should really take this lesson in if you haven't really ever considered something like this. If you know how to work with what you've got, you can still create a very good, pleasurable experience for you both.

In porn, you see men in all kinds of positions with girls. For the average guy, most of those positions won't work out quite the same way. It's better to forget all that and instead focus on your body and the experiences you are capable of creating. And remember, for her and for you, the moment of initial entry can be the sweetest. Which means, no matter the position, go slow and steady until you are all the way inside her. Firmly press yourself when all the way in, hold it for a bit to let that moment breathe, flex your dick if you can, and then slowly pull out a bit before starting to go in and out of her in whatever position you are in. And now that the essential first thrust is established, we go on to the positions themselves.

The two basic sexual positions that you can do will either have your partner facing you or facing away from you, generally. And you know the most basic of these as missionary – you in between her legs on top of her and facing her. The other is doggy style – her on all fours facing away from you. But the points I want you to consider have little to do with positions and more to do with how you can use angles and positions to rub her inside differently than your standard thrust.

The only downside to this is that it can also feel so good for you that it makes you want to cum as well. Or at least quicker than you might want. In that case, what you do is to change to a less pleasurable position. It will still feel amazing because you are so close to orgasm. She should be able to feel this, which will also increase her pleasure in that position. Ultimately, save the less pleasurable positions for when you are more sensitive and closer to orgasm, and the more pleasurable positions for when you either aren't feeling much or are perfectly in control of yourself.

The simplest explanation for how to improve the motion in your ocean with angles is to use your hands for what I'm about to share. Take your right hand and make it into a fist. Take your left hand and point with your index finger, but keep it rigid. Now insert your index finger into a small space in your fist between your thumb and curled index finger until it touches your pinky. As you keep the finger inside rigid, move your left hand to the left and right slowly. Now move it up and down slowly. If you did this right, you should have noticed that the tip of your index finger poked in one spot while the base of your finger pushed against the outer edge. Now, if you back out your finger halfway and again move your hand left and right and then up and down as you slide your finger in and out, you can feel how the tip of your finger slides across, then pokes the other side. Think about that – but with your dick completely hard inside a vagina.

It's much easier with the example of your hands, but more challenging when you are using your whole body and hips to achieve the same effect inside a vagina. That is what it means to have a 'good motion in your ocean'. The plus side of having an average-sized dick is that you can press your pubic area completely onto a girl's pubic area to get yourself as deep as you can go while providing new sensations from being pressed together like that. Then, as you change your hip angle or height angle, the rubbing of your skin together alongside the rubbing and thrusting you are now doing inside her, will give her some really good sensations. She may not have felt these often – or at all. Plus, it should feel good for you too.

You can rotate her left or right so that she's lying on her side when you try this. You can do it in doggy style, or missionary, and just see how it goes. You can also be standing next to the bed as she lies on it to give you the room you need to maneuver your hips for improving the motion in your ocean. This will, at a minimum, take you one step above the generic thrust in, thrust out as a lover.

If you can still get your dick totally hard but you're too long to get all the way in there, that doesn't mean you can't try angles in different positions. But it does mean you should be a bit careful not to stretch out the outer edge of the vaginal opening as you press against it with the base, or close to the base, of your dick. That part might be painful for her to stretch too much. So be sure to check and see with your sex partner. I've encountered this a couple of times, so it's worth remembering.

For you really hung men that can't really get it hard enough to do this, you can still try it and see. But if you are already filling her up completely inside, not much else can really make her feel something different. So, chances are you might be stuck with just the regular thrust in and thrust out. There isn't anything wrong with that. It'll just mean that your connection to her and her love for your size will matter most, probably.

12. Remember that there is an entire person there having sex with you, not just her pussy. So be considerate and give attention to her and her body as well. This is where going beyond what other mating animals can do starts to make a difference. I mean, if you just hop on in there as fast as you can after you bent her over and thrust yourself in and out till you finish, what is the difference between you and a horse or a dog?

When you're with a girl in a relationship, you end up doing quickies. Quickies are the sudden desire to have sex spontaneously, or due to limited time, where you get each other off quickly. Quickies are cool, fun, and exciting depending on the location. But if you hop on in there like a quickie is your usual in missionary, without any change, and that's how you do sex…then you aren't even acknowledging that there is someone else there for you to have sex with!

Look, a woman's body has so much potential for pleasure it's not even funny. Learning this and putting this into practice can be kind of mind-blowing in a good way. Even during sex, I would look for ways to give a woman's body as much stimulation as possible despite the multitasking challenge. In my head, I would think of it as finding ways to extrapolate as much pleasure as I could with all the tools at my disposal, if for no other reason than I enjoyed watching my lovers writhe and wriggle in ecstatic pleasure.

While you are having sex, be sure to make contact with as much of your skin onto her skin as possible. Don't just lean back and watch things go in and out the whole time like a porno. For example, use your hands. One to stimulate her breast and hold onto it, and the other to hold her close or grab a leg and wrap it around you. Your lips should be making contact with her in some way, depending on what you are doing, whether or not you are dressed, what position you are in, etc.

When having sex, you need to step up your game and stimulate more of her body parts like her ears, neck, cheeks, lips, shoulders, chest, hands, fingers, feet, or her nipples. Explore, play, discover, or even ask and see what she says about what she likes.

13. There is a real difference between making love, horny sex, just wanna fuck, passionate lovers, and electrifying chemistry. And honestly, some of the most intense, pleasurable sex is not just because

of electrifying chemistry. It can be because of the situation or circumstances. Are you in public? Are people in the other room? Can people see you, but they can't tell what you are doing? Maybe you are where you aren't supposed to be doing what you're doing with someone you're not supposed to be doing anything with? All these things can make sex unbelievably amazing and result in normal sex looking and feeling plain boring in comparison.

Making love is just sex with someone you are in romantic love with. It tends to be a bit more passionate and full of kisses and holds, but with love as the secret ingredient. There is something in that scenario that makes it magical. Horny is just when you feel the urge for sex or an orgasm or both, so you crave orgasmic satisfaction. When you just wanna fuck, you might be in a mood where sex, the act itself, the pleasure, and the nakedness are what you are looking for. You don't necessarily need it to be anyone in particular. You can just crave the act and the feeling of a woman in sex. Passionate lovers, on the other hand, likely rip each other's clothes off. They can't wait to rendezvous together and jump onto each other while releasing their hunger for each other whenever they can. Electrifying chemistry sex can be a momentary thing with a partner or a stranger. It can be spontaneous at first sight or touch, or something can happen that changes a mood or creates a vibe where you suddenly want to jump on the person. This type of sex is amazing. It can happen even after years of marriage, at the beginning of a relationship, or with a stranger whose name you don't even know. The sex can be terrible, but the energy does all the work because of the electrifying sensation combined with exhilaration that turns into extreme pleasure. Now your experiences of these types of descriptions may be different, and that's totally cool. I just wanted to make you aware of some of the different types you might experience if you haven't already.

Beware: Some of you may become prone to being sort of addicted to one of these types of sex or to a type I didn't mention here. Seeking thrills and adrenaline rushes are the reasons why some people get into extreme sports. The rush is amazing and like nothing else. If you apply that to sex and certain circumstances, then you might forego the less thrilling moments all in pursuit of that rush. Learn to appreciate the normal and to enjoy each experience on its own merits. Remember the memorable ones, but stay present. Don't try to live in the memory of past sexual relationships in hopes of recreating past passion or pleasures. I know it can be really difficult to readjust to regular sex if you are used to thrills and constantly crave that lightning and fire. But

I'm here to tell you that you can ruin a perfectly good chance at an amazing woman if you are constantly after sexual highs and thrills. Sexual urges can naturally wane over time in a relationship for various reasons. I just hope that if you are a sexual thrill seeker, you don't get addicted to that. Why? Because it won't always be possible, and you could ruin something beautiful with someone you can actually have a happy future with.

14. Do not try to get all BDSM-y or kinky right away, lover. Especially with someone you just met. Your kinky passions are better shared with someone you can actually explore that with over time. The only usual exception is if you happen to meet someone who is also into that stuff, or if you find each other through a kinky site or kinky group.

Again, this is something that is seemingly obvious but is worth mentioning because you might end up scaring away a good woman who is open to exploring those things if you go too fast. That's why it's important to pace yourself in a relationship in more than one way. You can also just ask, however. That way, if she's willing and has never done anything kinky, you can find out right away. Conversely, you ask, and she's already into it. Either way, asking or talking about it never hurts. And as I've said before, if you ask about it and the girl is put off for some reason – or expects you to be telepathic to discern how she feels about it – then she might not be the one for you.

15. Orgasms are not always possible for women through sex alone. So, if you came, then get to work on learning how you can let her have hers as well. But keep in mind that, as much as you may want to make her cum, you may not always be able to provide that.

Just to be clear: there is pleasure and gratification to be had still after you orgasm as a man. I know that for some of you, the moment you cum, you lose interest not just in sex but in her body and in more sexual activity, maybe even if you have feelings for her. I get that and understand. But, if the girl you just had sex with isn't yet satisfied or hasn't gotten off and looks like she is still hungry, then you get your head back in the game. Learn to enjoy sexual things beyond your orgasm, lover. You can still go down on her. Use your fingers. Use toys. You can still kiss her, and more. For those who still have sexual desire after orgasm, this shouldn't be too challenging at all unless you are physically tired. In which case, it is completely cool to take five, hydrate and rest a bit, then continue to see what you can do for her.

Even with foreplay and sex, sometimes it just takes a lot to get a girl to cum, if at all. Different things do it for different girls – so don't assume that what worked for one girl will always work for the next. If you happen to have had great foreplay, good sex, and then you cum and she still hasn't had an orgasm…and then you play more afterwards, and she still doesn't orgasm…you have to learn to take note of when to stop. Sometimes it's easy; you can see she's tired and ready to stop when you are. Other times, you might get caught up in your head thinking about video games. During those moments, it's important to just talk about it. Communicate with her and see what's up. She might just need to play with herself, and you assist. Or whatever. The point is that you at least take the time to a) Go beyond your orgasm and b) See what more she likes or wants to do, or even try to orgasm.

In the circumstances where no matter what you do or try, the girl still doesn't orgasm, and she hasn't said anything about it (this has happened to me more than once), then you really need to have a chat. Sit down, take your time, and talk and share to see if there is anything that can be explored or played with over time. I've met several women like this over the years. Some of them even had a hard time making themselves cum through masturbation. I found that for them, per their own words, "good sex is its own reward without the necessity for the orgasmic payoff", since even they couldn't make themselves cum consistently. This is even more reason to step up your game as a lover, so in case you run into such a woman, at least she walks away feeling great.

16. Pay attention to the mood, the connection, and the flow. Where you end up may not always be where you intended to go during sex, and that's not a bad thing.

Your instincts are likely to take over the moment you and a girl start to go at it. During those moments, you will have to make many instant decisions about what to do, how to touch, what to touch, and when. If nothing else, pay attention to her. Look for moments of wincing, like when something hurts, and look for moments of ecstatic pleasure in her voice and face. You never know what you might do or what you might touch that might incite one or the other.

Don't forget to keep an eye out for the face of boredom and of dissatisfaction either. Sometimes that happens. Typically, this can occur when a woman has expectations, she has secretly set that she wants to be met without saying anything – no matter how realistic or unrealistic they might be. Or you could just plain suck at sex, or maybe you talked a big game, thereby getting her hopes up, only to fall flat on your face with your performance. Just don't get so caught up in it that you aren't paying attention to the human you are sharing sex with, then you should be ok in catching those particular facial expressions.

No matter what you have read here, this chapter is no substitute for the real thing, and sometimes it takes the right woman to turn a boy into a man in bed. What I mean is that some women will actually take the time to teach you how to be a better lover in their own way. I, for one, sing praises to those women because they can see a man and what he might be able to become in bed – and then help you to reach that potential. I mean, it pays dividends both ways: you get more experience and sex, and she gets a better lover out of it.

These tips for this sex chapter may not at all be what you or others might have expected. In reality, through many conversations and experiences, this is more or less the essence of the fundamentals that I believe are a good idea for you to pay attention to if you truly desire to master the basics of being a good lover…and maybe even to getting that black belt level in dick-yoon-do.

With women, it can often be the most basic of things that turns them on or off. In that sense, getting all fancy or kinky isn't what is going to impress a woman in bed or get her to want seconds with you. Remember, learn to use what you got, pay attention, be attentive, enjoy the journey, don't make it all about the orgasm (though orgasms are important). Use your lips and hands to stimulate and touch as you have sex, and most of all, don't forget that if you are just doing basic sex, there's nothing wrong with that – but it doesn't make you anything special, so don't gloat. Essentially, you're just doing it like all the rest of us, and like all the other animals in the animal kingdom, so be humble about it.

The Epic Fail

How do you fail at sex? Forget the condom? Condom broke? Can't get it up? Woman gets bored and stops having sex with you? Thought you were all that, but the lady was unimpressed? Maybe you were humping away in missionary and slipped and hit her face with your face? Injure yourself perhaps? Maybe you got tired after just starting and had to stop from exhaustion? Well, feast your eyes and read this guy's epic fail.

On this particular occasion, I was invited to meet up with a girl I had previous experience with. We hadn't had sex yet, so I was thinking that I was finally about to have amazing sex and show this girl my qualities as a lover, when all of a sudden, reality hit my eyes after she took off her shorts. She was cute, a good kisser, really sexual and horny, great boobs, short and a bit thick, but when those shorts came off, I didn't know what to think.

I was super horny. Like so horny that I could feel each heartbeat in my dick. All the foreplay and anticipation had sensitized me to a point that I knew it wouldn't take me much to cum. Well, no longer standing and now spread-eagled before me was a giant bush. The biggest hairiest bush I'd ever seen. Not only did it spread along her inner thighs, to her butt, and over her mons pubis (i.e., her FUPA), but the hairs were so long that they had all joined forces like Voltron. But rather than forming a giant robot, they formed a big curly shield as if to protect her pussy at all costs from intruders. This wasn't here before and was definitely new.

The look of anticipation on her face was very real. Her bush didn't turn me off at all. Next thing I knew, she was grabbing at me, I was grabbing at her, kissing, squeezing, and as much as I wanted to go down on her, I was too horny for sex, and so was she. And I wasn't about to tackle that bush with my face either. There was just no way. At least not without a machete.

She embraced me as I leaned on her. I accidentally pinched her boob, missed a proper kiss and like some horny animal, I just went straight for her pussy with my dick without even trying to spread her pubes open for a clean entrance. My excitement got the better of me, and she embraced me while grabbing my ass, so I felt like she was as ready for it as much as I was. Our energies came together in such extreme excitement that I skipped all the things I would normally do to make sure it was a fulfilling experience for us both. And yet, I was overcome with horniness at her encouragement. As I poked more and more with my dick against her tropical Voltron bush, I felt more and more wetness. Thing is, like three or four pokes into the now-wet bush, I finally felt the edges of her vagina. I barely got a feel inside, but I was so sensitized from being horny that that small amount of pleasurable sensation made me about to cum, so I stopped abruptly and came on her belly. Elapsed time from entering the room and jumping on each other to this moment: approximately 32 seconds.

The look of disappointment on her face was clear and palpable. She was still super horny and wanted more of me, but with that giant Voltron bush, that she didn't want to help me with or do anything about, I wasn't too inclined to keep going either. Did that mean I wasn't horny anymore? Of course not. I came way too fast to be satisfied myself, so I wanted more, but I also didn't have any condoms at the time. So, going in again was a no-go – or I could have got her pregnant. And so, that's where we stopped.

Obviously if I could go back and do it again, I would do many things differently. I'm pretty sure that even if I did get another opportunity, the giant bush would still be there. Anyway, I failed big time on that one. Rarely had I ever cum so fast, and I didn't even make it in! It was just pure bush and lip rub! Not to mention I didn't pay attention to her boobs properly, messed up kisses, got overly anxious to fuck and allowed her eagerness to have me inside influence me from doing what I would normally do. The good thing is that I did reflect on what happened a lot and was able to improve my self-control from there onwards. It was also helpful that I never encountered a bush like that again. Whew.

The Epic Success

I had seen this one girl who completely fascinated me at a small beachside event I attended once. Being so captivated by her, I had to talk to her. One conversation led to another, and we ended up meeting a few times to get to know each other better. At some point, it became obvious that we were really interested in each other, and so we started dating. We hadn't had sex yet, but planned for it.

When the day came, I remember I was super excited and oh so ready. She showed up wearing soft, thin clothing and no bra. Very quickly, we got to it. At this point in my life, I was very confident as a lover and had my third-degree black belt in dick-yoon-do and went right to work on her body. Kissing, touching, going down on her etc. But the whole time, as much as I could tell it was enjoyable and pleasurable for her, it didn't feel right. Like I was somehow having sex with her the wrong way, despite it appearing ok on the surface.

After the sex was over, she felt really comfortable, and we talked. After some talk and some food, we started to have sex again. This time, though, I went with a completely different approach. Instead of being all about touching all the parts of her body, going down on her, doing different positions, and trying to poke her in different sweet spots inside, I decided to keep it simple and close and intimate. Somehow, I managed to figure out what I was sensing she needed as well as what her body would better respond to.

I slowed down, lowered my intensity and enthusiasm, paid more attention directly to her, squeezed her tightly and kept her close. I didn't try too many fancy positions, but rather just a couple of twists on missionary itself. I kissed much more and more slowly. I paid more attention to her neck and cheeks and slowed my strokes in and out of her to ensure that it was slow, methodical, thorough, and that I rubbed in the same spot inside her as I lay upon her while holding her close. Sure enough, that worked. Her reactions changed completely, she came to life more, her moans became deeper and more passionate, and suddenly she had an orgasm before I knew it and then had another right before I was ready to cum. That was great because she became rather limp and tired after the second orgasm.

We both came right after each other and then rested, laughed, and talked some more. It turned out to be really wonderful and an epic success in my book. Maybe some of you would have expected me to share a story about how I did everything right the first time or how I fucked a girl so awesomely in some other way. To me, what really makes an epic success in sex is the ability to stay flexible and adaptable enough to pay attention to a woman's needs and her body's needs to truly please her and yourself.

In my initial attempt at sex with this girl, I was just doing most of what I recommend here. I went for different pleasure spots, did oral, did different positions to hit different spots inside of her, etc. But none of it really felt right. It was only when I slowed down and just saw her as she was that it became clear that she was more about slow lovemaking and closeness than anything else. Sure, the sex we had at first was fine, but it didn't get her off even though she enjoyed it. And it didn't feel right to me because of the subtle ways her body reacted, or should I say, in the subtle ways it did not react.

I felt like this was an epic success because I was able to completely change how I had sex with her, and that not only increased her pleasure and satisfaction but mine as well. And the best part was I didn't have to try as hard or do as many things. I just made sure not to squish her with my body weight, kiss her passionately but slowly, held her close, and moved in and out of her with conscious intent rhythmically as her body reacted to mine. Whether having sex or making love, one of the most basic things is to pay attention to your lover so that you can adapt to keep the sex enjoyable and pleasurable for you both. If all you can do in sex is one thing or in one way, you won't be much good beyond those women who like exactly that. And if you are married, then at some point, your woman is bound to either get tired or bored with what it is that you do if all you do is the same thing while only paying attention to yourself.

It's also noteworthy that the sex was really basic. Missionary with little deviation essentially. The attention and focus I gave, on the other hand, had completely changed. Be attentive, stay adaptable, be considerate, communicate, don't gloat, and you'll do alright.

Chapter 16: Anal: The Forbidden Toot

My philosophy for anal has always been the same: make the girl desire, crave, and want anal from you, and it will almost always certainly be enjoyable for her. Once you get her to crave it from you, it sensitizes the area for pleasure even more. So long as you go slow and easy, have plenty of lube and be wary of not getting any anal fluids into her vagina, it should feel good for you both.

Highlights:

1. The number one rule of anal is: don't try it unless you're ready to potentially deal with some stink and some shit. Literally.

2. The most important tip I can give is that getting the woman you are with to crave or desire anal from you is the secret ingredient to making it as pleasurable for her as possible. This especially applies to first-timers.

3. Learn to look for the signs that indicate that anal may or may not be a good idea, as not all asses want to be done, can be done, and of those that do, many require good prep work.

4. Always think ahead and prep for the before, during, and after.

5. You must be gentler with her ass than with her pussy. (Contrary to most porn videos.)

6. Do not double dip. That is to say, as a general rule, don't go from anal to vaginal sex.

7. Be prepared to stop at any moment if she bleeds, becomes sore, or if it becomes painful or if she's just had enough.

8. If the woman you are with was already into it before you, ask her how she likes it.

9. Both of you getting tested for STIs, as well as condom use, is best. In the end, it's all up to you both as to how you wanna roll.

10. Be aware: dry anal, even slightly forced for any reason, can result in injury for you and or her. Lube. Plenty of it. Sometimes spit and saliva work, but a good lube is best. Even coconut oil works.

Anal sex can feel oh so good! At least when everything is going well, and you have a good woman with a good sphincter. But things can go oh so wrong so quickly, let me tell ya. Remember, anal sex isn't exactly natural. Lots of people, even myself, often talk like it is a perfectly natural thing to do, but when you look at the body, that area is clearly designed for one function alone. It just so happens that it is hackable, you might say. Even reprogrammable to a degree so that it can function similarly to how a vagina can when it comes to pleasure reception. That's only possible because there are so many nerve endings packed down there. So, pay attention and be attentive because, for whatever reason, not a single sex book I've read explores these details (which absolutely boggles my mind). Not to say other books I haven't read don't cover some of the things I write about here, but it's all basic stuff to me, so I have included it here for you, my aspiring lover, for both education and entertainment.

The basics in depth

1. The number one rule of anal is: don't try it unless you're ready to potentially deal with some stink and some shit. I would have thought that this was kinda obvious, and maybe for some of you it is. Yet you'd be surprised at how many people (and books) overlook this little tidbit of a detail. Look, just ask yourself this: how many situations in your life in general ever work out ideally? Where everything goes exactly as you hoped or planned. I'd venture to say, not that often. Maybe half for most of you. With that reality check in mind, you can go forth with eagle-eyed enthusiasm while full of desire, knowing well that anal comes with its own perils and you are ready for them.

The stink can come at you in a few ways. It can be from gas that was trapped that you let loose, from a clinger on the inside you keep pokin', or from something on the inside that you are bringing in and out with you. Dealing with her poop can happen randomly and will most likely be because she didn't prep or because her colon isn't naturally clean. And I'm here to tell ya, most girls colons nowadays aren't. Blame the Western diet. All that said, if you are still willing to go forth…

2. The most important tip I can give is that getting the woman you are with to crave or desire anal from you is the secret ingredient to making it as pleasurable for her as possible. This especially applies to first-timers. I cannot overstate this enough. The bonus is that if you succeed in this, it will truly feel even more amazing for her, which is a big bonus for you.

I did not start my sexual journey by craving or even being interested in anal. In fact, just being too close to a girl's butt hole when messin' around was a huge area of caution and worry for me. Eventually, I got more interested in playing around down there and very quickly realized that every girl I came across was even more apprehensive to try any anal play than I used to be. My first attempts, in retrospect, were clumsy and lacked any preparation. I always asked first, but it never went well. Even though the girl was open to it, it hurt, wasn't comfortable, or I was a bit too eager and didn't have enough lube.

One day at a club, I met a girl that I really liked, but after spending a bit of time together we really desired each other, and she wanted me to take her in every way possible. She went home for the holidays shortly thereafter. During that time, we chatted online regularly, and I took a chance and told her how I wanted to do anal with her. She had never tried it, but was curious, and we kept teasing each other with our desires to explore this the whole month she was gone. Long story short, she came back, we had anal sex, and it was amazing for both of us. Then I realized that the biggest and most important thing I could do to get a girl to enjoy anal was to get her to want to do it. And that to do that, I had to talk and tease and tantalize the girl in all the ways she could possibly want. That also meant getting to know each girl individually enough to be able to really trigger her curiosity and desire for it.

How then can you get a girl who is also curious about anal to desire experiencing it with you?

This has to be custom-tailored to each girl. Getting to know her is very important. There are, however, some general things I can share that may be of use to you as you try this:

First – talk about it. If you like to tease her with whispers or text messages about sex and the delicious things you want to do with her, go ahead and add how amazing it might feel, how you can't wait to be squeezed or how amazing it would feel to be filled up from that end. Or even how her pussy might ache and get super wet from being stimulated from the outside while feeling a different kind of pleasure.

Second – with touches. If you get good at foreplay, tease her pussy with some pats and rubs over her clothing or over her undies. Also take the time to go just a little farther and gently rub, with a finger or two, right over her ass and tell her how you crave it, how it might feel, how you look forward to it, and how hot it might be to be in her there while you also have fingers in her pussy. Then you can do this throughout the day. You can also pin her up against the wall, kiss her passionately, use your hands to gently go under her panties, play with her to get her wet if she isn't already. Then slide back a bit and rub her ass while telling her how hungry you are for her, and then stop there, kiss her gently, and say something like, "can't wait!"

Third – orally of course. When you go down on her, you can use your own saliva, or if she gets really wet, use her own wetness to gently rub her ass with a finger as you lick her. Do it in circles around the rim firmly but gently. You want to feel the relaxation of her ass. When you feel her relax, ask if its ok to gently put the tip of your finger inside. If she agrees, always wait for her to relax as you lick her slowly to then slowly and gently insert your finger. Once that happens, then you can try licking her in gentle circles down there as well and then slowly dip your tongue in. You'll be able to feel her sphincter tighten and relax. Time it so you only try to dip in when she's relaxed. Don't force your way in if she clenches and is tight. If you press your face up against her pussy as you do this, your nose and upper lip will likely be right at the opening of her pussy. You can use this to further make her feel good by gently rubbing your nose on and into her as well. Keep that up over the course of more than one sex session to build up her desire for it, and next thing you know (hopefully!) she'll be asking you for anal.

3. Learn to look for the signs that indicate that anal may or may not be a good idea, as not all asses want to be done, can be done, and of those that do, many require good prep work. I may have gotten a bit ahead of myself by talking about getting her to want it before trying it, because I assumed that you had already gone down on the girl or had sex with her. In that case, you have obviously had a good look at her ass, been close to it enough to sniff it, and therefore get a decent sense of it. Thing is, if you have little to no experience and are overwhelmed with desire, you might miss a few details that make it obvious that you might need to reconsider anal.

First and foremost is her smell down there. Look, ideally, if we all had perfectly functioning organs and great diets, every time we go to the bathroom, we would have a full bowel evacuations. All the poop in your colon would be excreted each time. Unfortunately, that does not happen for most of us. Many of us even have poop where it isn't supposed to be. Who knew that your poop isn't supposed to be waiting just inside your butthole to come out? It's actually supposed to be a bit higher in your colon than that. So if your girl, or lover, has a consistent smell of poop when you are down there right next to her bum, chances are you might wanna stop there because those aren't chocolates just on the other side of her sphincter. Note that she can look perfectly clean and hygienic, yet this can still happen. Just so you know.

The next thing is the sphincters of girls that have a mind of their own. In some women, no matter how much they might want or be in the mood for anal, for whatever reason, it just isn't going to happen. Maybe it refuses to relax. Maybe it's nothing but pain sensations that day, or maybe she's full of gas. Just think of it like when your dick won't get hard no matter what you do, despite being horny and ready in every other way. In that sense, how she feels down there dictates the anal desire, no matter how much you may tease or tantalize her.

Next, how does she look down there? Every asshole is different. Some look cleaner and nicer than others. That visual aspect will immediately affect whether you want be down there or not. Some look really nasty, others really inviting. If a girl doesn't shave down there, there can be little clingers randomly on the hair. It can look amazingly clean and inviting and yet just have an aura of shitty stink that is unavoidable. Some girls shave their pussies but not their asses. I had one that looked like a spider was trying to crawl towards her pussy from her ass, it was crazy lookin'. So yeah, there can be plenty of reasons why an ass is just not doable. I even had a girl once whose pussy was so beautiful to me and so damn tasty that it boggled my mind. And even more mind-boggling was the fact that the ass that neighbored that pussy was never, not even once, desirable to me because of the smell that emanated from it. It seemed like she always had a turtle head hiding just inside that sphincter of hers. That created a sense and aroma that, if not countered by her amazing pussy, would have just been plain too much to handle, and I wouldn't have been able to engage in oral with her at all.

Sometimes to get anal to work, it just requires prep work. I recommend prep work each time unless you happen to be with a girl who has a naturally immaculate ass, or you have a girl who takes care of herself in such a way that she's always ready. And yet, prep work can also be where you need to prepare yourself mentally because it's possible you're about to get into some shit.

4. Always think ahead and prep for the before, during, and after. The prep before means towels, paper towels, baby wipes, lube, and enemas or plain finger probing. If you don't know what an enema is (you have a phone, web search it for more details) basically it's where your girl will put some fluid in her butt to flush it out so she's clean on the inside. It can be done with an enema bag and tube or with a big fat syringe and tube, and can either be filled with warm water to let flow inside. After your girl gets the water inside, she can hold it for a bit and then let it all out in the toilet. This makes it so that your chances of encountering trapped gas or poop are greatly reduced, if not outright zero. Very important that the water is at least body temperature, though, because you don't want her or her insides to be cold.

During anal, it's always a good idea to have a towel underneath and to use plenty of lube. Be conscientious of the fact that any fluids that come out of her ass might accidentally make their way into her pussy. So, for starters, missionary or in a spoon position may work best. Though you don't have to be lying to spoon her. Just have her be in the spoon position on her side, and you can be upright. Once you get more comfortable with it all and get used to making sure her pussy is ok, you can try other positions.

After you are done, make sure to withdraw from her ass gently. Take the time to clean her up with the paper towels or wipes so she's good to go and can then go to the bathroom for any further clean up or just to use the toilet. Unless she wants to cuddle afterwards, which you should totally do if possible. Anal can make a girl feel vulnerable in good ways or new ways if she's new to anal. A good cuddle for a bit before the rest of the clean up can be good, so please be a considerate lover.

Apart from enemas, she can also prep by simply doing a check in the shower. One lover I had loved anal. To her, it was as pleasurable as vaginal sex. Her check consisted of merely going in the shower real quick, putting a finger or two in her ass and feeling for anything that might be hiding like a ninja in the dark. If she felt anything, she would sit on the toilet till it came out, back to the shower to probe further. If she felt nothing, she cleaned up and came out, and then it was on.

If your poop is loose, that is to say, close to diarrhea in consistency, it can end up lining the walls of your insides and you can then get coated in that as you do anal. When this happens, you clean with baby wipes and then try to go right back in, the chemicals from the wipes might not feel too good for the girl in her bum. Better to go and wash up and come right back than to just wipe.

5. You must be gentler with her ass than with her pussy (contrary to most porn videos). Obviously, her ass isn't her pussy – I know it can be hard for some of us to remember this when our hormones and desires are at peak, and you just want to get in there. It's even more of a challenge because for most of us guys, the whole sensation of going in and out of her is what keeps us hard. Suddenly, when having to go so slow, or to even pause for a bit to let her get used to us being in her ass, it can be challenging because we want anal, she wants anal, but it isn't going to happen if our dick goes down from lack of movement.

The solution to this is to make sure that you are super hard when you try it. Either towards the beginning of sex when you are primed and ready, or when you are really hard from being close to orgasm but not close enough to come. That sweet spot where you stay hard automatically in anticipation of the orgasm, but you keep yourself there for that sweet pleasure increase. That right there is the ideal time, if you ask me, to go for anal. Then you don't have to worry about getting soft, you can enjoy the slow insertion, the slow initial movements, and can even stay still a bit to let her adjust and have it still feel really good. Of course, this can work when you're partially soft as well. You'll just have to wait and try to see what works for you.

Remember that a bit of oral sex with some fingering and tongue in her butt will go a long way to relax her and get her and her butt in the mood – even if it's already planned. That way, you can ease into her with more pleasure. And do ease into her. Go slow with the insertion. Do it until you are all the way in and don't forget the lube! The only exception is if she gets ridiculously wet herself so that her wetness drips down and covers your dick as you insert (in missionary). Slow strokes, kiss her, gently touch her pussy, or encourage her to do so if it's at a bad angle for you. You'll be able to slowly speed up the pace, but remember this isn't her pussy, so you can't just outright fuck it unless she specifically asks you to. And did I mention lube?

The bottom line is that you cannot pound and fuck her ass like in the pornos. Well, at least not until she tells you that she wants you to go harder or faster or outright asks you to fuck her ass hard (which can happen). Anal is a bit more intimate and sensation-filled than vaginal sex is in a way. Not to mention that if you are in a good position, you can also play with and finger her pussy slowly to fill her up in both holes in a way that might be amazing for her to experience.

I've also had to where a girl asked me to fuck her really hard while I was in her ass. Naturally, this really turned me on and I was happy to oblige. Little did either of us know that afterwards she would suffer from excruciating pain in her as and lower abdomen at night from the intense anal. That turned her off of anal for a while and she became scared to try it again for fear of that terrible pain. For us lovers that means that we really need to take it easy as we start on that anal journey with a girl who isn't use to it or never done it. Pussy is made to take a pounding by design. Asses aren't. And yet the more anal you do the more her ass will get used to it. That means whether you are average sized or King Kong sized, be considerate.

6. Do not double dip. That is to say, as a general rule, don't go from anal to vaginal sex.

I'm taking a big breath and sighing here at this part because, well, this is my absolute favorite thing to do in all of sex. And I've only ever been able to do it with one girl. Why tell you not to do it when I did it and it became my favorite thing? Because she asked me to do it with her after telling me it was her favorite thing to do. And why would she do that, knowing how easily infected a pussy can become from going from anal to vaginal sex? Because this girl had a one-of-a-kind ass and vagina. Not saying there can't be others out there, but in my life, she is the only one I ever came across. Didn't matter how much double-dipping we did (keep in mind she always did enemas beforehand) at her request, her pussy never got sick.

Did I ever try that with anyone else? Once. And she developed an infection afterwards. But that was at her request because she didn't care about that and only cared about the amazing pleasure. To her, getting a urinary tract infection was a small price to pay for how good it felt to get fucked in both holes. Even so, she eventually stopped doing that because she got tired of dealing with UTIs.

I've been with some women whose little yonis got sick if they bathed in the wrong water, didn't pee after sex, if they had sex in the ocean or in any body of water, if they shaved their pussy completely, or even if they used the wrong condoms. This means that I have always been super careful to make sure that when I do anything anal with a girl, that I protect her pussy as much as possible. That means no using the same fingers, changing condoms from anal back to vaginal, going and actually washing my dick when going back to vaginal sex and even using the safest positions to prevent gravity from sneakily dropping bits into her pussy.

You can have all kinds of bacteria, viruses, and even parasites in your bum hole. And if neither you nor her have been checked or tested, you just don't know. So, as a general rule, never go from anal to vaginal without cleaning yourself up with soap and warm water first. And it should definitely go without saying to never try anal, much less double-dipping without her permission.

7. Be prepared to stop at any moment if she bleeds, becomes sore, or if it becomes painful or if she's just had enough. This can happen right after you start anal or just a minute into it, even if you have done anal before. If that's the case, don't question it or ask for just a few more strokes. Just stop, slowly pull out, clean her up real quick with a paper towel or a wipe, go clean yourself up with warm, soapy water, then come back and see if she would like to continue vaginally. Too easy.

8. If the woman you are with was already into anal before you, ask her how she likes it. That way, it makes things easier for you, and you can learn in the process. Since you are a different person with a different cack and balls, and a different motion to your ocean, it's possible you might even be able to get her to like anal slightly differently or in a new way. But whatever you do, don't make her like it less for your own sake. So don't get all weird on her when she tells you how she likes it and what to do.

9. Both of you getting tested, as well as condom use, is best. In the end, it's all up to you both as to how you wanna roll.

I've always leaned more towards getting tested. Granted, getting tested does not account for the types of bacteria you will be encountering with anal, nor does it account for parasites, which are a very real thing. That being said, that's why condoms are always best if you ask me when it comes to anal. With the plethora of condom options nowadays, it really should be a no-brainer. Now this is all predicated on whether you and your lover talk about it. For many women I've been with, condoms were the default, so there was no discussion. It was either that or leave. The opposite has also happened, where I wanted to wear a condom, and she didn't want me to because of how they irritated her pussy and ass.

Come to terms with however you decided to roll by respecting yourself and respecting her. Remember, it's ok if you don't see eye to eye and peacefully part. It's always better for you both when you do see eye to eye, as that always facilitates more joy and pleasure in the act. And don't assume that just because she's had more partners, or just a few partners, that she's safer for you one way or another when it comes to STIs. All it takes is sex with one person who's infected to pass stuff on.

10. Be aware: dry anal, even slightly forced for any reason, can result in injury for you and or her. Lube. Plenty of it. Sometimes spit and saliva work, but a good lube is best. Even coconut oil works.

It's true. Smoothly refined, not the gritty type, coconut oil can work as a cheap and effective substitute for anal sex, and it is oh-so natural. Beyond that, there is silicone-based lube, water-based lube, and oil-based. So, pick what feels best for you both and roll with that. If you let her get dry and you are dry, you can injure each other. For real. This gets even more important when you are doing anal, and she is on top. Do I really need to spell it out as to what can break or tear on you, or in her, in such a scenario? I mentioned dick injuries before, but not really anal injuries. If you are so inclined, take a moment to look that up on your device and see that it's a very real thing.

In the end...

Anal sex can be amazing. Some of the most intense pleasures I have ever felt have been from anal. The biggest bonus has always been that you can cum in a girl's ass without worry of getting her pregnant. That has led to many simultaneous orgasms through anal sex, which is something I hope you get to experience.

You never know how anal is going to be, regardless of how beautiful you find a girl. I say that because not all anal is the same. Just as your twig and berries can vary greatly from guy to guy, so can pussies and even asses vary to a great degree. Anal can sometimes feel like you're having sex with a fleshy, thick, tight ring and almost nothing else beyond it. Other times, it can feel like you're having sex with the smoothest, tightest, warmest velvet tube ever. It can even almost feel similar to a vagina, or it can feel so unique and pleasurable that it defies description. I'll even go so far as to admit that not all anal has been pleasurable. There have been times when it felt bad, it hurt, or I just plain didn't like it with that person.

What does that mean? Not all experiences will be the same. If you happen to have a bad experience, don't let it stop you or deter you from trying it again later or with someone else. And if you find that anal just isn't for you, that's perfectly OK too. Just be sure to always be considerate to the girl, watch out for her ass and pussy so they stay healthy, and so that she will always welcome you back into her pleasure centers.

The Epic Fail

One night, while I was imagining racing a light cycle on the grid while brushing my teeth and doing one-legged squats, I remembered that there was a girl in my bed waiting for me to have sex! As I rushed to finish what I was doing in the bathroom, I had no idea what was awaiting me in just a matter of minutes.

As I approached the glorious naked beauty in my bed, I noticed that she had already put a pillow under her hips as she lay there on her belly. Her ass was fantastic, and it was already being presented to me in such a wonderful state!

I made way around her body, kissing and nibbling along the way until I finally decided to give attention to the centerpiece she had presented to me. As I kissed, licked and nibbled her butt, I quickly made my way in between her cheeks, helped them apart, and started to tongue her in the way I knew she liked and was waiting for. Just as we were both getting into it, me with the rhythm of my tongue fucking her ass and her with gently leaning into each of my tongue jabs, the unexpected happened…

A huge fart came out of her ass. And not just any fart. Oh no, that would have been too easy. This fart was so full of gas, so powerful that the sudden outburst out of her ass filled my mouth full of said gas and expanded my cheeks completely. Ever take a hairdryer and aim it at your mouth, and it completely inflates your mouth and cheeks into balloons? Well, it was just like that. Except all fart gas.

Thankfully for me, there were no chunks or slimy bits that flew out. Just plain gas. Boy would have been partially traumatizing. Right after it happened, I immediately burst out laughing while coughing and trying to breathe at the same time. The sensations it filled my mouth with were so tickly in nature, and it was so unexpected yet sudden that I couldn't help but laugh. Oh, and surprisingly, it didn't stink. She had a clean butt.

She also started to laugh, but felt super embarrassed about it. Being one not to let things get me for long, I just laughed some more, caught my breath, spread her ass again and went right back to it. And wouldn't you know it, she farted again! And caught me again with a mouth full of puff blowing my cheeks out and all! She was already giggly and embarrassed from the first one moments ago, but we were both laughing so hard at this point that we had to stop. And then I jokingly, but also sincerely, told her maybe she should sit on the toilet for a bit and clean herself up again before we try again. And off she went. We ended up having a good time that day without any more issues, so it was all good.

That was an example of an epic oral anal fail. Here is an anal fail…

A long, long time ago. In a country far, far away, a new-to-anal-sex me was excited to have anal sex again with the lover I had at that time. We had had such mutual enjoyment that when she came to my room all bundled up in winter gear, I couldn't help but want to peel some of it, but not all of it, off of her. We started to kiss lying down, but I decided that I only wanted to pull her pants down just far enough for me to get access to her ass, so that we could go straight to anal.

I knew it was ok to go for it, but she didn't know that I wasn't going for her pussy. Not knowing I was going straight for the anal, she tells me that she was on her period, and I reply with, "That's ok, I'm going for your ass anyway." This turned her on instantly. I used a bit of saliva, lubed myself up and went in. Not only did I slip right in, but her moans of pleasure were nothing but music to my ears.

As we went at it in the spoon position, I lifted my head for a moment for some reason and caught a whiff of some strong smell that I couldn't quite place. I thought, meh, everything's fine, and just kept going. A minute later, I lifted my head again, and the smell was way stronger. I leaned up a bit and got a good, long whiff of what I was smelling as I kept having sex with her and realized that I knew that smell. I bet you can guess what it was too.

Once again, I thought to myself, meh, let's keep going till we finish anyway. And we did. I came inside her ass, stopped, leaned up and slowly pulled out…

She asked me what's up, and if I recall correctly, she wondered about feeling a bit wet down there. Well, not only was there a nice milk chocolaty wet ring around her butt, but my dick looked like it had just been dipped into a chocolate fountain – all shiny, glossy and brown. I looked at her and said I need to go clean up but before I went to the bathroom, I used the paper towels that were on hand to wipe her up and took them with me.

Needless to say, it was not a fun nor pleasant-smelling sight to behold. But with enough soap and water, I got myself all cleaned up. She came into the shower and cleaned herself up as well. We both thought it was gross, but laughed about it together the whole time. And let me tell ya, it did not deter us at all from doing anal again. It just made us more aware of what to look out for so that we could remain as clean as possible.

In the first example, despite her preparation, the unexpected happened. Not once but twice! That's the danger when doing oral to anal. In the second example, you can see that although mutual consent, desire, and anticipation were there, there was no proper preparation, nor were we really set up for success. Fortunately for us both, we were not put off by it enough to have it affect our desire to do it again with each other. We just considered certain things for next time, and it never happened again. I didn't even mention the time when I was having sex doggy style with a girl who, when I stuck my finger in her butt, left my finger coated thick chocolaty shiftiness. Needless to say, interact with asses at your own risk.

The Epic Success!

You ever just sit there and randomly think about someone you hadn't thought of in a long while? Well, one Tuesday I thought about an old friend and lover that I hadn't talked to in about five years. So, I thought, what the heck, let me reach out and see how she's doing. Well, we hit it off and started to chat regularly. We had great sexual chemistry, so the conversations started to drift more towards sex and eventually towards anal. She mentioned that she had only ever just barely tried it once and that it hurt a lot, but that with me she'd love to try again.

After a bit of time and some planning, I visited her. She was super
excited to have sex, as was I. But after all the talk we had about anal,
that first night was not just about sex but about anal sex. She had asked
me all that she should do to prepare, and I went into detail, and she was
completely on board. I should mention that not only had we both
gotten tested before we met up and came out clean, she also had her
tubes tied, which meant that we both felt it was safe not to use
protection.

Before we got started, she went into the bathroom and gave herself
an enema to clean herself out. She brought the towels and wipes, and a
roll of toilet paper instead of paper towels. Mostly because they are
easily flushable. Fortunately, we didn't need any lube because she gets
super wet easily, and that was all the lube we needed. Additionally,
because I had my black belt in dick-yoon-do already, I was confident
that things would go well.

We had sex for a bit till she was ready, the whole time talking to
each other about what we enjoy and how great it all feels. She was
lying down, legs up, towards the edge of the bed, towel underneath,
and I literally just wiped some of the wetness from her pussy onto
myself and slowly started to ease into her butt. She was very
communicative the whole time, and after a nice, slow start, she asked
me to speed up the pace until we were full-on fucking. She had I don't
know how many orgasms, got even more wet, which I didn't even
realize was possible and then came the biggest surprise…she squirted
all over me!

Apparently, something about anal with me set her off just right in a
way neither of us had experienced, and she came and squirted all over
herself and me. Kind of amazing to behold actually and also very
important to note that when a woman squirts, chances are she will also
pee to some degree. Not guaranteed but it does happen and in this case,
it sure did. We kept going until the towels were soaked and the bed
underneath as well, and then eventually, I came as well. Clean up took
a while, which was pretty funny. I had to mop the floor, while she had
to go into the bathroom and clean herself up inside and out. Then we
had to do laundry for the towels, and try to clean and dry up the bed, as
well as flushing the toilet multiple times to get rid of all the toilet paper
we used without clogging the toilet.

We not only talked about everything to do with anal, but we also
prepared thoroughly. Additionally, we also talked about how much we

wanted to do it and all the desires we had along with wanting to do it. This, of course, really built up the anticipation and made us want to have sex even more with each passing day until I came to see her. We communicated throughout, she had a wonderful experience, as did I, and even though the clean-up was a lot, it was totally worth it for both of us, and we ended up having anal sex every night!

Not all anal has required so much clean up and prep work, but sometimes, for both of you, there's just nothing like great anal sex.

Chapter 17: Orgasms: The Spice Of Life

Orgasms are a really interesting human phenomenon. It is considered the crescendo of sex. The peak. The payoff. And to some, the best part. Here is some info about orgasms for men and women, from my life meanderings and observations, so that you can get a better understanding of the differences between both sexes.

My simple philosophy when it comes to orgasms is to always figure out how to make the girl cum so that I can make her cum first. This serves two purposes. One, it gets her all fired up and hot so that she craves you and wants you inside of her urgently. (Which makes that sweet moment of first insertion that much more passionate and intense.) Two, so that the window is now open for her to potentially have another or for you and her to just enjoy the sex until you are about to cum, which just might get her worked up even more to experience, or help you with your orgasm.

Highlights: Your orgasms

1. Believe it or not, there is more than one type of orgasm that you can experience. There are normal/complete orgasms, partial orgasms, multiple orgasms, delayed orgasms, split orgasms, ghost orgasms, forced orgasms, surprise orgasms, pleasureless orgasms, premature ejaculation/orgasms and even nonstop orgasms.

2. Orgasms after sex can leave you feeling drained and tired, and also crystal clear with what I call the moment of clarity. They can leave you feeling normal, extra horny, or they can feel like you just did a warmup and are now ready for the main course!

3. Your diet, to some extent, can determine how your cum smells, looks, and even tastes. How well hydrated you are will also affect the look and consistency of your cum.

4. There are some benefits to holding back and having an orgasm every couple of weeks or so (if you're single).

5. If you don't know what blue balls are, well, it's when a girl gets you worked up but then you don't get to cum…leaving you with excruciating pain in your testicles.

6. Learning to feel and sense the very beginnings of when you are about to cum before you orgasm is essential for when you need to pull out. Timing and sensation are everything.

Her orgasms:

7. Women experience orgasms completely differently from men. It can last way longer, encapsulate the whole body, and sometimes open the door for many more. Orgasms need not even be based around you playing with her clit.

8. When a woman has an orgasm, it can be almost undetectable by you or so extreme that there is no way you can miss it.

9. Sometimes, when a woman has an orgasm, she can be totally done with sex, regardless of whether you are ready to stop or not or whether you have cum or not.

10. It is possible that you can discover multiple ways of stimulating your partner into reaching orgasm.

11. Sex isn't always enough to get a girl to orgasm.

12. Women can have an orgasm that also excretes fluid in some way. It can ooze out or squirt out.

13. The longer you have sex with the same woman, the greater the chance that your orgasms and hers will start to line up and trigger each other or happen at the same time. It's in these circumstances that it can be really difficult to pull out in order to prevent impregnating your partner.

The basics in detail

I'm sure many of you have taken the time to explore yourselves and get creative, so it's likely that you know yourself and your orgasms pretty well. And if you haven't, time and effort will fix that. But when it comes to exploring a woman and seeing what she's capable of in orgasm territory, I'm pretty sure that a good percentage of you know what you know from watching porn, not experience. So, to cover those bases, I will share my thoughts and ideas about those things here. And while this is no substitute for experience, at least having this knowledge will help to show you some of the possibilities you may not have thought of, as well as to help you not be surprised when you do experience something new.

1. Within you is also the potential to experience more than one type of orgasm. There are normal/complete orgasms, which are what most of us men have. You cum fully, you orgasm fully, you're done. Then there are partial orgasms, where you feel like you came, but you also feel like there was more orgasm left in you that wasn't pulled out, so to speak. This can leave you feeling like you want to keep going in masturbation or sex, or like you still want to have sex but need to wait to get hard again.

Then you can have multiple orgasms. Multiple orgasms have different triggers for different men. Sometimes intense pleasure can cause it, not having sex for a long time can do it, and being with an amazing girl that makes you feel fantastic can do it. It can just be inherent to you. Getting a blow job that uses different techniques to milk you for all your cum can also have this effect, or you can train your body to do it too.

In order to train yourself, it's relatively simple: just keep stimulating yourself after your orgasm. It will feel uncomfortable at first, and you won't be able to do it for very long, either due to your dick getting soft or to discomfort, but do it nonetheless. Do that each time after orgasm, and you'll find, over time, that you can both tolerate it longer and that pleasure will quickly start to return. Eventually, the discomfort and sensitivity can disappear completely, you'll stay harder longer, and you can pull out another orgasm from within. It may not work for everyone, but if you're curious, that's one way to do it. Another way is to deprive yourself of any pleasure or stimulation for say two weeks or more. After that, you use the absolute minimum sensation necessary to achieve orgasm. You can do this, or your woman can. As soon as you cum then you enhance the sensation a bit more, change techniques and continue on. Then keep the variations up until you are absolutely limp and done.

Next, delayed orgasms. Delayed orgasms, depending on how you experience them, can be where you cum first and then orgasm. Or it can be where you feel like you're going to orgasm, but it takes forever to actually happen, despite being right there on the verge of cumming. Split orgasms are when you have an orgasm, but it is half of what you normally experience. Because of that, you can have a feeling like there is more orgasm left in you. And then, with more effort, you can get the other half to happen as well, and you finally feel fulfilled or satisfied. This can be experienced as two smaller orgasms perceptively, which is very similar to partial orgasms but not quite the same. It can also feel like a multiple orgasm, although not quite the same.

Ghost orgasms are where you cum but feel no pleasure, or where you feel pleasure but nothing comes out. Forced orgasms are where either you or your partner manages to do something to force an orgasm to happen with little to no buildup (even when you didn't feel like you were able to cum or in the mood to cum). I've had this happen where a girl forced an orgasm out of me when I swore it wasn't possible, and I was quite surprised. Surprise orgasms can happen when you are being stimulated in a way that has never caused you to cum before, and yet there you are having an orgasm for whatever reason to your own amazement. Pleasureless orgasms are when you ejaculate and even feel the sense that you had an orgasm, but zero pleasure came from it. In that scenario, I always feel cheated. You can even have nonstop orgasms. Somehow, someway, something happens in that situation, and you start to have an orgasm…but it just doesn't stop. These orgasmic moments can feel like an eternity on their own when it finally happens, and the first time is the biggest surprise. And don't be surprised if you become exhausted afterwards and pass out.

Lastly, premature ejaculation and premature orgasms. They are usually tied together, but essentially, these happen with very little stimulation at all. It can be due to excitement, extreme sensitivity, deprivation of stimulation, a heightened and oversensitive nervous system, or you can just be wired that way for some reason. There are many simple ways to deal with this, however. As I wrote in Book 1 in the masturbation chapter, there are many things that we do that can cause us to lose sensitivity. Well, the reverse also applies in that if you are overly sensitive and cum prematurely, you can desensitize yourself through various means. First, use condoms. If that doesn't make any difference and you cum just as quickly in the condom there are desensitizing sprays that are sold for anal sex that you can use as well. You can masturbate more frequently and use a tighter grip. You can even use Viagra and plan for the premature ejaculation in that you go ahead and get the first orgasm out of the way, but the Viagra keeps you hard, and you just keep going on with a condom to enjoy the act of sex. Whether you try these things individually or combo is up to you, but if after all that nothing works, then it's time to go see a doc about it.

It is quite probable that you will experience a type that isn't on this list, so don't think that it is all-encompassing. I would encourage you to check which ones you've had, which ones you are interested in experiencing, and when you do experience one that isn't on this list, to add it. It's a big sexual world of pleasure out there, so I'm sure there are more variations that we men can experience.

2. Orgasms can leave you feeling any number of ways afterwards when with a girl. When you masturbate, you're usually ok. But when you have sex with a girl and then have an orgasm, you can feel drained and tired and so sleepy that you fall asleep. Orgasms after sex can leave you feeling drained and tired, and also crystal clear with what I call the moment of clarity. They can leave you feeling normal, extra horny, or they can feel like you just did a warmup and are now ready for the main course! They can leave you shaking, extra horny, or any number of other ways that apply to you specifically. Some of those ways you might feel could be age-specific or girl-specific.

When I was younger, I always felt like I was about to pass out for a nap after an orgasm with a girl. Then, when I got older, it completely changed to a feeling of just getting done with a great warm-up and like the real thing would start then. I even got to the point where I had to work so hard for an orgasm, it just didn't even feel worth it anymore! All of it is perfectly normal and perfectly ok, so don't sweat it. Don't freak out or beat yourself up if you don't feel the exact same all the time. You are allowed to feel different and have unique experiences; it doesn't need to be and won't be all the same. This means that when you are with a woman, and you become exhausted after having an orgasm, and she still wants more, that's perfectly ok. You don't need to soldier up if she's too selfish to be understanding. But – and this is a big but – if you have an understanding and patient woman who doesn't complain and you always just roll over and go to sleep after you get your orgasm, and she hasn't got much of anything, then you're just a lazy, selfish user of a man. If that applies to you, I say wake up because you might actually get better sex, and more sex, if you take the time to take care of her as well.

The moment of clarity can also come from orgasms. After you cum, suddenly, the fog of horniness and sexual desire can be lifted to the point where you can feel absolutely clear about the person lying next to you. In that moment, you'll know beyond a shadow of a doubt whether you want to remain or not, or whether you love this girl, like her, or whether it was just a one-time fuck. You can get clarity on other things, too, but that's the most common.

3. Your diet and hydration level also affect the smell, consistency, viscosity, and appearance of your sperm. I have spoken to women about this for decades, not to mention to my own lovers. Mostly because to engage in sex with a man is to engage with a man's cum. Since the majority of women I've encountered don't like the taste of it, or sometimes even to touch it, I would enquire about these details in person.

I experimented with this too myself. When my diet was clean with not much meat, no sweets or junk food, plenty of hydration daily, and fruits, not only was the semen pure white, but the consistency was good, and there was no smell. Some of the girls I spoke to mentioned how their husbands' cum stank to high heaven, or was always yellowish, looked like tapioca pudding, or was off-white. For the girls who actually tasted cum through oral sex or whatever, they also mentioned noticeable differences in the taste and intensity of cum depending on diet. Overall, the biggest factor that will affect your sperm (apart from tight underwear) is hydration, not pineapples.

4. When it comes to orgasms, depending on how horny you are, whether or not you are in a relationship, or just plain how often you like to masturbate, there is some benefit to holding off and masturbating every two weeks or so. The simple benefit is that the buildup will make you more sensitive, you'll have more cum, and likely a bigger orgasm. That also gives plenty of time for your dick to just chill without being choked. Now, is there anything behind this idea apart from my experiences and thoughts? Nope. It's just something that will help to maintain your dick ready for a girl should the occasion arise, and also give you the build-up for a good payoff. You could also do it once a week too. Up to you.

5. Blue balls. I hope that most of you are familiar with this term because it is something you do not want, but can get, and it sucks. The first time I got blue balls was when I lived in Louisiana. I was really getting into some touchy-feely stuff with the girl I was with at the time. Well, her parents came home early, and I had all this build-up and nowhere for it to go. Shortly thereafter, my balls started to ache, then hurt, then became so sensitive and painful that I could hardly walk. And so began my first experience with blue balls. If you let a girl get you all riled up without release, that is the prime scenario for your balls

to start to ache in a way like no other. In order to prevent that, better to go and give yourself some relief!

Also, having sex or getting a blowjob without release, masturbating, and not finishing and even from sex dreams that you didn't get release from, is never fun. So far, I have yet to find or hear of anything that will take it away apart from having a great orgasm. So, whatever you do, if you can't finish for one reason or another, excuse yourself and finish it off in the bathroom to ensure you do not get blue balls. Women tend to have varying amounts of sympathy when we experience this, but for the most part, they laugh and think it's funny. So don't expect much empathy from them. Either prevent it or take care of it right away. And if a girl sees you have blue balls and she gets right to work to milk you dry to give you relief, she's likely a keeper!

If you are in a relationship, there is some value in not masturbating that often to better enjoy your sex life. Unless you are already pretty sensitive, masturbation can help (as I've mentioned before). Anyway, the last thing I wanted to mention is about orgasm control. You know how we can stop peeing if we really want to, or need to, even though it can be uncomfortable? Well, you can do the same thing with orgasms to hold them back. Edging – bringing yourself close to orgasm and staying in that space – will help you to develop more orgasm control. I've gotten it to the point where not only could I hold an orgasm back long enough to pull out safely before orgasm, I can also stop the ejaculation if I want as the orgasm happens. I don't recommend that, though, as it is really uncomfortable and overall pointless. The point is that if you develop the strength to better control your orgasms, you can pull out more safely during sex so that you don't impregnate a woman. Sometimes the semen can be really sneaky, though, so you need to really practice awareness so you can sense anything traveling down your pee pipe a bit prematurely. It happens, which is why I'm mentioning it here.

6. Which reminds me, I know it feels unnatural to cum outside of the girl and not in her pussy, but you'd better get used to it if you don't want to create a baby that you don't want and aren't ready for. Even with a condom, practice orgasm discipline and pull out before you cum. Oh, and make sure it is your condom that you use during sex as well. It's rare, but some ladies out there will poke holes in condoms before they hand them to you. Pulling out and then cumming in the

condom is ideal, but if the girl gave you the condom to use, you have to check it for holes. The women who do that have their reasons, and it's usually about money and typically only the rich and famous encounter this issue. And there aren't that many that do, but to play it safe, always have condoms and use your own so you know they haven't been tampered with.

About women's orgasms:

7. Not sure if you ever gave it any thought, but you should know that women experience orgasms very differently than we men do. Their orgasms can last way longer, encapsulate the whole body, and sometimes open the door for many more orgasms to follow. Our orgasms tend to be solely focused in our penis or in that general area. A woman can experience it in her body, mind, in waves throughout her body, her breasts and pussy, and that's just to name a few.

It is possible that some of you men out there also have more profound orgasms that encapsulate more than intense sensation in your dick, but in comparison to women, our orgasms just don't match up. So don't be too surprised if you make some girl cum and she acts, moves, yells, screams, moans, or behaves in a way you've never seen before. Just be ready. I've had women act like cats who were trying to get away from the water while trapped in a bathtub, women who scream and moan like they were transforming into werewolves, and even women who were so still and silent it was like nothing I did could get them to come alive.

8. Some women can orgasm to such an intense degree that if you're not ready, her violent body spasms can catch you off guard and injure you! That happened to me during oral sex with one girl over two decades ago, and my jaw still isn't the same! There can be moaning, screaming, scratching, biting, squeezing, squirting, grunting, and her own body can even try to crawl away from you without her control. This also means that women having orgasms can be pretty funny as well. The ladies can make some funny faces and sounds, and more than once I had to laugh uncontrollably. So just roll with it. Literally.

Even though this may sound like a complete contradiction to what I just said, women can also have orgasms that are almost completely undetectable. These types of orgasms have often left me utterly confused to the point where the girl taps on my head to signal me to stop when I'm giving oral sex. Or she just asks me to stop if we're having regular sex…then tell me that she can't cum anymore and she's exhausted. With those ladies, I had to pay extra close attention to their subtle signs and signals that showed they were having an orgasm. Sometimes I even had to ask them to share what their signals were because I couldn't pick them up on my own. And for the rare ones that I had zero freakin' clue when they would orgasm, I just asked them to announce it right before it would happen so I would know. All that means, be ready. Life is not like a porno.

By paying more attention to the woman's body instead of mine, and not being in my head the whole time, I began to notice the signs that were there all along. There is usually some tension in the body or the vagina itself. Her pussy will get wetter, or the wetness will change in taste and viscosity to some degree. Then the breathing will change alongside the body language. If you can read between the lines here, obviously, I was pretty ignorant for quite a while. I just couldn't help it. I was in my head the whole time trying to focus on not cumming, and on being the best lover that I could be, all the while trying to keep sex fun and interesting for myself. Not to mention some women felt so good that I could keep my mind on little else!

It is true that many women will often fake orgasms for whatever reason. Based on various accounts, it's usually due to either the guy's expectations, to make the guy feel good about his hard work, or to hurry up and get the sex over with. But in all likelihood, there are more reasons. Just try to create such a comfortable and honest atmosphere that she feels comfortable telling you, or that she feels good enough not to have to fake it. Apart from doing the best you can and taking the time to be considerate and to improve over time, not much else you can do. If she feels she needs to fake it despite your best genuine efforts, she'll fake it.

9. In certain circumstances, but usually after orgasm, a woman can be completely done with sex. As in, worn out and ready to rest. When she has these types of orgasms, or for any reason that requires it, you stop having sex with her, and you change gears to cuddle her unless she just needs space to relax, breathe, or cool off. Unless you were super close to finishing, to prevent blue balls go finish in the bathroom, come back and then cuddle her. Or you can see if she will finish you off. Most good lovers would do this if you ask. But with the best lady lovers, you won't have to say anything because they will jump on it like white on rice, in a glass of milk, on a paper plate in a snowstorm, just to make sure you are taken care of.

Remember, a woman literally lets you inside her whole being when you have sex. Add to that all your thrusting and pumping, as well as the intensity of your energy completely directed towards her and well, sometimes they can be done way before you, so please be understanding and patient when that occurs.

10. Women can also orgasm from other types of things like nipple stimulation, being teased in the right ways, being stimulated over her clothing, teased on the right parts of her body, mind games and saying the right things in her ear, and even from kinky play. But this book is not about advanced things like kink, so don't bank on that one. I even met a girl once who could have orgasms just depending on how you played with her nipples and areolas, which was pretty amazing to witness.

Purely accidentally, I even made a girl cum from just sticking my tongue into her vaginal opening repeatedly because I was starving (she tasted really good, and it had been a while since I tasted her). All I did was strive to taste and drink all that wetness that came out without touching her clit, and sure enough, after about 30 to 45 seconds, she had a huge orgasm. Apparently, after some discussion, turns out that my hunger, in combination with the whole situation, made it so that I literally sucked an orgasm out of her to her complete surprise. Women really can orgasm in a myriad of ways, and it's your duty, and delight, to discover what those ways are for the individual woman you are with and for your pleasurable gratification.

11. Continuing on, in case you didn't know, sex is usually not enough to make a lot of girls reach an orgasm. Often it can be that they need a few things going on at the same time to reach that point. Whether it's a proper warm-up she needs, tons of foreplay, sweet whispers in her ear, or additional stimulation, you have to remember that there are two of you at play here. So even if you cum first because she feels too amazing, you'd better regroup and then pay attention to her body in other ways to see if you can give her the same thing. At a minimum, stimulate other parts of her body simultaneously, including her clit, if she can tolerate it, during sex, so that she can cum around the time you do. If all else fails, talk to her about it. It's her body after all. If she knows, she can share. If she doesn't know, then play together and discover. Just don't let your efforts to satisfy her start and end with sex and your orgasm.

There was a girl I was really in love with some time ago, and when she and I had sex in the beginning, I remember I came too fast on one occasion. But I was still really horny and really hungry for her. So right after I came, I went right back down on her and continued as though we hadn't had sex yet. Not only was she super happy that there was more after my orgasm, but I managed to make her cum as a result. The reason I got used to doing things like that was because there were women in my past who took the time to make me cum after they were satisfied as well, and I really appreciated that. So, keep that in mind.

12. Women can also cum in their own juicy ways. I'm sure you have seen it in porn where the girls squirt like crazy. Well, not all girls can do that, and not all do so with the same technique you see in porn. Sometimes the girl may just get really, really wet or may start to slowly ooze out some wetness, and even pee a little. So be ready. But also, don't be disappointed if nothing comes out. I can think of a couple of females off the top of my head that didn't get really wet until after they came and were done with sex. Either way, an orgasm is enough. No need to make her pee herself or squirt wetness all over. Anyway, just be aware that that can happen and that the goal is simply for her to have a satisfying orgasm.

Now, having said that, there are two little things you need to keep in mind as well. First, sometimes, not always and certainly not with most girls, but sometimes, when a girl comes, she can pee or let out squirts of pee. You'll feel it if not smell it because the pee is not a lubricant. Which means that as it comes out, apart from being extra warm, it will feel like water was suddenly added to the lubricant equation. Second, and this is extremely rare because I only learned about this one through a close friend of mine when we were swapping stories, on rare occasions, a girl can shit herself as she orgasms. Yes. You read that right. My friend had a lover once who had a sister whom another friend had also had sex with. Turns out that as they were talking about sex with the sisters, they both inexplicably shit themselves as sort of a reflex action every time they orgasm. Inexplicably, they both had sex with these girls more than once! Which made me laugh to no end. Apparently, apart from really liking them, the sex and pussy were great. Anyway, be ready just in case something rare like this happens.

13. The last thing to remember about women and orgasms is that they can often be directly tied to your orgasm if you have bonded enough and/or your bodies can feel each other enough. Your orgasm

can trigger hers; she can trigger yours, or you can just start feeling it at the same time. This is important to note because when you reach this state, this is the most challenging time to pull out if you don't want to impregnate a girl. She may even beg you to stay in, wrap her legs around you, or beg you while she moans to keep going so you can cum together. Personally, I only ever allowed that if the girl was on birth control of some sort, if I was wearing a condom, and I knew she was outside her ovulation window, while at the same time having full trust in her. If those things weren't in place, I always pulled out. So, if you are bonded, or your bodies react to each other to the point where you can feel and trigger each other's orgasms, make the decision that doesn't end up with an unwanted human nine months later. I'm tired of seeing single moms because so many of my fellow men out there are cowards and can't commit to raising their offspring. So, resist and pull out for children's sake.

Hopefully you now get the idea about how different our orgasms can be. The stimulation is really basic. For us, up and down with something that wraps around our dick. (And yes, I am aware that we men also have many other ways we can cum, but to the vast majority, that statement applies.) With women, something that goes in and out and also stimulates her clitoris in some way, but potentially many other parts of her body. We both can have various parts of our bodies that can be linked with our genitalia, causing great arousal to be possible without even touching the genitals. In a lucky few, you may even be able to make yourself or her cum by stimulating these points on the body. They could be ears, neck, tongue, throat, nipple, breasts, back, or even fingers.

Orgasms are an awesome function of the body, and I personally believe that a woman's body is designed in such a way as to be able to feel pleasure in any given part if done right by the right person. As such, I always looked forward to discovering the various places and ways that I could make a woman writhe and wriggle into an orgasm in a way she hadn't before. To me, there is nothing like that look of ecstasy on their face, both during and after. Especially since they possess the only organ whose sole purpose is for pleasure.

The last thing to remember about orgasms is that you can't force them. Sometimes it just isn't going to happen for you, for her, or both. It could be stress, bodily changes, not turned on enough, feeling off, not the right chemistry, already came enough for one day, work shit, family shit or constipation, or any number of innumerable reasons.

Whether you can't get hard enough to cum, or she just isn't sensitized enough, that is ok. Orgasms are not a prerequisite for sex to happen and for sex to be enjoyed. Think of orgasms as a nice bonus. Not to mention that it is perfectly possible to have sex that is so pleasurable that you prefer to keep going rather than end the sex through orgasm. If you haven't had sex like that yet, you are in for a treat! Just remember not to give yourself blue balls.

As a man, if you really just want to have an orgasm, you can masturbate. But if you want to experience the pleasure and joy that comes from intertwining yourself with a woman's body, then the journey of it is the key, not the orgasm. If you keep that in mind, you will most likely enjoy the process of sex and foreplay more and worry about orgasms less. You just might make yourself a better lover in the process.

The Epic Fail

One day, I was inside the 101st Airborne Division Band Barracks, face-first into a clarinet player's pussy and trying to hum the national anthem, when all of a sudden, she grabs fistfuls of my hair with both hands, locks her legs around my head and neck and immediately proceeds to both flex and roll left to right. Naturally, that placed me in a precarious position. Why? Because (a) her bed was elevated, so I was actually mostly standing up while my head was buried between her legs; (b) because my head and neck could not turn to match the full rotations that this girl was performing in both directions so quickly. That meant that I either allowed my neck to be snapped – or that I rolled with what she was doing to preserve my life. Her body weight and momentum were by far stronger than my mere neck could resist in her orgasmic stupor.

Thank goodness for the fact that I was already a brown belt in dick-yoon-do.

As she rolled to her left, I completely turned and rolled my entire body, complete with fancy footwork worthy of the best dancers, to match her speed and momentum. I managed to do this successfully the first two times. And it's worth mentioning that women orgasm longer than men. But alas, this particular woman was a virgin up until the year before I met her and she had never really had an orgasm because, and get this, somehow, someway, she would manage to resist them due to their intensity. What did that mean for my head, neck, jaw, and tongue?

Well, unfortunately, after spin number three, she zigged, and I zagged, and that meant ouch.

The sounds my jaw made from my first-person point of view, while having my ears completely covered by rock-hard thighs, was not pretty. Thank the heavens that she let go immediately after that because that's when I truly felt the pain and discomfort on the right side of my jaw. What made it worse was the fact that she successfully fought off and resisted the orgasm she was having that I worked and sacrificed to give her!

I just couldn't get her to relax enough, and tiny barracks beds aren't the best places to have such tugs of war. Not only did I fail to give her an orgasm but what I did manage to give her she resisted…to the detriment of my jaw. Due to this fail on my part, my jaw would not quite be the same for over a decade after that. Fortunately for my jaw, this type of situation did not repeat itself again because I never again allowed myself to be locked into such a leg lock.

The Epic Success

So, no shit there I was, in a foreign country, in the big bedroom of this girl's apartment, knee deep in sex, wishing I had some sort of magical powers while harnessing my inner chi, when I suddenly realized that I had tried everything I could think of to make this girl I was with cum. Nothing was working. Oral sex, check. Oral sex with fingers, check. Tons of foreplay, check. Teasing throughout the day, check. Sex, check. Plenty of clitoral play, check. Vaginal play, check. Different tongue and mouth techniques, rhythms, speeds, and pressures, check. Fingers and mouth and tongue, check. Penis and fingers, check. Talking in Spanish while doing the sex, check. Different positions, check.

Starting to sound like an epic failure, right? Nope. Not yet. I didn't give up even after we had long, sweaty sex till I came. She was genuine and said that she loved the sex and didn't really feel the need to have an orgasm. I believed her because I could tell she was tired from the sex and that she was radiating satisfaction. (Plus, she said she'd never really had an orgasm before, so she was used to not cumming and just enjoying the process). But me, being the ever-explorative lover that I am – while simultaneously wishing to keep my black belt in dick-yoon-do – and still a bit hungry, I pinned her up against the doorway on a whim. I held her arms behind her back, made out with her while I fingered her using the cum here technique, something I suddenly realized I hadn't tried yet. And as I did that, out of nowhere, a look of utter surprise came from her eyes and face, and she had a huge orgasm and dripped all over the place. But sensing that I could do it again, I went for another quick round, and she came even harder than the first time and then almost immediately collapsed to the ground! I had to hug her to keep her upright until she could recover her strength but, in that moment, I felt victorious! In my head, I thought, mwahahahahaha!! Even if you don't know your own body, I will learn it for you!

And so, in my head at least, that day went down in infamy. Mostly because there were some women I was not able to give an orgasm to in the past. That always left me feeling a bit down, or like I just didn't know enough and hadn't earned my belts in dick-yoon-do. But in this situation, just when I thought I wouldn't be able to give her what no one before was able to give her, I pulled it off and made it happen. Of all my experiences, this was the one that felt the most genuinely epic. I cheered and laughed and jumped for joy afterwards in front of the girl, to her joyful amusement, because I worked really hard for that victory and the payoff, in the way she reacted and her body responded, was totally worth it. Granted, I prefer to not have to work so hard to make a girl cum by far, but that one felt so earned it was definitely epic for me.

In the End: What is a Casanova's Code?

A Casanova's Code is the individual process, philosophy, and techniques you, as a true to yourself man, embody as you go about striving to be a good lover to those women that choose to share themselves with you or to the one woman you share your life with. And this book is my code.

It's also just me having fun figuring out how to sexually please women in order to maximize their pleasure because of how gratifying it is for me to do so.

Remember, mastering the basics of being a lover will be helpful to almost every lady you come across and may turn you into your own Casanova. And don't take this seriously. This was all written in good fun just to help out those to whom this type of advice applies to. Thank you for reading. I hope it was fun and enjoyable. And always remember to have clean hands when touching lady parts. They appreciate that. And so do the ladies.

FIN

About the Author

Javier Ocasio is a US Army Aviation Veteran from Puerto Rico. After his Army career, he did some activism, ran for public office, traveled around a lot, and became a spiritual seeker. He's never won any awards worth noting, but he did receive a certificate from three random girls voting him best looking guy in tenth grade once. He treasured that but lost it. This is his first book, with more to come. When he's not writing books or poetry, he paints, goes to the gym, trains others, gives massages, plays his ukulele, plays video games, watches anime, goes to the movies, and loves to have sexy time with his girl.

Go to www.javierflair.me for all my links, future books, and my art.

www.ingramcontent.com/pod-product-compliance
Lightning Source LLC
LaVergne TN
LVHW010502200726
843506LV00013B/2497